A Beginner's Guide
to the
STEINSALTZ
TALMUD

A BEGINNER'S GUIDE
to the
STEINSALTZ TALMUD

JUDITH Z. ABRAMS

JASON ARONSON INC
Northvale, New Jersey
Jerusalem

The author wishes to thank Random House, Inc., New York, NY for permission to reprint material from *The Talmud: The Steinsaltz Edition, Volume III, Tractate Bava Metzia, Part III* by Rabbi Adin Steinsaltz (translation copyright © 1990 by The Israel Institute for Talmudic Publications and Milta Books, Inc.), *The Talmud: The Steinsaltz Edition: A Reference Guide* by Rabbi Adin Steinsaltz (translation copyright © 1989 by The Israel Institute for Talmudic Publications and Milta Books, Inc.). The complete edition of the *Steinsaltz Talmud* is available at local bookstores or by calling Random House, Inc. at 1-800-733-3000. The author also wishes to thank the Jewish Theological Seminary of America for permission to reprint material from Leiberman's *Tosefta* (1988) and Jason Aronson Inc. for permission to reprint material from *The Strife of the Spirit* by Rabbi Adin Steinsaltz (1996).

This book was set in 10 pt. Leawood by FASTpages of Montebello, NY and printed and bound by Book-mart Press, Inc. of North Bergen, NJ.

Library of Congress Cataloging-in-Publication Data

Abrams, Judith Z.
    A beginner's guide to the Steinsaltz Talmud / by Judith Z. Abrams.
        p. cm.
   Includes bibliographical references and index.
    ISBN 978-0-7657-6047-0
    1. Talmud. Bava Metzia II—Outlines, syllabi, etc. 2. Steinsaltz,
Adin—Contributions in the study of the Talmud. I. Title.
BM506.B33A28 / 1999
296.1'25061—dc21   98-41125

Printed in the United States of America. Jason Aronson Inc. offers books and cassettes. For information and catalog write to Jason Aronson Inc., 230 Livingston Street, Northvale, NJ 07647-1726, or visit our website: http://www.aronson.com.

To my friends...
teachers and fellow travelers on the
road toward eternity.

Contents

Acknowledgments

"All beginnings are hard," say the sages (Mekhilta, Parshat Bachodesh 2). This is true even—perhaps I should say *especially*—when it comes to the study of Talmud. We know we ought to want to study, but the Talmud often feels foreign despite our knowing that it belongs to us. This book is designed to help ameliorate the first pangs of Talmud study by presenting Rabbi Steinsaltz's translation with explanations and insights from learners who began with no adult knowledge of Talmud and who became knowledgeable of the text. It is my heartfelt hope that this book will serve as a life preserver for those just learning to swim in the sea of the Talmud.

A book is never just the product of the author's efforts and this fact is particularly true in the case of this book. I would like to thank God for the opportunity to do this work. My great gratitude goes to Arthur Kurzweil for asking me to write this book. I also want to thank the students to whom I have taught this material, especially the Talmud classes at Congregation Emanu El, the Jewish Community Center, and the Federation, all in Houston, Texas; and PARR, the Pacific Association of Reform Rabbis. As usual, I have learned more from them than they have learned from me. Thanks also go to Marsha Schneider for her assistance in typing and for helping Maqom to grow and become more efficient. I'd like to thank Michael Rubinstein of Houston for his "because I'm your father, that's why." Finally, I thank my husband, Steven, and our children, Michael, Ruth, and Hannah, for their love and support.

I would like to especially thank the contributors whose insights you'll find on these pages. Here are the students you will meet:

Shirley Barish has been in the field of Jewish education for over thirty years. She has authored several books for teachers and writes a teachers' newsletter six times a year.

Ken Carr is the assistant rabbi of Congregation Beth Am, Los Altos Hills, California. He endeavors to integrate continuing study into his rabbinic life.

Mark Frydenberg is a software developer and educator. He is a member of the Progressive Chavurah of Boston and Temple Beth Israel of Waltham, Massachusetts, and is currently working on a Siddur project with members of chavurot across North America.

Naomi Mara Hyman is the editor of *Biblical Women in the Midrash: A Sourcebook* (Jason Aronson Inc., 1997) and a rabbinical student in the ALEPH Simcha program.

Robert E. Reichlin is a clinical psychologist specializing in problems of adulthood and aging. He is particularly interested in Talmud, Biblical Hebrew, and the integration of historical and traditional approaches to the study of Torah.

H.J. Stern is an attorney practicing primarily probate and family law in Houston, Texas. He has been studying Talmud for several years.

Stephanie Rosenthal Odle is on a spiritual journey toward a Primary Jewish Life by engaging in the study of Torah, immersion in prayer, and the performance of mitzvot.

Elizabeth Weinberg is a psychodynamically oriented psychiatrist living in Houston with her husband, a lawyer and musician, as well as two cats and an iguana. She has been studying Talmud for several years.

Except where Rabbi Steinsaltz's edition is cited, or unless otherwise noted, translations are the author's own. Side notes concerning sages, concepts, and language come from Rabbi Steinsaltz's other English language volumes of the Talmud or from his *Reference Guide*.

Introduction

Congratulations! You have in your hand what is likely to be one of your first tastes of Talmud. This is one small section of Rabbi Adin Steinsaltz's translation of the Talmud into English; a passage from Bava Metzia about the importance of feelings, about how to deal with conflict, and about business ethics. Along with pages from Rabbi Steinsaltz's translations, there are comments made by myself and others to help make your Talmud study easier and more enjoyable.

You are taking an important step and you should feel great about getting started. Before you begin the actual study of this passage, I'd like to give you some information and a few rules that will make Talmud easier to study.

What Is Talmud?

Let's quickly review the development of rabbinic literature to put the Babylonian Talmud in perspective. When the Temple was destroyed in 70 C.E., the Jewish people were devastated spiritually and emotionally. In addition, after the failure of the Bar Kokhba revolt in 135 C.E., the Jews of the Land of Israel were subjugated militarily and politically by the Roman conquerors. What does a people do when they are defeated spiritually, emotionally, physically, and politically?

They dream. Powerless to change the world in which they live, they imagine an orderly, meaningful world in which human relations, commerce, and politics run according to tidy paradigms. This is precisely what the sages did. The document they formulated to express this neat world vision is called the Mishnah. It is spare, rhythmic, cleanly organized, and idealistic; in a word, poetry. You could memorize it easily, just as you would memorize a poem. (Another analogy you might find helpful is this one: Mishnah is Martha Stewart's house; Gemara is your house.)

In fact, there is much to be said for memorizing the three mishnahs presented in this book. (When we refer to the Mishnah with a capital *M*, we mean all six volumes of the Mishnah, which covers the topics of agriculture, holidays, women, civil law, holy things, and pure things. When we refer to a mishnah with a lowercase *m*, we mean one small segment of this large work.) First of all, they are meaningful and important in and of themselves, beyond the Gemara's commentary on them. Second, one acquires spiritual merit and a sort of "insurance policy" by memorizing some of the Mishnah. Imagine how great it would be if, in a moment of anxiety, you could pull out of your memory bank a few *mishnayot* (the plural of mishnah) to recite. Not only would the content guide you but the practice of recitation would calm you. According to Jewish mysticism, the memorization and recitation of text offers protection in this world and merit in the world to come. One of the ways you might want to use this book is to memorize its three mishnahs (on Steinsaltz's pages 223, 241, and 247) and try reciting them at different times.

But Talmud is obviously more than just the Mishnah. There is commentary to the Mishnah called Gemara. Together, the Mishnah and Gemara equal the Talmud. The Gemara consists of several components. We will name them in turn and look at how they developed. The Mishnah was compiled around 200 C.E. as a collection of teachings by famous sages. However, many teachings were excluded from this collection. (Think of a greatest hits album purporting to represent the music of the 1980s, for example, which must leave out many excellent songs.) Some of the teachings that were left out of the Mishnah were soon collected into a larger compilation called Tosefta, which means "Additions," in 220 C.E. (This would be analogous to a four-volume set of 1980s music meant to supplement the first greatest hits album.) Still, there were many wonderful teachings left out of both collections. These teachings are often quoted in the Gemara and are called *baraitot* (singular: *baraita*). (This would be analogous to including the "uncollected" recordings in an authoritative history of the music of the 1980s.) In addition to these early teachings (they are called tannaitic because they were taught by *tannaim*, "repeaters," who would recite the traditions of different schools—something like living CD-ROMs) there were commentaries on the Mishnah composed after 200 C.E. by sages called *amoraim* (singular: *amora*) that form the earliest layers of the Gemara. The Gemara also includes stories of how the sages lived, folk sayings, and expositions of Biblical texts as well as secular knowledge of the day, such as business and medical practices.

There are two Talmuds: the Yerushalmi, composed in the Land of Israel by about 400 C.E., and the Bavli, composed in Babylonia by around 500 C.E. How do these two Talmuds differ from each other? (1) They comment on different parts of the Mishnah. (2) There is far more midrash in the Bavli than in the Yerushalmi (one-third and one-sixth of total content, respectively). In Israel, separate midrash collections were formed, some of which will be cited in this volume. In

Babylonia, these midrashim i.e., expositions of the Torah, were included in the Talmud itself. (3) The Bavli has a layer that the Yerushalmi does not have to the same extent: the layer of the *stammaim*. The Babylonian Talmud was composed over a period of some two hundred to five hundred years. The later layers of this composition are clearly distinguishable from the earlier layers. The first generations' comments on the Mishnah are short insights, often using named sources. For example, look at Rabbi Steinsaltz's page 231, line 5–7, for two examples of short teachings attributed to specific sages. A later layer of the Gemara is called stammaitic material. *Stamma* means anonymous; stammaitic material does not name its source, hence its name.

The *stamma* has a distinctive, recognizable quality that, once identified, practically proclaims itself to you every time you see it. It expresses a sort of "split the difference/reconcile all the views" perspective that is clearly distinctive. A classic example is the one found on page 231, lines 8–9. In lines 5–7 there is a legitimate difference of opinion between Rav and Rav Pappa: one counseling that a man shouldn't listen to his wife's advice and the other suggesting the opposite. We could very well have let these two opinions stand as legitimately different points of view. Instead, the stammaitic commentator jumps in and tries to resolve the differences between them in lines 8–9. Stammaitic material is in Aramaic, while earlier components of Talmud are often in Hebrew.

Now, why should you like the stammaitic layer of the Gemara? Because the *stamma* brings in information from other places in the Talmud, resolves problems in the texts that can be beneficially resolved, and gives the Babylonian Talmud its extraordinarily complete and beautiful nature. Some suggestions for dealing with the stammaitic material as you study are provided below.

How Might I Study Talmud?

Everyone has different study habits and you will develop your own personal style of learning. However, here are some guidelines for establishing an environment that will facilitate your study of Talmud.

1. Study with a group. Discussion is probably the best way to study Talmud. When people bounce their ideas off of each other, the energy starts flowing and everyone ends up more enlightened than if they had studied alone.

2. Study out loud. It helps enormously to read the passage under study out loud, often more than once. Talmud study takes patience.

3. Study on a table to make it easier to write in your book. Writing in the margins is your way of making the Talmud your own—so go ahead and mark up the text and fill in those blank margins with your own thoughts.

The Rules

Here are six basic rules that may make your Talmud study easier. They reflect scholarly insights into the Talmud as well as simple, common sense rules that could apply to any learning situation.

1. Talmud is a waltz. "One two three, one two three." That's how the Talmud is organized. The Talmud is not composed according to Western literary patterns, which leads some people to think it is disorganized or merely stream-of-consciousness writing. Nothing could be further from the truth. You'll see that the Babylonian Talmud is a carefully composed and closely edited document once you understand its rules of composition. The Talmud tends to have a pattern of three statements grouped together. The second statement in such a tripartite group is usually the one that the sages wish to highlight.

2. Think of the *stamma* as a footnote that found its way into the text. Stammaitic passages can be some of the least satisfying for a novice to study. You can think of such material in the following way. The *stamma* has the voice heard in footnotes today: It provides extra source material and resolves issues that interest only real devotees of a subject. You can usually adopt a "take it or leave it" attitude toward footnotes not struggling with them to the extent that you would if that same material were in the body of the text. Stammaitic passages may be thought of as footnotes that found their way into the main text. Do not struggle too hard with this material if you will become so discouraged that you stop studying. This concept leads to the next rule . . . .

3. You have permission to skip. You'll come back. Although there is almost nothing in these pages of Talmud that is so difficult that you will be tempted to skip it, there are some relatively difficult sections, e.g., the midrash about King David, pages 228–229, and the one about the plumbline, pages 232–233. These midrashim can be hard to understand and even once understood may not seem too meaningful if you are just beginning to learn Talmud. Get what you can out of this material and then move on. You can (and almost certainly will) come back to this passage and each time you do, after you've acquired more knowledge, it will have more significance to you.

This particular section of the Talmud is one of rabbinic literature's most important and famous passages. It teaches us how to deal with feelings and conflicts. It can help us enormously as we conduct our daily business and personal affairs. Many of the principles expounded in psychology and self-help books can already be found in this ancient passage: principles of consideration, honor, due process, honesty, and so forth. As you study the text repeatedly, it will have increasing meaning for you. Even if it never becomes very meaningful, that's alright. Talmud is enormous and not every single sentence in it will ring true for every individual. Just as one may not love every single thing one's spouse or best friend does, one need not love everything in Talmud for one's connection to it to remain viable.

One other matter is related to skipping parts of Talmud. Don't skip things because they're uncomfortable, only do so when they're too difficult to grasp. Why? Because there are some things in this passage that don't have pretty, symmetrical, "made for the movies" endings. These are, however, extremely important passages with which to grapple. Embrace the deep learning that comes from struggling with such material.

4. Apply it to your life. Talmud teaches its students to balance idealism and realism. In real life, values vie with each other for primacy, so "cookbook" ethics—"In situation *A* apply value *B* with outcome *C*"—don't work. The Talmud recognized that we hold many values dear and have to juggle them in any given situation, dropping as few as possible.

The best way to study Talmud is to *live* Talmud; that is, apply its principles to your own life through discussion and debate about the text. In such a process, you'll almost surely hear the mix of theoretical considerations, case histories, stories, and insights from the secular world that you find in the Talmud. When you engage in this sort of discussion, you're creating the newest layer of the Talmud. That's why there is a blank space on many pages of this book, so you can write down your insights and your analogies.

5. The self-esteem issue. I can almost hear you thinking, "Yeah, right! Who am I to write down insights? I don't have any background. I'm not that observant. How could what I think about Talmud be important?" Please stop thinking this way. You need an appropriate level of self-esteem to study Talmud. If you don't have enough, you'll stifle your voice unnecessarily. On the other hand, if it's too high, you'll fall into the classic Talmud trap: thinking that because you are smart or observant that you are somehow above the Talmud. Learning Talmud requires a balance of humility, bravery, wonder at the glory of the document in your hands, and a pride in ownership, knowing that the texts are yours to explore and enjoy.

6. The parallel text issue. The Babylonian Talmud is not the only example of rabbinic literature. Sometimes, there will be a parallel to our primary text in Bava Metzia from another work of rabbinic literature that can shed light on the material we are studying. Those texts will be presented here as, often, seeing a text in a different setting and/or different version can be enlightening. As always, if this is an approach that helps you, use it. If it does not aid you now, put it by for another time.

The Ingredients: What Goes Into a Passage of the Bavli

There are many ways to enjoy Talmud study. You can concentrate on the simple historical and anthropological insights the text gives you or on its spiritual or halakhic aspects. One of the most enjoyable ways for many people to study Talmud is to examine how it was put together. That is what this section is about.

The creators of rabbinic literature inherited a set of traditions and teachings. This was the basis for their creative activities. How they culled those original materials and shaped them is a great part of their art and tells us much about their perspective. Imagine it this way: If you went to a painting class where all the students were painting one model, you could tell a great deal about each student's artistry by comparing a photo of the model with their individual paintings. When we look at the earlier texts upon which the sages drew, we are engaging in a very similar process. Each of the works listed below is a work of art and meaning that represent Judaism from slightly different vantage points.

	Date Finished	Place Finished	Abbreviation
Mishnah	200 C.E.	The Land of Israel	M. + tractate name
Tosefta	220–230 C.E.	The Land of Israel	T. + tractate name
Yerushalmi	400 C.E.	The Land of Israel	Y. + tractate name
Midrash	c. 350 C.E.	The Land of Israel	full name used
Bavli	427–560 C.E.	Babylonia	B. + tractate name

The two midrash collections we will draw on here, Mekhilta de-Rabbi Ishmael and Sifra, are among the earliest composed. They were probably redacted in the second half of the third century. Midrashic interpretations of selected Torah verses form the basis for the Mishnah and Tosefta themselves. ("How can this be?" you ask. "I look up at the chart and see that the Mishnah and Tosefta were composed earlier than the midrash collections!" "Yes," I'd answer, "but the midrash collections contain material from earlier eras, like leaves that fall into a stream way up on a mountain but are only collected in the valley.")

NOTES

N O T E S

Mekhilta de-Rabbi Ishmael Nezikin 18 on Exodus 22:20–23

(See p. 249, line 8 to p. 251, line 8 in the English Steinsaltz Talmud)

מסכתא דנזיקין משפטים פרשה יז–יח

וגר לא תונה ולא תלחצנו כי גרים הייתם בארץ מצרים. לא תונגו, בדברים, ולא תלחצנו, בממון, שלא תאמר לו אמש היית עובד לבל קורס נבו, והרי חזירים בין שיניך, ואתה מדבר מילין כנגדי; ומנין שאם הוניתו שהוא יכול להונך, תלמוד לומר כי גרים הייתם, מכאן היה רבי נתן אומר. מום שבך אל תאמר לחבירך – חביבין הגרים שבכל מקום הוא מזהיר עליהם °וגר לא תלחץ. וגר לא תונה °ואהבתם את הגר, °ואתם ידעתם את נפש הגר. – רבי אליעזר אומר, גר לפי שסיאורו רע לפיכך מזהיר עליו הכתוב במקומות הרבה.

"And others say . . ."

Mekhilta de-Rabbi Ishmael Nezikin 18 on Exodus 22:20–23

The Torah, time and again, warns the Jewish people to be kind to strangers because the Jews were strangers. The word for stranger, *ger*, can also mean "convert to Judaism." Mekhilta, an early midrash on Exodus, provides several interpretations of one verse in the Torah that urges Jews not to oppress the *ger*.

"Neither oppress (*tonu*) nor pressure a stranger (*ger*) for you were strangers (*gerim*) in the land of Egypt." (Exodus 22:20)

You shall not oppress him with words, neither shall you put pressure on him in money matters. Do not say to him, "Yesterday, you worshipped Bel, Kores [and] Nevo and until now pork was stuck between your teeth, and now [who are] you [to] stand up and to speak to me [about righteous behavior]!"

And from whence [do you know] that if you oppress him that he would be able to oppress you? [From the verse in] which it is said, "Neither oppress (*tonu*) nor pressure a stranger (*ger*) for you were strangers (*gerim*) in the land of Egypt." (Exodus 22:20) And from [this very verse] Rabbi Natan used to say [teaching]: "Do not mention to your fellow a defect from which you [also suffer]."

Beloved are the *gerim* for everywhere Scripture cautions [us] about them: "Neither oppress (*tonu*) nor pressure a stranger (*ger*)." (Exodus 22:20) "Love you therefore the *ger* . . ." (Deuteronomy 10:19) "For you know the soul of a *ger* . . ." (Exodus 23:9) Rabbi Eliezer says: "[The] *ger* [is mentioned so many times in Scripture] because his original immoral condition [is still a factor] and therefore Scripture cautions [us] about him so much."

First, Mekhilta gives a straightforward explication of what appears to be a redundancy in the Torah text. Why does it say "Neither oppress nor pressure" instead of simply "Don't oppress"? Mekhilta assumes that it is because the verbs refer to different things: the former to oppression with words and the latter by means of money. Then, it gives an example of hurting with words: one ought not bring up something shameful in a person's past to discredit him today if he has repented.

Mekhilta then comments on the next part of the verse. Why is oppression of a *ger* linked to the Israelites having been strangers in Egypt? Mekhilta suggests that this verse is a reminder that every Jew is on an equal footing with a *ger*. If we are tempted to oppress a *ger*, we ought to remember that a *ger* could oppress us since we have also held that status at certain times.

Finally, Mekhilta wonders why we are warned in so many passages to be kind to the stranger. On the one hand, it could be because it is a simple matter of justice and hospitality to treat strangers in our midst with kindness. On the other hand, Rabbi Eliezer's argument is equally logical: the

Torah warns us against *gerim* because they pose a threat. It stands to reason that the more dangerous something is the more warnings we need about it. (How often have you heard the warning, "Never talk to strangers"?) Thus, Mekhilta offers straightforward explanations of obscurities in the text. These midrashic explanations underlie much of the Mishnah and Gemara we will study. (It's also ironic that Rabbi Eliezer, who does not hesitate to condemn the *ger*, will be condemned himself.)

NOTES

N O T E S

Sifra Behar Sinai 4:1–2

(See p. 223, line 2 to p. 225, line 7 in the English Steinsaltz Talmud)

תורת כהנים פרשת בהר סיני פרק ד

(א) ולא תונו איש את עמיתו זו אונאת דברים יכול זה אונאת ממון כשהוא אומר אל תונו איש את אחיו הרי אונאת ממון אמורה א] הא מה אני מקיים ולא תונו איש את עמיתו הרי אונאת דברים: (ב) כיצד אם היה בעל תשובה לא יאמר לו זכור מעשיך הראשונים מה היו ואם היה בן גרים לא יאמר לו זכור מה היו מעשה אבותיך ב](כיצד) היו חליים באים עליו יסורים באים עליו היה קובר את בניו לא יאמר לו כדרך שאמרו חביריו לאיוב הלא יראתך כסלתך תקותך ותום דרכיך זכור נא מי הוא נקי אבד ואיפוא ישרים נכחדו. ראה חמרים מבקשים תבואה מבקשים יין לא יאמר להם לכו אצל פלוני והוא לא מכר חיטה מימיו ר׳ יהודה אומר אף לא יתלה עיניו על המקח ולא יאמר לו בכמה חפץ זה והוא אינו רוצה ליקח. וא״ת ג] עיצה טובה אני מוסר לו הרי הדבר מסור ללב נאמר בו ויראת מאלהיך

מאלהיך כל דבר שהוא מסור ללב נאמר בו ויראת:

"And others say . . ."

Sifra Behar Sinai 4:1–2

The midrash collection Sifra covers the book of Leviticus. We will look at its expositions of the following Torah verses:

And when you sell anything to your neighbor, or buy anything from your neighbor's hand, *let a man not oppress* (tonu) *his neighbor*: According to the number of years after the Jubilee [year] shall you buy [property at a certain price] from your neighbor; according to the number of crop years [remaining between now and the next Jubilee year] shall he sell [property] to you. The greater the number of years, the greater [the property's] price and the fewer the number of years, the lower [the property's] price will be, for it is the number of crop years he sells to you. *[So] let not a man oppress* (tonu) *his neighbor and you shall fear your God for I am the Lord your God*. (Leviticus 25:14–17)

The issue under discussion in the Torah is selling land and how the Jubilee year, during which land returns to its original tribal owner, affects such transactions. According to this system, one really only sells a lease and its value is related to how many years the lease will last until the next Jubilee year occurs. The words in italics, above, form a sort of frame for the law. Anytime we have this sort of framing it means (1) that the message within the frame is extremely important and (2) that the words in the frame themselves are wide open for later interpretation by the sages. The

midrash takes these verses to apply to hurting both with words and with money in a way quite similar to Mekhilta's.

"And men should not wrong one another." (Leviticus 25:17) This refers to *ona'ah* with words. [You might think] it's possible that [it refers to] *ona'ah* with money. [However,] when it [Scripture] says, "A man should not wrong his brother," (Leviticus 25:14) it [already] refers to *ona'ah* with money. So how do I establish [that the verse] "A man should not oppress his neighbor" (Leviticus 25:17) [applies to] *ona'ah* with words [since Leviticus 25:14 is already taken to refer to *ona'ah* with money]?

How [does one oppress with words]? If [a person] was a repentant sinner, one should not say to him, "Remember your earlier deeds which you did." And if he was the child of converts, do not say to him, "Remember the deeds of your ancestors." How [does one oppress with words]? If illnesses came upon him [or] trials came upon him [or] he buried his children, do not say to him, in the way that Job's friends said to him, "Is not your fear of God your confidence and your hope the integrity of your ways? Remember, please, who that was innocent ever perished or where were the upright cut off?" (Job 4:6–7)

[If] he saw ass-drivers seeking produce or seeking wine, he should not say to them, "Go to So-and-so," and [So-and-so] never sold wheat. R. Yehudah says,

"He shouldn't even cast his eyes on a product nor say to him [the merchant] 'How much does this cost?' if he does not wish to buy [it]. And if you will say, 'Good advice do I give to him!' behold the matter is given to the heart, as it is said in [Scripture], 'You shall fear your God.' (Leviticus 25:17) And everything that is given over to the heart, it is said of it, 'You shall fear.'"

Sifra first gives a straightforward explanation of the repeated admonition not to oppress people, similar to Mekhilta's: One may oppress with neither words nor money. Then is asks how, specifically, one might oppress with words. One does so by taunting repentant persons or the children of converts to Judaism about their own or their parents' deeds or by attributing their suffering to sin or by "buck passing" with a customer. It would seem that both the Sifra and Mekhilta are making a conscious effort to link monetary and verbal wrongdoing. After all, they could have made these "superfluous" words in the Torah refer to different sorts of monetary transactions, but that's not what they did. Instead, they emphasized the importance of feelings and words.

The answers to the question, "How does one oppress with words?" all have one thing in common: they all have to do with remembering inappropriately. Holding on too strongly to the past is the strongest way to oppress someone. You aren't allowed to carry old baggage around with you forever. There are some things, Sifra says, of which you must release possession. What, specifically, is oppressive remembering? Remembering a person's past sins; remembering a convert's former religion; and remembering, however kindly, in a conventional but untrue way are oppressive remembrances. Job's "friends" come to comfort him after his children have died and he's been stricken with illness. They urge Job to remember the misdeeds he must surely have done to bring such suffering on himself. They want him to subscribe to conventional thinking and remembering when those techniques won't work in his situation.

Verbal ona'ah can be prospective as well as retrospective. We can oppress someone with words that raise their hopes unrealistically. One may either raise a buyer's expectations of finding produce they hope to buy or cause a merchant to hope that they will be able to sell their merchandise. Raising such false hopes is prohibited in both directions, as it were. These two broad categories—inappropriate remembering and raising false hopes—cover the time continuum. We may not oppress with words that recall the past or shape the future with emotional pain.

The exposition is wrapped up by an answer to the inevitable objection, "Well, how can you tell whether you want to buy an item before you've asked its price?" Only the one asking the price knows whether there was an intention to buy. This, Sifra suggests, is why the Torah "frame" from Leviticus ends with the words, "and you shall fear God." Only God could judge such a matter and thus one has only God to fear in this case.

Sifra, like Mekhilta, links verbal and monetary ona'ah. Sifra mentions taunting converts with their past as a form of verbal ona'ah. Unlike Mekhilta, however, Sifra ends with an exposition that points to the importance of motivations that only God may discern. This last theme, along with the previous ones, will be examined by the Bavli at length.

N O T E S

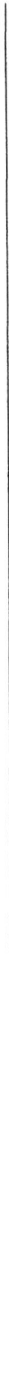

Tosefta Bava Metzia 3:25–29

(See p. 224, line 1 to p. 246, lines 2–3, and p. 249, lines 8–9 in the English Steinsaltz Talmud)

בבא מציעא פ״ג

כשם שאונאה במקח וממכר, כך אונאה בדברים. ועוד מרובה אונאת דברים מאונאת ממון, שבאונאת אחיו הוא אומ׳ ולא תונו איש את אחיו, ובאונאת דברים הוא או׳ לא תונו איש את עמיתו ויראת מאליך, ויראת ממי שפיקד על אילו. היו חמרין מבקשין יין, ושמן, לא יאמר להן לכו אצל פלני, והוא לא מכר יין ושמן מעולם, היו חלאין באין עליו, וייסורין באין עליו, וקובר את בניו, לא יאמר לו כדרך שאמרו חביריו לאיוב הלא יראתך כסלתך זכר אתה אין כת׳ כאן, אלא זכר נא וגו׳. ר׳ יהודה או׳ אף לא יתלה את עיניו ויאמר לו בכמה חפץ זה, והוא אין רוצה ליקח. ראה גר שבא ללמוד תורה, לא יאמר לו ראו מי שבא ללמוד תורה, שאכל טריפות ונבלות שקצים ורמשים, וכן הוא או׳ ויען איש משם ויאמר ומי אביהם, וכי יש אב לתורה, והלא כבר נאמ׳ מה שמו ומה שם בנו כי תדע, ואו׳ בית והון נחלת אבות ומה׳ אשה משכלת. 26. אין מערבין פירות בפירות, ואפי׳ חדשים בחדשים וישנים בישנים, ואין צריך לומ׳ חדשים בישנים וישנים בחדשים. אפי׳ סאה בדינר וסאה בדינר וטריסית, לא יערבם וימכרם סאה בדינר. אין מערבין יין חדש בחדש וישן בישן, ואין צריך לומ׳ חדש בישן וישן בחדש. ולא קשה ברך, ור׳ יהודה מתיר קשה ברך, מפני שהוא משביחו. וכן היה ר׳ יהודה או׳ מין אחד המשביח את חבירו, מותר. שני מינין המשביחין את אחד אסור. 27. אין מערבין שמרי יין ביין, אבל נותנין לו שמריו. כיצד, היה שופה יין לחמרין נותן לו שמרי אותו יין, אבל לא שמרי יין אחר. אף כשאמרו נותן לו שמריו, נותן לו של היום היום, ושל מחר למחר, אבל לא של היום למחר, ושל מחר להבא. לא יערבם חנוני וימכרם בחנותו, אלא אם הודיע. לא ירביץ חנוני לתוך חנותו יין ושמן, מפני שגונב דעת הבריות. מקום שנהגו להטיל מים למחצה, לשליש, ולרביע, יטילו, ואין משנין ממנהג המדינה. 28. חומטון בתבואה, קב בכור, ואינו חושש. ובעלי בתים מטילין כל צרכן. חנוני צורר ומניח על פי המגורה. 29. אין מסרטין את הבהמה, ואין נופחין בקרבים, ואין מטילין בשר לתוך המים.

"And others say . . ."

Tosefta Bava Metzia 3:25–29

Tosefta, a supplement to the Mishnah, was composed only twenty years after the Mishnah was finished. In this passage from Tosefta, you can see how texts from Mekhilta and Sifra are used and, when you read the Bavli, you'll see how this Tosefta passage forms the basis of the Gemara there.

Just as there [may be] *ona'ah* when buying and selling, so there [may be] *ona'ah* when [using] words. And more, *ona'ah* when [using] words is worse than *ona'ah* by means of money, for about [monetarily] oppressing his brother [Scripture] says, "Let not a man oppress his brother." (Leviticus 25:14) And about oppression by words [Scripture] says, "Let not a man oppress his neighbor and you shall fear your God." (Leviticus 25:17) "And you shall fear" the [One] who remembers [and metes out judgment] on these [offenses].

[If] ass-drivers seek wine and oil [at your place of business], do not say to them, "Go visit What's His Name," [when] he [What's His Name] has never sold wine or oil.

[If] illness were to come upon him and sufferings were to come upon him, and he buried his children, do not say to him, in the way that Job's friends said to him, "Is not your fear [of God] your confidence? [Is not your hope the perfection of your ways? Remember, now, who clean (i.e., virtuous) perished and where

are the upright who were destroyed?]" (Job 4:6–7) It is not written here [in Job 4:7, simply] "Remember you" rather, "Remember *now* [who clean (i.e., virtuous) perished.]"

R. Yehudah says, "[And] also, let him not raise his eyes and say to him [a seller], 'How much does this cost?' when he has no wish to buy."

[If] he saw a *ger* that came to study Torah, he should not say to him, "Look who came to study Torah [the one] that ate animals torn by a beast, animals that died a natural death, unclean animals and creeping things," and thus [Scripture] says, "And a man from there answered and said 'And who is their father?'" (I Samuel 10:12) For is there a father [necessary to determine lineage] for [the one who learns] Torah? For has it not already been said, "What is His [God's] name and what is his son's name, if you know?" (Proverbs 30:4) And it says, "A house and riches are the inheritance of fathers but a wise wife [Torah] is from God." (Proverbs 19:14)

One should not mix fruits and even new fruits with new fruits and old ones with old ones, and it goes without saying [mixing] new [fruits] with old or old with new. Even a *seah* [of wheat that sells] for a *dinar* and a *seah* that [sells for] a *dinar* and a *trisis*, one shouldn't mix them and sell them for a *dinar* per *seah*. (// Sifre Deuteronomy, Piska 295)

One should not mix wine; [not] new

wine with new nor old with old and it goes without saying, [mixing] new [wine] with old and old with new. And one does not [mix] strong [wine] with weak [wine]. But R. Yehudah permits strong [wine to be mixed] with weak [wine] because this improves it. And thus would R. Yehudah say, "One kind [of produce] that improves another, one is permitted [to mix them]. [But the mixing in of] two kinds [of produce] that improve one [kind is] forbidden."

One should not mix the lees of wine into [another cask of] wine but one may sell [wine with] its own lees. How [would one ideally observe this concept]? He would pour the wine out slowly for ass-drivers [traveling in a caravan and stopping at an inn; people who are unlikely to be frequent customers. He thereby gives them only the wine with very few of their lees]. He [may] give the lees of that very wine [with the wine itself] but not [with] the lees of some other wine. But if they said, "Give [us the wine with] its lees," he gives today's [lees] with today's [wine] and tomorrow's [lees] with tomorrow's [wine] but he doesn't give today's with tomorrow's or tomorrow's with the next day's.

A shopkeeper should not mix them and sell them in his shop unless he makes it known [that he has mixed them]. A shopkeeper may not sprinkle wine and oil in his store because he deceives people [thereby]. [In] a place where they usually mix water [with wine] by half, [or] by a third [or] by a quarter, they may [so] mix [wine and water] and they should not differ from the custom of the district [in regard to the proportions of wine and water].

[Regarding] salty earth in produce, one *kav* per *kor* is nothing to worry about [and is not considered a violation of the prohibition against mixing kinds of produce]. And housekeepers put in as much as they need. A storekeeper binds it and leaves it by the opening of the [wheat] bin.

One does not stiffen a beast['s hair] and one does not inflate their intestines and one does not put meat in water [to cause these items to appear better and/or larger than they truly are].

In general, this passage reflects the midrashim we have already studied, and extends the guiding principles of the Torah into far more—and more specific—cases. Tosefta's first four paragraphs seem to be only slightly rearranged versions of the expositions we found in Sifra.

The material on Torah and lineage is important in light of the main passage in Bava Metzia we will study. In the sages' days, lineage was quite important. One could only be a Cohen or Levite by being born with the right blood. The sages were thus at a disadvantage in that their elite had no distinction in blood. The sages solved this problem by fostering the idea that learning was a form of fertility (B. Bava Metzia 32a, volume II, p. 179, line 6 through p. 181, line 4), which trumped blood in determining membership in the Jewish people's elite (see the commentary to Rabbi Steinsaltz's pages 240–241).

One's parents and children may not be great Torah scholars yet one may become a great Torah scholar oneself. The symbolism of the prooftexts here is that one needs no lineage to study Torah. Torah, indeed, is depicted both as the sages' "wife"—the vehicle of their fertility—as well as their own mother. By teaching others, the sages made their students their spiritual progeny, and the relationships among such "parents" and "children" were as intense as any between blood relatives. Adding this dimension to our understanding of the sages' relationships with each other also sheds new light on the fierceness with which they supported their viewpoints. Theirs were not just intellectual or legal debates. No, each teaching, not just each student, is a sage's progeny, his stake in immortality and continuity.

Tosefta then goes on to explore the extent to which one must be scrupulous in trade. A *seah* is about 2 gallons; a *dinar* is a large coin (for the sake of argument let us say it is worth $100) and a *trisis* is a small one (we'll postulate that it is worth $1). It would be as if one had small lemons that sold at ten for a dollar and larger lemons that sold at ten for one hundred dollars. One is not even allowed to mix the large lemons with the small lemons and sell them at ten for a dollar. There is a minority opinion noted here. According to Rabbi Yehudah, one may mix two kinds of produce together but two items added to one item is prohibited. Why? Because the consumer may want one of the added items but not the other. In our example, let us say one mixed large lemons, small lemons, and limes from the Florida Keys, which are much smaller than ordinary lemons and limes— about one inch in diameter. Rabbi Yehudah allows either the large lemons or the limes to be added to the small lemons but not both, since the consumer may not want both kinds. One may be making lemonade and want only lemons; or one may be making Key Lime Pie, in which case small lemons would go best together with the limes. Rabbi Yehudah wants to place the power to make this decision in the hands of the consumer.

The issue of fairness is well illustrated by the wine examples. Grapes were an economically important crop and were used symbolically by the sages. Wine has within it a component called "lees." This is the concentrated, solid wine "sludge" found in bottled wine. Indeed, today when fine wine is being decanted it is poured out slowly over a candle's flame so the one pouring can pinpoint the moment when these lees are entering the decanter and stop before that happens. Today, when we order wine by the prepackaged bottle, we buy the wine and its lees and discard the lees. But what if we were ordering wine in a tavern some 2,000 years ago, when wine was stored in great casks and ladled out for consumers? Would it not be fair that we should have to buy some of the lees as an expected byproduct of the wine? Would it be fair if the tavern keeper skimmed clearer wine off the top for friends and scooped larger portions of lees off the bottom for strangers? We would all agree that anyone buying from a given cask of wine has to accept that it comes with the lees that settle out of the drink. Likewise, we would probably all agree that consumers need only buy lees from the wine they are purchasing. In other words, it's unethical for the wine merchant to take yesterday's lees and pour them into today's cask of wine. If the merchant didn't succeed in selling off those lees then they should be put to some other use, but not sold to consumers.

Tosefta mentions the "candling" approach to wine. The ass-driver is mentioned as the archetypal customer with the least amount of influence over the vendor. People traveling then were more vulnerable to subtle disadvantages. In ancient days, before credit cards, picture ID cards, checks, and airplanes, this was probably even more true than it is today. People had to carry cash with them and might be taken advantage of at any moment. The ass-driver stops at a tavern and orders some wine. Nobody's seen him before nor are they likely to see him after this. There is every temptation in the vendor's heart to give the ass-driver wine with its own lees and yesterday's lees and almost no commercial motivation to give him carefully poured out wine with a minimum of its own lees.

However, even a native could be duped. To prevent false advertising, Tosefta forbids merchants to sprinkle wine and oil throughout their shops. This would give potential customers the impression that the merchant is measuring out oil and wine liberally and thus must be selling it cheaply. This practice is only designed to mislead the consumer and so is forbidden.

Tosefta rules that even a practice designed to help consumers must be regulated with great strictness. The salty dust mentioned in Tosefta preserves the produce from worms. A *kav* is 2.5 pints (1.4 metric liters) and a *kor* is 7 bushels (246.2 metric liters) so the preservative is quite a small proportion in relation to the produce. In order to be sure that his wheat will be preserved, the merchant may wrap the dust and leave it at the mouth of the bin so that it shouldn't be mixed into the wheat. This preserves the produce but ensures that the weight paid for this product will not include the weight of the preservative. The cost of the preservative is overhead, which must be paid for by the merchant. Today, it might be likened to the cost incurred by grocers who put out plastic bags with which people collect their produce. The cost of these bags is one of the prices of doing business.

Livestock, like crops, must be presented in honesty to the consumer. One may not fluff up an animal's hair or stuff it full of feed so that it looks larger, nor may one soak meat in water to make it appear larger because of the liquid it has absorbed. These are deceptive practices that increase the distance between perceived value and received value; the very distance that causes hurt feelings when discovered.

The sum of Tosefta's arguments results in an ideal of extraordinary honesty and protection for the consumer. We are to oppress others neither by words nor by money, neither by hurtful remembering nor by irresponsible commercial practices that effect the future. We must present our salable goods with scrupulous honesty, neither with the intent to cheat the consumer nor even with the intent to profit the consumer. The rights of both the merchant and the consumer are guarded by Tosefta's rulings.

NOTES

N O T E S

Mishnah Eiduyot 7:5–7

(See p. 234, line 5 to p. 235, line 1 in the English Steinsaltz Talmud)

ה הֵעִיד רַבִּי יְהוֹשֻׁעַ וְרַבִּי יָקִים אִישׁ הֲדַר עַל קָלָל שֶׁלְּחַטָּאת שֶׁנְּתָנוֹ עַל גַּבֵּי הַשֶּׁרֶץ, שֶׁהוּא טָמֵא; שֶׁרַבִּי אֱלִיעֶזֶר מְטַהֵר.
הֵעִיד רַבִּי פַּפְּיַס עַל מִי שֶׁנָּדַר שְׁתֵּי נְזִירִיּוֹת, שֶׁאִם גִּלַּח אֶת הָרִאשׁוֹנָה יוֹם שְׁלֹשִׁים – שֶׁמְּגַלֵּחַ אֶת הַשְּׁנִיָּה יוֹם שִׁשִּׁים; וְאִם גִּלַּח יוֹם שִׁשִּׁים חָסֵר אֶחָד – יָצָא, שֶׁיּוֹם שְׁלֹשִׁים עוֹלֶה לוֹ מִן הַמִּנְיָן.
הֵעִיד רַבִּי יְהוֹשֻׁעַ וְרַבִּי פַּפְּיַס עַל וְלַד שֶׁלִּשְׁלָמִים, שֶׁיִּקְרַב שְׁלָמִים; שֶׁרַבִּי אֱלִיעֶזֶר אוֹמֵר: שֶׁוְּלַד שְׁלָמִים לֹא יִקְרַב שְׁלָמִים. וַחֲכָמִים אוֹמְרִים: יִקְרַב. אָמַר רַבִּי פַּפְּיַס: אֲנִי מֵעִיד, שֶׁהָיְתָה לָנוּ פָּרָה זִבְחֵי שְׁלָמִים, וַאֲכַלְנוּהָ בַּפֶּסַח, וְאָכַלְנוּ וַלְדָּהּ שְׁלָמִים בֶּחָג.
הֵם הֵעִידוּ עַל אֲרוּכוֹת שֶׁלַּנַּחְתּוֹמִים שֶׁהֵן טְמֵאוֹת; שֶׁרַבִּי אֱלִיעֶזֶר מְטַהֵר. הֵם הֵעִידוּ עַל תַּנּוּר שֶׁחִתְּכוֹ חֻלְיוֹת וְנָתַן חוֹל בֵּין חֻלְיָא לְחֻלְיָא, שֶׁהוּא טָמֵא; שֶׁרַבִּי אֱלִיעֶזֶר מְטַהֵר.

"And others say . . ."

Mishnah Eiduyot 7:5–7

One of the most dramatic parts of the passage we will study in Rabbi Steinsaltz's translation of Bava Metzia is the story about Rabbi Eliezer and his fight with the other sages. There are different versions of this story. One early form that provides some essential background comes from the Mishnah tractate Eiduyot. This tractate differs from almost all others in that it is arranged not according to subject but according to the authorities who issued the individual rulings. Thus Eiduyot ("Opinions") is a book that expresses the importance of personality as well as of halakhah (Jewish law). It is fitting that some of the many disputes between Rabbi Eliezer and Rabbi Yehoshua are included in this tractate of the Mishnah.

Rabbi Yehoshua and Rabbi Yakim of Hadar testified about the pitcher [containing the ashes] of the [red heifer] sin offering that if it were set on top of an [unclean] reptile that it is ritually impure whereas Rabbi Eliezer declares it ritually pure . . . .(M. Parah 10:3)

Rabbi Yehoshua and Rabbi Pafyas testified about the fetus of a peace offering that it is also offered as a peace offering and Rabbi Eliezer says that the fetus of a peace offering is not offered as a peace offering. And the sages say it is offered . . . . (M. Temurot 3:1)

They [Rabbi Yehoshua and Rabbi Pafyas] testified about the long boards of bakers—that Rabbi Eliezer declared unsusceptible to ritual impurity—that they are susceptible to ritual impurity . . . .(M. Kelim 15:2)

They testified that if an oven was cut into segments and sand was placed between the segments—that Rabbi Eliezer declared unsusceptible to ritual impurity—that it is susceptible to ritual impurity. (M. Kelim 5:10)

Before we examine the somewhat complicated details of the cases mentioned here, we can first look at the general dynamics between the sages in dispute. Rabbi Eliezer, in each of these four cases, rules to limit the effects of ritual impurity and the claims of the priesthood over a specific category of livestock. Rabbi Yehoshua, along with two far less well known colleagues, rules extending the effects of ritual impurity more broadly as well as finding the future beholden to the Temple as well as the present. In each instance, Rabbi Eliezer rules one way and is overruled by two sages. Notice, too, that Rabbi Yehoshua is the most consistent contender with Rabbi Eliezer. If these are only a sampling of the times that Rabbi Eliezer disagreed with other sages in his rulings, then the dramatic nature of the final confrontation between Rabbi Eliezer and the sages in the Bavli makes more sense. That isn't the first time such a disagreement had happened. Apparently, this sort of thing has gone on consistently. No wonder a fight erupts about something that seems as innocuous as whether an oven is pure or not!

The first rulings here involve the ashes of the red heifer, which are used to purify a person.

Numbers 19:9 says that the ashes must be kept in a pure place. The pitcher itself is made of stone and does not receive ritual impurity (M. Kelim 10:1). However, it should be kept in a pure place, according to the Torah, and standing on an impure reptile is surely an impure place. Such a position would make the ashes themselves, which are in the pitcher, impure. But Rabbi Eliezer says that since the ashes are in the pitcher, which is not susceptible to ritual impurity (M. Kelim 2:1), then the ashes are in a pure place.

The second ruling concerns peace offerings. These were cattle or sheep that were brought on Festivals and voluntarily on special, personal occasions. (For a modern situation, imagine that you held a wedding in Texas and bought an entire cow to barbecue for the occasion. After you buy the cow for this purpose, you discover that she is pregnant. Do you own the fetus? Are you bound to serve it at your wedding feast? Or does it belong to the rancher? Or may you raise the calf as your own?) Such offerings were to be brought promptly (Deuteronomy 12:5–6 and 23:22) and Rabbi Eliezer worried that, if the fetus were declared eligible for sacrifice, people might delay making their peace offering at the appropriate time. Therefore, he rules that the fetus is not part of the peace offering. However, he is overruled by Rabbi Yehoshua, who rules that one offers the peace offering and later makes an offering of its young which, being inside the mother when it was promised to the altar, was part of the promise.

The third case involves bakers' boards on which dough was rolled out, rose, and shaped into loaves. Rabbi Yehoshua and Rabbi Pafyas declare it impure, i.e., a complete cultural item that can accept ritual impurity even though it might appear to be just a board. Rabbi Eliezer holds that such an item is not susceptible to ritual impurity. Similarly, Rabbi

Eliezer believes that an oven that has been broken up and reassembled is not susceptible to ritual impurity while Rabbi Yehoshua believes that it is.

All four of these disagreements, brought together from other places in the Mishnah, have to do with fire: the ashes are its product, the animal will be consumed by it, the board is made of fire's kindling (wood), and the oven is fire's locus in the home. Fire civilizes, turning raw food into cooked and dough into bread. Fire purifies, turning blood into sacrifice. Fire transforms, turning wood into heat and light. Fire also destroys. Fire and light are metaphors for Torah. With this meaning, it is clear that Rabbi Yehoshua wants to validate the interconnectedness of entities in the world while Rabbi Eliezer would limit the same by ruling against the ability of items to accept ritual impurity.

There may also be an economic dynamic at work in these differences of opinion. Rabbi Eliezer, who was quite wealthy, saw only whole, unbroken, specially made items as capable of accepting ritual impurity, i.e., being real in a cultural and functional way. Rabbi Yehoshua, who was quite poor, saw far more things as whole and would have been likely to cobble broken items, or pieces of different items, together and use them in ways perhaps unintended by their original makers.

Thus, in Eiduyot a picture is delineated of two ends of the sages' spectrum just after the Temple was destroyed. Fire, blood, and ashes are apt symbols for the destruction of the Temple and two paradigms for dealing with its aftermath: interconnectedness and improvisation (Rabbi Yehoshua) and conservatism and constriction (Rabbi Eliezer). Both hands, in Bava Metzia, are played out in full and the logical consequences are extended to their farthest reach.

N O T E S

Bavli Berachot 19a

(See p. 234, line 5 to p. 238, line 9 in the English Steinsaltz Talmud)

מי שמתו פרק שלישי ברכות יט ע״א

ט חֲתָכוֹ חוּלְיוֹת וְנָתַן חוֹל בֵּין חוּלְיָא לְחוּלְיָא, רַבִּי אֱלִיעֶזֶר מְטַהֵר, וַחֲכָמִים מְטַמְּאִים, וְזֶהוּ תַּנּוּרוֹ שֶׁל עַכְנַאי; מַאי עַכְנַאי? אָמַר רַב יְהוּדָה אָמַר שְׁמוּאֵל: מְלַמֵּד, שֶׁהִקִּיפוּהוּ הֲלָכוֹת כְּעַכְנַאי זֶה וְטִמְּאוּהוּ; וְתַנְיָא: י אוֹתוֹ הַיּוֹם הֵבִיאוּ כָּל טָהֳרוֹת שֶׁטִּיהֵר רַבִּי אֱלִיעֶזֶר וּשְׂרָפוּם לְפָנָיו, וּלְבַסּוֹף בֵּרְכוּהוּ!

"And others say . . ."

Bavli Berachot 19a

In the Bavli we find a different retelling of the main story in its core form. A version of Rabbi Eliezer's story is included in a discussion of the excommunication of sages:

"If he cuts it [the oven into which an impure animal fell] into segments and puts sand between the segments, Rabbi Eliezer [says] it is not susceptible to ritual impurity but the sages [say] it is susceptible to ritual impurity. And this [such an oven] is [called] the oven of Akhnai. Why Akhnai? Rav Yehudah said [in the name of] Shmuel: [This name] teaches [us] that they surrounded [this issue and Rabbi Eliezer's decision on it] with legal teachings as a serpent [surrounds its prey and squeezes it to death] and [were able to legislate that] it is susceptible to ritual impurity. And it has been taught: On that day they brought all the things that Rabbi Eliezer had declared not susceptible to ritual impurity and burnt them before him and in the end they "blessed" him [a euphemism meaning they excommunicated him].

Here, we have a more dramatic version of the personal dynamics between the sages than the one hinted at in M. Eiduyot. In this retelling, the sages burn everything that Rabbi Eliezer has declared clean and excommunicate him as well. These ideas were missing from the version in M. Eiduyot.

The context for the story's retelling in this tractate of the Talmud is significant. It is part of a long passage on excommunication and forgetfulness (the worst enemy of knowledge in an orally transmitted system) brought as commentaries to M. Berachot 3:1. This mishnah explores the relationship between duties related to burial and the obligation to recite the Shema and perform other mitzvot. When one's dead lie unburied, one is exempt from the obligation to recite the Shema, wear tefillin, or say the Amidah (Judaism's central prayer).

Rabbi Eliezer, because of his excommunication, occupies a very odd role. It is as if a corpse continued to walk and speak. He has been excommunicated and should no longer be seen or heard from but neatly disappear from the sages' society. However, his spiritual power is so vast and his teachings so potent that he refuses to die (so to speak). In this way, he is something like a corpse that continually disrupts the sages' prayer and study. This is particularly so since the sages are the ones who pronounced Rabbi Eliezer's sentence, in effect attempting to kill him socially, intellectually, and spiritually. By placing this story in its commentary to this mishnah, the Gemara gives us a message, emphasizing the power of the sages to excommunicate those who defy them. In this version of the story, Rabbi Eliezer is quite passive (corpse-like, we might say). He accedes to his excommunication submissively and has almost no role in the story at all. In other versions of this story, Rabbi Eliezer plays a far more active role.

Yerushalmi Moed Katan 3:1, 81c–d

(See p. 234, line 5 to p. 238, line 8 in the English Steinsaltz Talmud)

פני משה ואלו מגלחין פרק שלישי מועד קטן

מנדין ועל כמה דברים מנדין. *ביקשו לנדות את רבי ליעזר אמר אמרין מאן אזל מודע ליה אמר רבי עקיבה אנא אזל מודע ליה. אתא לגביה א״ל רבי ר׳ חביריך מנדין לך. נסתיה נפק ליה לברא אמר חרוביתא חרוביתא אין הלכה כדבריהם איתעוקרין ולא איתעקר׳. אין הלכה כדבריי איתעוקרין ואיתעקרת אין הלכה כדבריהם הוזרין ולא חזרת. אין הלכה כדבריי חוזרין וחזרת. כל הדין שבחא ולית הלכה כר׳ אליעזר. א״ר חנינה משניתנה לא ניתנה אלא אחרי רבים להטות. *ולית ר׳ אליעזר ידע שאחרי רבים להטות לא הקפיד אלא על ידי ששרפו טהרותיו בפניו. *תמן תנינן היתכו חוליות ונתן חול בין חולייא לחולייא רבי ליעזר מטהר וחכמים מטמאין זה תנורו של חכיניי. אמר רבי ירמיה חכך גדול נעשה באותו היום כל מקום שהיתה עינו של רבי ליעזר מבטת היה נשדף ולא עוד אלא אפילו היטה אחת חצייה נשדף וחצייה לא נשדף והיו עמודי בית הוועד מרופפין. אמר להן ר׳ יהושע אם חברים מתלחמים אתם מה איפכת לכם ויצאה בת קול ואמרה הלכה כאליעזר בני. א״ר יהושע לא בשמים היא. ר׳ קריספי ר׳ יוחנן בשם ר׳ אם יאמר לי אדם כך שנה ר׳ ליעזר שונה אני כדבריו אלא דתניא מהלפין. חד זמן הוה עבר בשוקא וחמת הדא איתא סחותא דביתא וטלקת ונפלת נו רישיה אמר דומה שהיום חביריי מקרבין אותי דכתיב °מאשפות ירים אביון.

"And others say . . ."

Yerushalmi Moed Katan 3:1, 81c–d

One of the foremost principles of literary organization in rabbinic literature (and Jewish Scriptures as well) is parallelism. A story can be shaped like a pyramid. Each layer is homogeneous (i.e., reflects parallelism) and all layers focus attention on the center peak. The point of the story is made not at the end, as in English literature, but in the middle. The version of the story about Rabbi Eliezer's excommunication in the Yerushalmi is no exception. To make identifying these parallel portions easier, the story is marked here to show how it builds and is resolved through this "parallelism pyramid" structure.

A. EXCOMMUNICATION BEGINS: [The sages] wanted to put Rabbi Eliezer in *niddui* [a form of excommunication]. They said, "Who will go and let him know [that he is in *niddui*]?" Said Rabbi Akiba, "I will go and let him know." He [Rabbi Akiba] went to him [Rabbi Eliezer] and said to him, "My teacher, my teacher, your colleagues (*chaveirecha*) are putting you in *niddui*."

B. DRAMATIC DEMONSTRATION: [Rabbi Eliezer resolved to test the correctness of the sages' decision] and took [Rabbi Akiba] outside [and] said, "Carob tree, carob tree, if the law is according to their words, be uprooted!" And it was not uprooted. "If the law is according to my words, be uprooted." And it was uprooted. "If the law is according to their words, return." It did not return. "If the law is according to my words, return." It returned. All this praise [sung by the very trees; i.e., all these signs] and the law is [still] not according to Rabbi Eliezer?!

B1. IS RABBI ELIEZER'S WORD LAW? Said R. Hanina, "Since it [the Torah] was given, it was not given except to incline [i.e., follow] a majority [opinion]." (Exodus 23:2) [But is it possible that] Rabbi Eliezer does not know that we follow the majority?! [So why would he make such a vigorous demonstration, knowing that the majority must rule?]

C. BURNING: [Rabbi Eliezer] did not lose his temper until they burned [all the things cooked in an Akhnai oven that he had declared] insusceptible to ritual impurity before his [very eyes]. [For] there (M. Kelim 5:10) they taught, "If he cuts it [the oven into which an impure animal fell] into segments and puts sand between the segments, Rabbi Eliezer [says] it is not susceptible to ritual impurity but the sages say it is susceptible to ritual impurity. And this [such an oven] is [called] the oven of Akhnai."

C1. BURNING: Said Rabbi Yermiyah, "A great visitation happened on that very day: Every place upon which Rabbi Eliezer cast his eyes was burned. And not only that but even one grain of wheat [would be] half burnt and half unburnt [depending upon which half of the grain of wheat he had looked at with his glaring gaze].

B1.   DRAMATIC DEMONSTRATION: And the pillars of the sages' meeting place vibrated. Rabbi Yehoshua said to them [the walls], "If colleagues (chaveirim) are arguing with each other—you [walls]—what does it matter to you?" And [then] a Heavenly Voice came forth and said, "The law is according to Eliezer, my son." Said Rabbi Yehoshua, "It [i.e., Torah] is not in heaven!" (Deuteronomy 30:12)

B1.1.   IS RABBI ELIEZER'S WORD LAW? Rabbi Krispi, Rabbi Yohanan in the name of Rabbi [who redacted the Mishnah in 200 C.E.], "If a person would say to me that thus did Rabbi Eliezer teach I would have taught according to his words but [now] the Tanna have switched [the attributions of the teachings so I cannot do Rabbi Eliezer this honor; to make Rabbi Eliezer's teachings the authoritative ones in the Mishnah because they are said in his name]."

A1.   EXCOMMUNICATION IS OVER: One time he [Rabbi Eliezer] was passing through the market place and he saw one woman cleaning her house and she threw out the dirt from her house and it fell on his head. He said, "It appears to me that today my colleagues (chavraya) will bring me close [to them soon and lift the ban of excommunication so that I might fulfill the following verse], as it is written, 'From the ash heap He lifts up the needy. [To sit him with princes, with princes of His people. He sets the barren one (akeret) of the house [as] a happy mother of [many] children].' (Psalm 113:7)"

In this version of the story, as opposed to the one in B. Berachot, Rabbi Eliezer and the sages seem equally matched. There, Rabbi Eliezer barely entered the account as a person. He was simply dispatched and banished. In this version, Rabbi Eliezer comes off as a far more sympathetic character. He resorts to supernatural demonstrations only in private, with his closest student, Rabbi Akiba, instead of making them part of a public showdown (as is the case in the Bava Metzia passage we will study).

In A and A', Rabbi Eliezer is excommunicated and then restored to the community of sages. Rabbi Eliezer, usually portrayed as an extraordinarily severe man, at the end of this story displays flexibility and perhaps even some levity. Instead of interpreting having garbage dumped on him as a sign of God's wrath, he sees it as a good omen. The word that is used to describe excommunication (lindot) comes from the same root, nun-dalet-hey, as the word that describes a woman who is ritually impure because of a menstrual flow (niddah). Both a niddah and Rabbi Eliezer are cut off from communion in different ways: the wife from sexual relations with her husband and Rabbi Eliezer from the life of the Academy that represents his spiritual posterity.

The second tier of the story, the B level, is the level of "dramatic demonstrations," which have a supernatural aspect to them. Rabbi Eliezer causes the tree to move as a demonstration that his view is the correct one. The demonstration is even more effective because the tree explicitly does not move to prove the sages' point of view. The use of a carob tree is highly symbolic. First of all, carobs, which grow among rocks, give off a sort of honey when they are ripe and so fulfill the verse "And He made him to suck honey out of the crag." (Deuteronomy 32:13 // Y. Peah 7:4 20a) This is usually interpreted as one of the greatest signs of God's benevolence and generosity. Interestingly, the carob tree is also associated with poverty that leads to repentance, for carob is what poor folk ate in those days (Leviticus Rabbah 35:6). A story about Rabbi Shimon bar Yohai and his son Rabbi Elazar, who were forced to live in a cave for thirteen years because of Roman persecution, tells that their only food came from a heaven-sent carob tree (B. Shabbat 33b). The word carob, *cheruv*, may also be the subject of literary allusion here. The letters of this word, rearranged, spell *chaver*—the very word used in this story to describe Rabbi Eliezer's colleagues. A *chaver* was not just a friend or study partner, as the word is used today, but a person who punctiliously observed the laws of Judaism, particularly as they applied to ritual purity and agricultural taxes. Of course, this root is also associated with the word *charav*, which means to destroy or make desolate, and *cherev*, the sword that destroys. In a fascinating parallel, a carob tree opened itself and swallowed the prophet Isaiah when his life was being sought by the evil king Menasseh. When the tree was cut open, blood flowed from it (Pesikta Rabbati 4:3). So the carob tree has rich symbolic meanings that form a backdrop of collegiality and cut-offness, posterity and prosperity.

The word *itokrin* means "to be uprooted" but also "to become impotent." Indeed, the verse from Psalms that ends the Yerushalmi's version of Rabbi Eliezer's story promises the barren one (*akeret*, from the same root, *ayin-kuf-reish*) a house full of children. Since sages

considered their students to be their spiritual children and students considered their teachers their parents (M. Bava Metzia 2:11), the issues of fertility and membership in the Academy are far from academic, so to speak. Just as a *niddah*, a woman in a state of ritual impurity, cannot conceive a child and is thus linked with the *akarah*, the barren one, so is a sage in *niddui* (excommunication) unable to conceive spiritual children, destroying his own stake in posterity.

One last pun on this theme might be noted. Rabbi Eliezer takes Rabbi Akiba outside (*bara'ah*, from the root *beit-reish-alef*). This word is linked to the word that designates an "outside" teaching, *baraita*. Such teachings are often cited in rabbinic literature: teachings from the age of the Mishnah that were not included in that document. In addition, in Aramaic *beit-reish-alef* can also mean "son." Thus, we might imagine that Rabbi Eliezer takes his spiritual son, Rabbi Akiba, into the world of mystical beginnings and shows him how, at an advanced state of development, all the conventional truths of this world are turned on their head when seen from a mystical perspective. With such an outlook, trees may dance and having ashes dumped on one's head can be a good omen.

From a strictly spiritual perspective, Rabbi Eliezer's story demonstrates a great truth: only the humble, who are willing to have ashes placed on their heads in the service of a higher spiritual or communal goal, can learn Torah and lead. In Rabbi Steinsaltz's translation of tractate Taanit 7a, part 1, volume 13, p. 83, he states:

> Pride is not only considered a contemptible quality, but also a sin. With respect to Torah study, pride is regarded as an obstacle to success. A proud person is not

willing to accept anything, nor is he capable of studying the truth. Moreover, he is incapable of correcting judgments that he erroneously holds to be true. Pride also involves an inability to criticize oneself or to accept criticism from friends. Therefore if one is not humble, not only does one have a bad character trait, but one's spiritual capacities are also impaired by it.

One of the ways this is concretely symbolized is when, on fast days that are days of communal repentance, the leaders of the community put ashes on their heads first and then on those of the rest of the congregation (B. Taanit 15b, Rabbi Steinsaltz's edition, volume 14, p. 13). Rabbi Eliezer, for all his wealth and intellectual power, is taught a lesson in what it takes to teach Torah by a woman cleaning her house. The wise, it is said, learn from everyone (M. Pirkei Avot 4:1).

The balance to Rabbi Eliezer's demonstration is provided by Rabbi Yehoshua, his traditional opponent and opposite. Rabbi Yehoshua stops the walls of the Academy from falling, thereby physically preserving the majority of sages who are ruling against Rabbi Eliezer. He refutes the Heavenly Voice as well, thereby spiritually preserving the sages' authority. It may have been that the "shock waves" that followed Rabbi Eliezer's excommunication were so great that they seemed to rock the foundations of the Academy. One need only think of times when one has been in an institution during a period of great emotional turmoil and turnover and think how little stability there was (and how little productivity, for that matter!) to understand this situation. Rabbi Yehoshua, who is notoriously shy about standing up for his own rights before human beings (e.g., B. Berachot 27b), has no hesitation when it comes to speaking up before a heavenly court. Rabbi Yehoshua and

Rabbi Eliezer represent opposing sorts of wisdom and position in the sages' culture. Rabbi Eliezer, for all his flamboyance and spiritual power, his social standing and his wealth, is still on the outside. Poverty-stricken Rabbi Yehoshua is a quintessential insider, protecting his institution from harm and even defying a voice from heaven to do so.

These "dramatic demonstrations" lead the Yerushalmi to address a pressing question. If Rabbi Eliezer is right, as affirmed by the Heavenly Voice, how can the law not be decreed according to him, even if he didn't follow the majority? This problem is introduced in B1 and resolved in B1'. The sages must, for obvious reasons, uphold the idea of majority rule, however they have no desire to flaunt the manifest decrees of heaven. Therefore, according to B1', they developed a loophole. The tannaim, the people who repeated the traditions in the names of different teachers, concealed the fact that Rabbi Eliezer's teachings were, in fact, his own, thereby allowing people to follow the dictates of the Heavenly Voice despite this incident.

In section C, we finally learn what the fight was all about. It involves the susceptibility to ritual impurity of an oven into which something impure has entered. The word *chachinai* means "snake." Of course, this brings to mind the Garden of Eden but also the way some earthenware looks in its first stages of production, when long ropes of clay are coiled together to make the vessel's basic shape. According to P'nei Moshe, an important commentary to the Yerushalmi, the sages and Rabbi Eliezer disagreed about the nature of this oven. The sages saw it as an earthenware vessel that can receive impurity. Rabbi Eliezer ruled that it was like a building made of dung or earth and therefore could not receive impurity.

At the very center of this telling of Rabbi Eliezer's story is fire. The sages shame Rabbi Eliezer, burning goods baked in the oven that he considered pure. The way the story is told, it is almost as if the sages put the fire into his eyes and he then reciprocates their act of burning. The sages burn bread and Rabbi Eliezer burns wheat in retaliation and pain.

We can see the structure of the story graphically, as follows:

C. Burning   C1. Burning

B. Dramatic Demonstrations   B1. Dramatic Demonstrations

A. Excommunication begins   A1. Excommunication ends

This story in the Yerushalmi is balanced. Actions bring equal reactions. Rabbi Eliezer is cast off and brought back. Rabbi Eliezer makes demonstrations that are countered by Rabbi Yehoshua. Rabbi Eliezer's teachings are rejected because he did not accept majority rule yet they are preserved and followed. The sages burn Rabbi Eliezer's bread and he burns theirs in return. This demonstrates a principle that underlies much of biblical and rabbinic literature: *midah k'neged midah* (measure for measure). That is, the energy that one sends forth is the energy that one receives.

This is not the only time that the fire of Rabbi Eliezer and Rabbi Yehoshua is so powerful that it is destructive. At the circumcision celebration of Elisha ben Abuya, one of the sages' greatest disciples and a man who later apostatized, Rabbi Eliezer and Rabbi Yehoshua left the party, went into a side room, and began to study. At that moment, as they tapped into Torah's essential energy, fire came down and surrounded them (Y.

Hagigah 2:1, 77b). The fire of Torah (and of the Temple where it was stored for so long) is everywhere, just below the surface. It can bring people together and it can keep them apart. A connection through the texts to God is available to these two sages.

How, then, is the Yerushalmi's version of the "Oven of Akhnai" different than the Bavli's? One major clue is where it is positioned within the Talmud. The story in the Bavli is part of the commentary to a mishnah concerned with the gravity of hurt feelings, the *beginning* of separation. In the Yerushalmi, it is part of the commentary to a mishnah that concerns the *end* of separation and excommunication. Ordinarily, according to the Mishnah, people did not cut their hair during the intermediate days of a festival. However, the following people were allowed to do so:

> And these are they [who may] cut their hair during the intermediate days [of a festival]: the one who comes from a country [located across] the sea, and the one who [comes out of] captivity, and the one who leaves prison, and the one who was excommunicated that the sages [just] released him [from his state of separation]. (M. Moed Katan 3:1)

Actually, the story makes a great deal of sense in the context of this mishnah. It discusses what happens at the end of a period of excommunication: One immediately resumes participation in normal life, signified by the cutting of one's hair. The Bavli, too, could have put the "Oven of Akhnai" story in the commentary to this mishnah. However, it wanted to underscore a different point, the seriousness of hurt feelings, in its retelling of this tale.

Yerushalmi Bava Metzia 4:7, 4:9, 9d

(See p. 249, line 8 to p. 251, line 8 in the English Steinsaltz Talmud)

תנא רבי יעקב עמסונייא מהו אין מפרקסין דלא יימא ליה צור גרמך:

הדרן עלך פרק הכסף

:גמ' רבי אבדימא מלחא הוה מפתר סרדוותי' א"ל יעקב בר אחא והתנינן אין מפרקסין. מילתיה אמרה שיש פירקום באוכלין. ר' זירא הוה עסק בהדא כיתנא אתא גבי רבי אבהו אמר ליה מה אנא משפרה עיבידתיה. א"ל איזיל עביד מה דאת ידע. רבי אבהו הוה עסיק באילין לסוטיא אתא שאל לרבי יוסי בן חנינה אמר ליה מנן באילין לסוטיא. אמר ליה איזיל עביד מה דאת ידע. רבה שקר טהר.

חנא

"And others say . . ."

Yerushalmi Bava Metzia 4:7, 4:9, 9d

What does the Yerushalmi's commentary on Mishnah Bava Metzia 4:10–12 say if it does not mention the material about Rabbi Eliezer and the oven of Akhnai? The answer is that the Yerushalmi has surprisingly little to say!

Rabbi Avdima, from Milcha, would steep his lean meat [in water to improve its appearance]. Said to him Yaakov bar Ahah, "Was it not taught, 'One doesn't [deceive by] beautifying [merchandise]'?" From here [the words of Yaakov bar Ahah] we can learn [that the prohibition of] beautifying applies to food.

Rabbi Zeira who worked with flax came to Rabbi Abahu. He said to him, "May I beautify my work?" Said he [Rabbi Abahu] to him [Rabbi Zeira], "Go and do what you know [i.e., act according to your understanding of the law]."

Rabbi Abahu was weaving veils. He came and asked Rabbi Yose ben Hanina and said, "What can we do with these veils?" He said to him, "Go and do what you know [i.e., act according to your understanding of the law]."

Rabbah painted a bath red [to beautify it]. Rabbi Yaakov Amsonya taught, "What does it mean, 'One doesn't [deceive by] beautifying [merchandise]'? That one doesn't paint one's body."

The brevity of the Yerushalmi's comments here, especially when compared with the length of the Bavli's parallel passage, is remarkable. Only the very last sentence of all three *mishnayot* (i.e., M. Bava Metzia 4:12) seems to be explored. Some brief cases of law are cited, liberalizing the degree to which one can beautify one's merchandise. This parallel is offered merely to show how the two Talmuds emphasized different aspects of the traditions they received to make different rhetorical points.

Rabbi Eliezer's Life Story

The strongest character we meet in these pages of the Babylonian Talmud is Rabbi Eliezer. It may help you to know something about his biography before you study his story in Rabbi Steinsaltz's translation of Bava Metzia. He was fabulously wealthy, though not greedy. He and his wife, Imma Shalom, were said to have a beautiful intimate relationship (B. Nedarim 20a–b). Not only was he at odds with his colleagues on halakhic issues but on theological ones, as well. He was tried for *minut* by his colleagues, which may mean he was linked to Christian or Zoroastrian practices (T. Hullin 24:2). When he was dying, his disciples gathered around his bed to apologize for excommunicating him from the Academy he had so loved. Rabbi Eliezer, saddened, chastened, but still adamant, taught his Torah till the very end, dying with the word "*Tahor!* (Pure!)" on his lips— the very ruling that caused him to be driven out of the Academy (B. Sanhedrin 68a // Sifre D., Piska 34).

What's on Rabbi Steinsaltz's page? What's on the facing page?

This book is designed to make it easy for you to jump into the study of Talmud. Each set of facing pages will present you with different perspectives on the primary text of the Talmud. First, let's explore what is on a page of Rabbi Steinsaltz's translation. The main thing you're going to study, if you don't know Hebrew, is the *Translation and Commentary*, which is on the left-hand part of the page. Each sentence in the actual text of the Talmud, which is in the middle of the page in Hebrew letters, is numbered. The numbers in the *Translation and Commentary* and *Literal Translation* are coordinated with this central text. The boldface type in the *Translation and Commentary* is the translation of the text. The rest, in plain type, is the commentary. It is occasionally fruitful to read the *Literal Translation* and compare it with the *Translation and Commentary* to see how much "filling in" needed to be done to bridge the gap between the sages' days and our own.

The Notes at the bottom of the page are Rabbi Steinsaltz's digested form of a large number of commentaries to the text. A list identifying these commentaries can be found in this volume (the List of Sources). If you are a beginner, it may be advisable to ignore who said what for now and just concentrate on *what* they said. You can always go back and figure out who the *Ra'avad* and the *Rosh* were later. If you don't understand something in the *Translation*, check the bottom or side of the page to see if Rabbi Steinsaltz has written a note on it. You'll know there's a note because the boldface type at the beginning of each Note matches the line in the text to which it refers.

Under the Notes is a section entitled Halakhah. Halakhah is Jewish law and here Rabbi Steinsaltz summarized the "bottom line," as it were, from the topics on the page. If you are interested in Jewish law, read these sections. If you are not interested in Jewish law now, you may want to skip these entries until it becomes a subject that interests you.

On the outer margins are various sorts of notes that Rabbi Steinsaltz provided to help us study. Some of these will be more helpful to the beginning student and some to the advanced student. If you are a beginner, stick to the entries marked Background, Sages, and Realia. If you are advanced, i.e., you are starting to read the text in the original Hebrew and Aramaic, then go ahead and start reading the entries entitled Terminology and Language.

There is another Hebrew text on this page entitled Rashi. This is the classic medieval commentary to the Talmud, presented in a script different from standard Hebrew letters. If you want to learn to read this script, look in the back of this book for the Rashi script alphabet. Unless you are well advanced, you probably won't even be attempting to read this commentary in Hebrew. In many cases, Rabbi Steinsaltz's commentary includes Rashi's insights, so don't feel that you're losing too much by not reading Rashi separately.

Now, what is on the facing page? There will be some comments designed to help you understand the literary, psychological, and spiritual characteristics of the material. Additional insights about Talmudic Concepts are provided from Rabbi Steinsaltz's *Talmud Reference Guide* as well as his biographies of sages found in other volumes of his Talmud translation. In addition, several students of Talmud have been asked to provide their comments on this famous passage. These contributors, and their backgrounds, are listed in the Preface. Finally, there is room for you to write your insights, ideas, remarks, and so forth on each page. That way, you become part of the never ending process of Talmud study.

NOTES

N O T E S

The Text and Notes: Bava Metzia 58b–60b

Author's Note: The following two pages are the actual introduction by Rabbi Steinsaltz to the Talmud chapter we will be studying.

Introduction to Chapter Four

הַזָּהָב

"And if you sell something to your neighbor, or buy something from your neighbor's hand, do not oppress one another" (Leviticus 25:14).

"And you shall not oppress one another, but you shall fear your God, for I am the Lord your God" (Leviticus 25:17).

"You shall neither vex a stranger nor oppress him, for you were strangers in the land of Egypt" (Exodus 22:20).

"And if a stranger sojourns with you in your land, you shall not vex him" (Leviticus 19:33).

The two principal themes of this chapter are the rules governing the acquisition of movable property, and the laws of *ona'ah* (which concern financial and verbal wrongdoing). One of the general questions arising in connection with the laws of acquisition is how and when acquisition takes place — i.e., at precisely what point does the transfer of ownership take effect when property is purchased? Does the buyer gain title to the property as soon as he pays for his purchase, or only after he takes physical possession of the merchandise? If monetary payment cannot effect a sale, does it have any legal validity? And is a verbal agreement between the buyer and the seller in any way binding? The chapter opens with the specific issue of the rules governing an exchange of coins, and deals with a fundamental problem: How is money defined? Is "money" an absolute concept, which invariably refers to a particular means of acquisition, or is it a relative notion, the definition of which changes with the circumstances? This question has ramifications with regard to the laws of acquisition and of *ona'ah*, as well as to the laws of interest (discussed in the next chapter).

The laws of *ona'ah* fall into two categories: (1) Monetary wrongdoing, whether because the seller overcharged or the buyer underpaid. (2) Verbal wrongdoing, i.e., taunting other people and hurting their feelings.

Numerous questions arise in connection with the Torah's prohibition against financial wrongdoing: Precisely what is considered overcharging? Does the prohibition apply only if one overcharges a fixed sum (or by a fixed percentage), or even in a case of minimal overcharging? What legal remedies exist when one overcharges or underpays? Is fraud in business an offense punishable in court, or is it merely subject to civil litigation? And is a sale entailing fraud valid, or void? Must the party who was defrauded be reimbursed, and if so, to what extent? Does the prohibition against *ona'ah* apply equally to all people and transactions, or not?

Verbal oppression is also examined. Precisely what is considered verbal wrongdoing? Are there cases where this is permitted, and if so, what are they? Does this prohibition apply equally to all people?

These general issues, along with their specific applications, are dealt with in this chapter.

N O T E S

"And others say . . ."

Rabbi Steinsaltz's Introduction

There are six orders in the Mishnah, six basic areas that are covered: (1) Seeds, (2) Seasons, (3) Damages, (4) Women, (5) Holy Things, and (6) Pure Things. The tractate, or book, called Bava Metzia is in the third order concerning civil and criminal law. Bava Metzia means "The Middle Gate." The tractate before it is called Bava Kamma "The First Gate," and it is followed by Bava Batra "The Last Gate." There were so many *mishnayot* on the topic of civil law that they had to be divided into three sections, i.e., "The Gates." (There is no Bava Meiseh, "an old wives' tale tractate," though!)

According to the Mishnah, business laws and rules have to take the feelings of both buyer and seller into account. Feelings were considered quite real and influential by the sages and the passage we will study deals with feelings, as well as rules for honesty in business, how much initiative a merchant can take to attract customers, and where to draw the line between promotion and deception (a

tough boundary to ascertain in any era). Indeed, this passage would be a good one for those engaged in business to study together. It explains a fundamental business idea about how recognizing the importance of feelings and doing business with scrupulous honesty can positively influence commercial transactions.

The sages demand a surprisingly high level of integrity when someone's feelings and/or money are at stake. As you study, you may question whether anyone could attain such a level of absolute honesty in any relationship. The sages assume everyone *can* achieve this kind of integrity, at least some of the time. In fact, the study of this passage could serve as the impetus for an important spiritual exercise. You know when your inner voice tells you that something isn't quite true or fair. Listening to that voice, and acting on its promptings, is one proven path to spiritual enlightenment. The more you are guided by that "inner accountant" the closer you will come to the goals of honesty, fairness, and consideration the sages have set.

NOTES

TRANSLATION AND COMMENTARY

the laws of ***ona'ah* do not apply to** such a transaction, [1]**because** during a war a person's very **life depends on these** items, and people are willing to pay considerably more than what they are really worth." Thus Rabbi Yehudah ben Betera's opinion parallels Rabbi Yehudah's, as both Tannaim maintain that the laws of *ona'ah* do not apply if a buyer is willing to pay more than the ordinary market value of the merchandise.

MISHNAH כְּשֵׁם שֶׁאוֹנָאָה בְּמִקָּח [2]Having completed its discussion of the laws of fraud, the Mishnah now turns to laws governing human relationships. The connection between these two topics is the Hebrew word *ona'ah* (אוֹנָאָה), which means not only fraud or overreaching but also the causing of anguish to others. The Mishnah declares: **Just as there is** a law prohibiting *ona'ah* — fraud **in buying and selling — so too there is** a law prohibiting verbal *ona'ah* (אוֹנָאַת דְּבָרִים), in which anguish is caused to other people by hurting their feelings.

לֹא יֹאמַר לוֹ [3]The Mishnah now shows how words may cause pain. The first example is related to the previous topic — buying and selling: A customer **may not say to a merchant:** "How **much is this** article" **if he does not** in fact **wish to buy it,** as this arouses false hopes in the seller, who will be upset if the questioner does not purchase the item.

אִם הָיָה בַּעַל תְּשׁוּבָה [4]The Mishnah now considers examples totally unrelated to the previous discussion: **If someone is a repentant sinner,** other people **must not** remind him of his past by **saying to him: "Remember your earlier deeds."** [5]Likewise, **if** someone is **the son of converts,** other people **must not** remind him of his origins by **saying to him: "Remember the deeds of your fathers."** In fact, there is a special prohibition against causing anguish to converts, [6]**for the verse** (Exodus 22:20) **says: "You shall not wrong** (*tonu*, from the same Hebrew root as *ona'ah)* **a stranger** (i.e., a convert) **nor shall you oppress him."**

אוֹנָאָה, [1]מִפְּנֵי שֶׁיֵּשׁ בָּהֶן חַיֵּי נֶפֶשׁ".

משנה [2]כְּשֵׁם שֶׁאוֹנָאָה בְּמִקָּח וּמִמְכָּר, כָּךְ אוֹנָאָה בִּדְבָרִים. [3]לֹא יֹאמַר לוֹ: "בְּכַמָּה חֵפֶץ זֶה"? וְהוּא אֵינוֹ רוֹצֶה לִיקַּח. [4]אִם הָיָה בַּעַל תְּשׁוּבָה לֹא יֹאמַר לוֹ: "זְכוֹר מַעֲשֶׂיךָ הָרִאשׁוֹנִים". [5]אִם הוּא בֶּן גֵּרִים לֹא יֹאמַר לוֹ: "זְכוֹר מַעֲשֵׂה אֲבוֹתֶיךָ", [6]שֶׁנֶּאֱמַר: "וְגֵר לֹא תוֹנֶה וְלֹא תִלְחָצֶנּוּ".

LITERAL TRANSLATION

ona'ah for them, [1]because life depends on (lit., "is in") them."

MISHNAH [2]Just as there is *ona'ah* in buying and selling, so too there is *ona'ah* in words.

[3]One may not say to him [a merchant]: "How much is this object," if one does not wish to buy [it].

[4]If [someone] was a repentant [sinner], one may not say to him: "Remember your earlier deeds." [5]If he is the son of converts, one may not say to him: "Remember the deeds of your fathers," [6]for it is said: "You shall not wrong a stranger, nor shall you oppress him."

LANGUAGE

אוֹנָאָה **Fraud, wrongdoing, overreaching.** This word, generally translated "fraud" (i.e., overcharging and underpaying, financial dishonesty), is derived from the root ינה or אנה, whose basic meaning in Biblical Hebrew is "to cause distress." The primary meaning of this root also plays a part in Mishnaic Hebrew, as we see from our Mishnah where we read: "Just as there is *ona'ah* in buying and selling, so too there is *ona'ah* (i.e., causing distress, or hurting other people's feelings) in words."

BACKGROUND

אוֹנָאַת דְּבָרִים **Verbal *ona'ah*.** As the Mishnah indicates, verbal *ona'ah* includes a wide variety of activities, from intentionally disappointing others (by pretending that one wants to buy something when one in fact does not), to insulting them outright. Verbal *ona'ah* of this sort is not grounds for lawsuits to be adjudicated in court, although it is considered an extremely grave offense which is punishable at the hands of Heaven.

אִם הָיָה בַּעַל תְּשׁוּבָה **If someone was a repentant sinner....** If a person sincerely and completely repents for his misdeeds, they are forgiven, and he must thereafter be treated as a righteous man. Hence, it is considered a gratuitous insult to remind a penitent of his past.

NOTES

שֶׁיֵּשׁ בָּהֶן חַיֵּי נֶפֶשׁ **Because life depends on them.** It is not clear whether Rabbi Yehudah ben Betera's view is accepted or not. On the one hand, no one disputes this opinion, so it would appear that it should be accepted. On the other hand, the Gemara implies elsewhere (see, for example, *Yevamot* 106a and the commentators there) that a person who overcharges for objects or services necessary for survival is only entitled to the true value of the object or service he provided. Following this reasoning, it would appear that the prohibition against *ona'ah* should apply to military implements in wartime, contrary to the viewpoint of Rabbi Yehudah ben Betera (*Remakh*).

אוֹנָאַת דְּבָרִים **Verbal *ona'ah*.** Verbal *ona'ah* means insulting others, hurting their feelings, or putting them to shame (compare, for example, Isaiah 49:26, "I shall feed them that oppress you with their own flesh," where the same Hebrew root is used). *Meiri* suggests that two types of transgression are subsumed under the category of verbal *ona'ah*: (1) Causing a person financial loss through one's words, and (2) putting another person to shame. Indeed, both types of offense are discussed in the Mishnah. In the first case, the seller thinks the buyer did not buy the merchandise because he felt it was overpriced (and not because he did not want to buy it in the first place); hence the seller is likely to cut prices. Thus, the buyer's conduct is liable to cause the seller an unnecessary financial loss. And the next two cases in the Mishnah (where one reminds a penitent or descendant of proselytes of their origins) constitute verbal *ona'ah* because they involve putting others to shame.

כְּשֵׁם שֶׁאוֹנָאָה בְּמִקָּח **Just as there is *ona'ah* in buying and selling, so too there is *ona'ah* in words.** *Baḥ* explains that the Mishnah had to teach us that verbal *ona'ah* is prohibited, because we might not otherwise have inferred this from the Biblical text, which ostensibly refers to financial fraud and not to verbal wrongdoing.

לֹא יֹאמַר לוֹ בְּכַמָּה חֵפֶץ **One may not say: "How much is this object?"** This is forbidden because it causes the seller distress, since he mistakenly thinks that he will be able to conclude the sale. Moreover, such behavior may even cause the seller financial loss (see *Rashbam, Pesaḥim* 112b).

"And others say . . ."*

p. 223 Commentary

We begin with the Mishnah; the dream. Here we have the orderly progression of concepts. The mishnah before this one examined the oppression of people by means of money. In this mishnah, we move on to the idea that we can oppress people by means of words as well. The first example is clearly related to laws of commerce: You shouldn't raise the hopes of the seller if you have no intention of buying.

But the next two examples would appear to have nothing to do with commerce. Rather, they are simply ways that you could hurt another person with words. They have at least one factor in common: We should not remind people of their past deeds once they have changed their ways.

In other words, God's gift of t'shuvah (repentance, "return") is mercifully complete: One does not have to live with a cloud over one's head because one once sinned. In that sense, then, these two examples are not so far from the world of commerce. Once a spiritual debt has been paid (through repentance and righ-

teousness) we don't have to see ourselves as debtors anymore.

Note how the "waltz" appears here, with three examples of oppressing a person with words: (1) asking about an item as though one were going to buy, (2) reminding a sinner of his/her past sin, and (3) reminding a convert of his/her past faith.

—JZA

Verbal Ona'ah—The Subtle Sin

At this point, the Talmud makes what appears to be a significant departure. The bulk of Bava Metzia concerns property law and revolves around the same type of financial transactions, property disputes, and concerns about fraud we would expect to find in our own civil courts. Verbal ona'ah, on the other hand, cannot be prosecuted in court and can only be identified by knowing the intentions of the speaker. These crimes are the most subtle expressions of universal human failings—greed, jealousy, envy, and pride. The Talmud tells us that to hurt another person's feelings

---

* . . . And others say . . .

One of rabbinic literature's most salient, and endearing, qualities is its ability to allow many voices to speak. Sometimes these are our greatest sages arguing passionately about a text. Sometimes these are later sages and their students clarifying the text. This process, which continues to this day, is what makes Talmud study a living document rather than simply a book on a shelf.

When we study the Talmud, we often encounter the phrase ". . . and others say . . ." to introduce another interpretation of the text. Here, it is the name given to a new commentary to Rabbi Steinsaltz's English Edition of the Talmud. The students of Talmud who wrote the interpretations found in ". . . And others say . . ." use their own life-wisdom and professional insights to shine their own, unique light on this text and illuminate it with love and reverence.

is indeed a serious crime, although only we can judge our own guilt. We are responsible for holding ourselves as accountable as though we were impartial judges faced with criminal evidence.

—*Elizabeth Weinberg*

Verbal *ona'ah*: putting others to shame or causing anguish to others by hurting their feelings.

Much of Talmudic commentary on social interaction is directed specifically towards potential or actual harm of others. Not surprisingly, post-modern philosophers in this century also have been deeply concerned with the vicissitudes of violence. In their efforts to characterize the essential elements of such violence to personhood, the term "desubjectification" is used to refer to the treatment of the Other—in thought, speech, or other action—as if that person is without a sense of self, volition, or sensibility. It is the psychological equivalent to destroying the humanity of the Other, and the opposite of Buber's I-Thou relation. Interestingly, the Talmud's concern with the maltreatment of the Other, whether through verbal or monetary *ona'ah,* assumes that the Other (and, hence, ourselves) is always a subject, always possessing aself who can enact good or evil actions. Only someone who is embodied with a sense of self can act ethically, or be redeemed.

—*Robert E. Reichlin*

Rabbi Yehudah says: "One may not even cast one's eyes on merchandise when one has no money. For the matter is entrusted to the heart, and concerning any matter that is entrusted to the heart, it was said, 'And you shall fear your God.' "

Not only should one not ask a merchant the price of an item without the intention to buy it, one should not even go "window shopping," for it is possible that such behavior will disappoint the merchant whose expectations are that a customer is interested in purchasing a particular product. In a time before super-stores and sales circulars, it was especially important not to mislead the merchant whose livelihood depended upon each individual's purchase. This is a matter "entrusted to the heart" for it involves acting in a way that takes into consideration the possibility of hurting the feelings or hopes of another person.

Why does Rabbi Yehudah include the phrase from Leviticus "And you shall fear your God" in this statement? It is a reminder that God is watching us as well as watching over us. The Torah uses this phrase on occasions when it instructs us on how to treat one another with dignity, kindness, and respect:

Regarding purchasing land before the fiftieth year, the Torah teaches, "So you are not to wrong one another, rather you shall fear your God." (Leviticus 25:17) About the treatment of slaves, we read "You shall not rule over him with rigor, but you shall fear your God." (Leviticus 24:43) In dealing honestly with others, "You shall not curse the deaf or put a stumbling block before the blind, but you shall fear your God." (Leviticus 19:14) Listening to the voice within, "the midwives feared God and did not as the king of Egypt commanded them but they saved the male children." (Exodus 1:17) Abraham realized that "the fear of God is not in this place" (Genesis 20:11) if he were to be killed after representing Sarah as his sister to Avimelech. The antithesis is found in the story of Amalek, who showed no concern and smote the weary stragglers among the Israelites: "Remember what Amalek did to you . . . he feared not God." (Deuteronomy 25:18)

To fear God is to be in awe of the One and the Wonder that comes when I reach out in moments of compassion.

To fear God is to acknowledge the true Judge when I treat others with fairness and honesty.

To fear God is to bless the Heart of the World when I spend time with a loved one who is ill.

To fear God is to call upon the Source of Strength for help that I not give up and let others down.

To fear God is to recognize the Knower of Secrets, aware of the intentions of my heart and the direction of my spirit.

To fear God is to connect with the One and the many around me, who support me so that I am not afraid.

B'yado afkid ruchi. . . . Adonai li v'lo ira.

In God's hand I entrust my spirit;
God is with me and I do not fear.

—*Mark Frydenberg*

Times Past

T'shuvah mastered,
Past no longer is her truth.
Speaking it is fraud.

Name and livelihood—
One does not trifle with these.
They are of essence.

—*Naomi Hyman*

Verbal *Ona'ah*

Trust, mutual respect, and affection build solid relationships. If a person speaks recklessly about the character of a friend or a spouse, harm is caused and trust begins to wane.

A spouse might allege an untrue act of abuse against his or her mate to gain advantage regarding financial or parental control. The pain caused by the falsity destroys the relationship. The Levitical prohibition **"You shall not wrong one another"** was a command intended, I think, to use words wisely and accurately to avoid the destruction of relationships.

Rabbi Yehudah, the sage, speaks of the prohibition against one looking silently at merchandise if he has no money to purchase the merchandise. It arouses false hope in the seller. Subjective intent of the viewer, the Talmud says, cannot be enforced by a human court because no one can know another's thought.

A person convicted of shoplifting in a department store cannot be free from suspicion when he looks silently at merchandise in a store with no money in his pocket. Intent cannot be positively identified without action, although a person's history can circumstantially impute intent. Courts in America have found and often find persons guilty of theft, without a direct witness to the theft, because of the person's prior similar conduct, together with other factors.

—*H.J. Stern*

TRANSLATION AND COMMENTARY

GEMARA תָּנוּ רַבָּנַן [1] **The Rabbis taught** the following Baraita, which discusses a verse in Leviticus (25:17): "The verse says: **'You shall not wrong** (*tonu*, from the same Hebrew root as *ona'ah*) **one another,** but you shall fear your God, for I am the Lord your God.' **The verse is speaking of verbal** ***ona'ah.*** It is prohibiting the use of words that cause other people anguish." [2] The Baraita defends its interpretation of the verse by asking a rhetorical question: **"You say** that the word *ona'ah* appearing in this verse **refers to verbal** ***ona'ah.*** **But might it not be referring to monetary** ***ona'ah*** overcharging and underpaying — and causing people anguish is thus not prohibited by the Torah?" [3] The Baraita explains: "The verse cannot be referring to monetary *ona'ah*, for there is an earlier **verse** (ibid., 25:14), **which says: 'And if you sell something to your neighbor, or buy something from your neighbor's hand,** do not oppress (*tonu*, from the same root as *ona'ah*) one another.' [4] Thus we see that **the case of monetary** ***ona'ah*** **has** already **been stated** explicitly. And since the Torah has already explicitly forbidden fraudulent business dealings in verse 14, the verse cited at the beginning of the Baraita (verse 17) must be intended to teach us something different. [5] **How then do I interpret** the expression **'You shall not wrong one another'** in verse 17? **This** verse must **be referring to verbal** ***ona'ah.*****"** [6] The Baraita now explains the law in detail: **"How so?** What constitutes verbal *ona'ah*?" [7] The Baraita explains: **"If someone is a repentant sinner,** other people **must not** remind him of his past by **saying to him: 'Remember your earlier deeds.'** [8] Likewise, **if** someone **is the son of converts,** other people **must not** remind him of his origins by **saying to him: 'Remember the deeds of your fathers.'"** [9] The Baraita now adds several examples not found in our Mishnah: **"If a convert came to study Torah,** other people **must not** insult him by **saying to him:** [10] **'Shall the mouth that** once **ate carrion and forbidden animals,**

גמרא [1] תָּנוּ רַבָּנַן: ״׳לֹא תוֹנוּ אִישׁ אֶת עֲמִיתוֹ׳. בְּאוֹנָאַת דְּבָרִים הַכָּתוּב מְדַבֵּר. [2] אַתָּה אוֹמֵר בְּאוֹנָאַת דְּבָרִים, אוֹ אֵינוֹ אֶלָּא בְּאוֹנָאַת מָמוֹן? [3] כְּשֶׁהוּא אוֹמֵר: ׳וְכִי תִמְכְּרוּ מִמְכָּר לַעֲמִיתֶךָ, אוֹ קָנֹה מִיַּד עֲמִיתֶךָ׳, [4] הֲרֵי אוֹנָאַת מָמוֹן אָמוּר. [5] הָא מָה אֲנִי מְקַיֵּים ״לֹא תוֹנוּ אִישׁ אֶת עֲמִיתוֹ״? בְּאוֹנָאַת דְּבָרִים. [6] הָא כֵּיצַד? [7] אִם הָיָה בַּעַל תְּשׁוּבָה אַל יֹאמַר לוֹ: ׳זְכוֹר מַעֲשֶׂיךָ הָרִאשׁוֹנִים׳. [8] אִם הָיָה בֶּן גֵּרִים אַל יֹאמַר לוֹ: ׳זְכוֹר מַעֲשֵׂה אֲבוֹתֶיךָ׳. [9] אִם הָיָה גֵּר וּבָא לִלְמוֹד תּוֹרָה, אַל יֹאמַר לוֹ: [10] ׳פֶּה שֶׁאָכַל נְבֵילוֹת וּטְרֵיפוֹת,

LITERAL TRANSLATION

GEMARA [1] Our Rabbis taught: "'You shall not wrong one another.' [2] The verse is speaking of verbal *ona'ah*. You say [it refers] to verbal *ona'ah*, but might it not be [referring] to monetary *ona'ah*? [3] When [the verse] says: 'And if you sell something to your neighbor, or buy something from your neighbor's hand,' [4] the case of monetary *ona'ah* has been stated. [5] How then do I interpret (lit., 'establish') 'You shall not wrong one another'? [It refers] to verbal *ona'ah*. [6] How so? [7] If [someone] was a repentant [sinner], one may not say to him: 'Remember your earlier deeds.' [8] If he was the son of converts, one may not say to him: 'Remember the deeds of your fathers.' [9] If he was a convert and he came to study Torah, one may not say to him: [10] 'Shall the mouth that has eaten carrion and forbidden (literally, 'torn') animals,

BACKGROUND

פֶּה שֶׁאָכַל נְבֵילוֹת וכו׳ **Shall the mouth that has eaten carrion, etc.** The various types of food mentioned here are considered repulsive, and not just forbidden. Indeed, a non-Jew may eat such foods, and Jews are explicitly permitted to sell animal carcasses to non-Jews (see Deuteronomy 14:21). Thus reminding a convert that he once ate forbidden foods has emotional rather than Halakhic significance. Other Talmudic passages, too, indicate that eating non-kosher food (even unwittingly) exerts a deleterious influence on those who do so.

NOTES

אִם הָיָה גֵּר **If he was a convert.** The commentators ask why the Gemara does not speak of wronging converts by reminding them of their former deeds. *Maharsha* answers that this is not considered *ona'ah*. On the contrary, the fact that a convert was able to abandon his former ways and draw near to God demonstrates his spiritual greatness. *Pnei Yehoshua*, however, explains that the convert's deeds before he converted are not attributable to him, since a convert is Halakhically considered "like a newborn child" who has no connection with his past.

HALAKHAH

אוֹנָאַת דְּבָרִים **Verbal** ***ona'ah.*** "Just as it is prohibited to wrong other people in business by overcharging or underpaying, so too it is prohibited to wrong others verbally by hurting their feelings. Indeed, verbal *ona'ah* is a graver offense than fraud in business, since it is directed against the person himself rather than against his property. Moreover, someone who shames another person cannot rectify the wrong by paying money. Moreover, if the offended party demands Divine retribution from the person who humiliated him, his prayers are answered immediately." (*Shulḥan Arukh, Ḥoshen Mishpat* 228:1.)

כֵּיצַד אוֹנָאַת דְּבָרִים **What is considered verbal** ***ona'ah?*** "It is forbidden to ask how much something costs if one does not intend to buy it, or to send ass-drivers to someone who does not sell produce. It is forbidden to remind a repentant sinner of his past deeds, or to remind the son of proselytes of his ancestors' deeds. Similarly, it is forbidden to tell a person afflicted in any way that he deserves to suffer as punishment for his sins." (Ibid., 228:4.)

שְׁקָצִים וּרְמָשִׂים, בָּא לִלְמוֹד תּוֹרָה שֶׁנֶּאֶמְרָה מִפִּי הַגְּבוּרָה?׳ [1]אִם הָיוּ יִסּוּרִין בָּאִין עָלָיו, אִם הָיוּ חֳלָאִים בָּאִין עָלָיו, אוֹ שֶׁהָיָה מְקַבֵּר אֶת בָּנָיו, [2]אַל יֹאמַר לוֹ כְּדֶרֶךְ שֶׁאָמְרוּ לוֹ חֲבֵירָיו לְאִיּוֹב: ׳הֲלֹא יִרְאָתְךָ כִּסְלָתֶךָ, תִּקְוָתְךָ וְתֹם דְּרָכֶיךָ? [3]זְכָר נָא מִי הוּא נָקִי אָבָד?׳ [4]אִם הָיוּ חַמָּרִים מְבַקְּשִׁין תְּבוּאָה מִמֶּנּוּ, לֹא יֹאמַר לָהֶם: [5]׳לְכוּ אֵצֶל פְּלוֹנִי, שֶׁהוּא מוֹכֵר תְּבוּאָה׳, וְיוֹדֵעַ בּוֹ שֶׁלֹּא מָכַר מֵעוֹלָם. [6]רַבִּי יְהוּדָה אוֹמֵר: אַף לֹא יִתְלֶה עֵינָיו עַל הַמִּקָּח בְּשָׁעָה שֶׁאֵין לוֹ דָּמִים. [7]שֶׁהֲרֵי הַדָּבָר מָסוּר לַלֵּב, וְכָל דָּבָר הַמָּסוּר לַלֵּב נֶאֱמַר בּוֹ: ׳וְיָרֵאתָ מֵאֱלֹהֶיךָ׳״.

LITERAL TRANSLATION

abominations and creeping things, come to study Torah that was uttered by the mouth of the Almighty?' [1]If suffering befell someone, [or] if illness befell him, or if he was burying his sons, [2]one should not say to him in the way that [Job's] friends said to Job: 'Is not your fear [of God] your confidence, your hope and the uprightness of your ways? [3]Remember, I pray you, whoever perished, being innocent?' [4]If ass-drivers were seeking produce from someone, he may not say to them: [5]'Go to so-and-so, who is selling produce,' when he knows that he has never sold [produce]. [6]Rabbi Yehudah says: One may not even cast one's eyes on merchandise when one has no money. [7]For the matter is entrusted to the heart, and concerning any matter that is entrusted to the heart it was said: 'And you shall fear your God.'"

TRANSLATION AND COMMENTARY

abominations and creeping things (such as insects and rodents), all of which are types of non-kosher food, **come** now **to study Torah that was uttered by the mouth of the Almighty?'** [1]Also, **if** a person **is suffering, or has become ill, or if his children** have died and he **is burying** them, [2]it is wrong to suggest that the tragedy might have been averted had the person been more scrupulous, **in the manner of Job's friends** after tragedy befell him. The suffering person's friends **should not say to him: "Is not your fear of God your confidence, your hope and the uprightness of your ways? [3]Remember, I pray you, who ever perished being innocent?'** These words spoken to Job (Job 4:6-7) imply that God does not allow innocent people to come to harm. Speaking in this way to a bereaved or suffering person is forbidden as verbal *ona'ah*, since it is tantamount to accusing the sufferer or the deceased of being a sinner. [4]An example of another kind: **If ass-drivers are seeking** to buy **produce from** a person, and he does not have produce to sell them, **he must not say to them: [5]'Go to so-and-so who is selling produce,' when he knows that** the other person has **never sold produce**, for by speaking in this way, he is causing the ass-drivers (and the person to whom he sent them) needless distress. [6]**Rabbi Yehudah said:** A person **may not even cast his eyes on merchandise if he has no money** to purchase it. Even though he does not say anything, he arouses false hopes in the seller merely by staring at the merchandise." Having described a number of examples of verbal *ona'ah*, the Baraita concludes by explaining the last words of the verse in Leviticus (25:17) on which the Baraita is based: "And you shall fear your God, for I am the Lord your God." The Baraita points out that there is no objective definition of hurtful words: "**For** the same words may be helpful or destructive, depending on the circumstances, the tone of voice, and the speaker's intent. Thus, practically speaking, it is impossible to enforce this law, because the speaker can always claim that he really meant no harm. If he sent the ass-drivers to another merchant, he can pretend that he really thought that the other had produce to sell. If he stared at merchandise, he can claim that he was considering buying it, but decided not to. [7]**In cases** such as **these, the matter is entrusted to the** person's own **heart.** This law cannot be enforced by a human court, because no one can know another person's thoughts. However, the person himself knows whether his intentions were good or evil. **And concerning any matter that is entrusted to** a person's own **heart the verse says: 'And you shall fear your God.'** For He who knows a person's innermost thoughts and intentions will enforce His law." This concludes the Baraita.

RASHI

שהרי דבר המסור ללב – ולפיכך נאמר בו "ויראת מאלהיך". האי "שהרי" – ליתן טעם למה נאמר בו יראה נקט ליה, והכי קאמר: שהרי כל הדברים הללו אין טובתן ורעתן מסורה להכיר אלא ללבו של עושה, הוא יודע אם לעקל אם לעקלקלות, ויכול הוא לומר: לא עשיתי כי אם לטובה, הייתי סבור שיש לך תבואה למכור או הייתי חפץ לקנות מקח זה. **וכל דבר המסור ללב** – של אדם, נאמר בו הוי ירא מן היודע מחשבות, אם לטובה אם לאונאה.

BACKGROUND

אִם הָיוּ יִסּוּרִין בָּאִין עָלָיו If suffering befell someone. While many statements are found in Rabbinic literature to the effect that suffering is a punishment for sin (although the Rabbis admitted that there were exceptions to this rule), it is improper to accuse sufferers of wrongdoing, since only God knows what other people's merits and transgressions are.

לְכוּ אֵצֶל פְּלוֹנִי Go to so-and-so. From here we may infer that not only are outright insults forbidden, but so are remarks made facetiously, if they are likely to cause others distress.

אַף לֹא יִתְלֶה עֵינָיו עַל הַמִּקָּח One may not even cast one's eyes on merchandise. From here we learn that even actions that are likely to arouse false hopes in the seller (such as "casting one's eyes" on merchandise) are forbidden as verbal *ona'ah*.

NOTES

הֲלֹא יִרְאָתְךָ כִּסְלָתֶךָ "Is not your fear of God your confidence?" *Maharsha* explains that the word כִּסְלָתֶךָ — here rendered "your confidence" — means "your fortune." Thus, the verse as a whole would mean: "As long as you were blessed with good fortune you feared God, but in fact you are not a God-fearing person."

NOTES

"And others say . . ."

pp. 224–225 Commentary

What's going on here? We said before that the Gemara comments on the Mishnah, but that's not what is happening here. As it often does, the Gemara immediately supplants the mishnah with a *baraita*. The citation of a *baraita* is often prefaced by the phrase, *Tanu Rabbanan*, "Our Rabbis taught." Any time you see this phrase you should automatically think, "*baraita.*" This particular *baraita* is the Tosefta passage that in turn was based on the midrash collection Sifra, both of which we explored in the "Ingredients" section earlier.

If you are curious about the word *ona'ah*, which is being thrown about quite a bit on these two pages, please refer to the section later in the book entitled "How to Use Dictionaries and Other Tools of the Trade."

—JZA

Concepts
Ona'ah/Overreaching, deception, fraud.

In civil law this term refers to the prohibition against deceiving or taking unfair advantage of another person in a business transaction (Leviticus 25:14). If either the buyer or the seller takes unfair advantage of the other, the wronged party has the right to be reimbursed according to the true value of the article. According to rabbinic law this right may be exercised if either party has overcharged or underpaid to the extent of one-sixth of the article's true value. If the *ona'ah* is greater than one-sixth of the article's true value, the sale is annulled. (*Talmud Reference Guide*, p. 159)

Our Rabbis taught.

A term used to introduce a *baraita*, usually a longer anonymous passage from the Tosefta, Mekhilta, Sifra, or Sifrei (see Berakhot 16a). (*Talmud Reference Guide*, p. 144)

Beyond the requirements of the law.

The strict "line" or letter of the law is the limit to a person's obligations as set by the Halakhah. "Beyond the requirements of the law" implies the exercise of restraint in claiming one's due, so as to fulfill a religious commandment. In the context of a person's duty to God, such a contract is generally called *hiddur mitzvah*—the beautification of a commandment—and usually involves carrying it out with extra scrupulousness. But in commercial relationships the expression "beyond the requirements of the law" is used to describe a situation where one person does a favor for another although he is not strictly obliged to do so by the Halakhah. Generally the sages are of the opinion that the greater a person is, the more he is morally obliged to behave "beyond the requirements of the law" and to exact less than the full to which he is legally entitled. (*Talmud Reference Guide*, p. 209)

Baraita/External.

A general term for a tannaitic source that is not part of the Mishnah, the collection of *mishnayot* edited by Rabbi Yehudah HaNasi. (*Talmud Reference Guide*, p. 107)

Window Shopping

Have you ever gone window shopping? Have you ever wanted to know the price of something even if you have no intention of buying it? We are in the furniture business. In the early days my husband often asked me to call our competition to get their price on a specific piece of merchandise. This I did without giving it too much thought since I knew we needed to keep our prices in line with our competition. But is what I did to be considered a sin? Who did I cause distress? How would my inquiry cause pain?

—*Shirley Barish*

NOTES

NOTES

[1]אָמַר רַבִּי יוֹחָנָן מִשּׁוּם רַבִּי שִׁמְעוֹן בֶּן יוֹחַאי: גָּדוֹל אוֹנָאַת דְּבָרִים מֵאוֹנָאַת מָמוֹן, [2]שֶׁזֶּה נֶאֱמַר בּוֹ: ״וְיָרֵאתָ מֵאֱלֹהֶיךָ״, [3]וְזֶה לֹא נֶאֱמַר בּוֹ: ״וְיָרֵאתָ מֵאֱלֹהֶיךָ״.
[4]וְרַבִּי אֶלְעָזָר אוֹמֵר: זֶה בְּגוּפוֹ, וְזֶה בְּמָמוֹנוֹ.
[5]רַבִּי שְׁמוּאֵל בַּר נַחְמָנִי אָמַר: זֶה נִיתָּן לְהִישָּׁבוֹן, וְזֶה לֹא נִיתָּן לְהִישָּׁבוֹן.
[6]תָּנֵי תַּנָּא קַמֵּיהּ דְּרַב נַחְמָן בַּר יִצְחָק: ״כָּל הַמַּלְבִּין פְּנֵי חֲבֵירוֹ בָּרַבִּים כְּאִילּוּ שׁוֹפֵךְ דָּמִים״.
[7]אֲמַר לֵיהּ: שַׁפִּיר קָא אָמְרַתְּ, דְּחָזֵינָא לֵיהּ דְּאָזֵיל סוּמָּקָא וְאָתֵי חִוָּורָא.

LITERAL TRANSLATION

[1]Rabbi Yoḥanan said in the name of Rabbi Shimon ben Yoḥai: Verbal *ona'ah* is a greater [sin] than monetary *ona'ah*, [2]for concerning this one it was said: "And you shall fear your God," [3]but concerning that one it was not said: "And you shall fear your God."
[4]And Rabbi Elazar says: This [applies] to [the victim's] person, and that to his money.
[5]Rabbi Shmuel bar Naḥmani said: This can be restored, but that cannot be restored.
[6]A Tanna taught before Rav Naḥman bar Yitzḥak: "Anyone who shames (lit., 'whitens the face of') his fellow in public is as if he sheds blood."
[7]He said to him: You said well, for we see in him that redness goes out and whiteness comes.

TRANSLATION AND COMMENTARY

אָמַר רַבִּי יוֹחָנָן [1]The Gemara now cites a number of other statements made by the Sages about the importance of not inflicting anguish. **Rabbi Yoḥanan said in the name of Rabbi Shimon ben Yoḥai: Verbal *ona'ah* is a greater sin than monetary *ona'ah*.** [2]**For concerning** the former **the verse** (ibid.) **says: "And you shall fear your God,"** [3]**and concerning** the latter **the verse** prohibiting monetary *ona'ah* (ibid., 25:14) **does not say: "And you shall fear your God."** This shows that the Torah considers causing people anguish a sign of disrespect for God, in a way that monetary *ona'ah* is not.

וְרַבִּי אֶלְעָזָר [4]**Rabbi Elazar** suggested a further reason why verbal wrongdoing is considered more heinous than monetary fraud, and **said: The former applies to the victim's person,** whereas **the latter** applies only **to his money.**

רַבִּי שְׁמוּאֵל בַּר נַחְמָנִי [5]**Rabbi Shmuel bar Naḥmani** added yet another reason and **said:** Monetary *ona'ah* is less severe because it **is subject to restitution.** If someone overcharges or underpays, he can recompense the victim by simply paying the difference. **But** verbal *ona'ah* **is not subject to restitution.** Even if the wrongdoer tries to atone for his sin by compensating the victim, the anguish he caused can never be completely undone.

תָּנֵי תַּנָּא [6]**A Tanna** (Baraita reciter) **taught** the following Baraita **before Rav Naḥman bar Yitzḥak: "Anyone who shames another person in public is as if he sheds his blood."** The Hebrew expression for shaming someone is *malbin panim* (מַלְבִּין פָּנִים), which literally means "whitening the face." The connection between shaming a person and shedding his blood is based on this literal meaning.

אֲמַר לֵיהּ [7]Rav Naḥman bar Yitzḥak **said to the Tanna: You say well.** The Baraita you cited expresses a profound truth. **For** when a person is publicly shamed, **we see that the red** color of his face as he blushes **disappears and whiteness takes its place** as he pales. In this sense it may truly be said that the shamed person's blood is being shed.

BACKGROUND

כְּאִילּוּ שׁוֹפֵךְ דָּם **Is as if he sheds blood.** In a sense, putting another person to shame is tantamount to assassination, since it destroys his social status and personal honor.

NOTES

גָּדוֹל אוֹנָאַת דְּבָרִים מֵאוֹנָאַת מָמוֹן **Verbal *ona'ah* is more serious than monetary *ona'ah*.** In addition to the reasons suggested by the Gemara, *Maharsha* explains that verbal *ona'ah* is particularly serious because it reflects an attitude of contempt towards God. Specifically, a person who commits verbal *ona'ah* attempts to convey the impression that he did not mean to hurt the victim's feelings. Thus such a person shows that he is attempting to deceive God, even though he is afraid to deceive other people. By contrast, if a person defrauds another person financially, other people realize that he has done so, and thus his conduct does not imply that he fears man more than God.

HALAKHAH

הַמַּלְבִּין פְּנֵי חֲבֵירוֹ **One who shames his fellow in public.** "A person who puts other people to shame in public, or calls other people derogatory names, has no share in the world to come unless he repents." (*Rambam, Sefer HaMada, Hilkhot De'ot* 6:8; ibid., *Hilkhot Teshuvah* 3:14.)

"And others say . . ."

p. 226 Commentary

The *baraita*/midrash/tosefta ends on p. 225 and now we have some further comments on *ona'ah*. Three "attributed" comments about the seriousness of *ona'ah* with words and why it is a more serious sin than *ona'ah* with money are brought forth. The segue is accomplished smoothly by relating Rabbi Shimon ben Yohai's interpretation of the verse just discussed about fearing God (Leviticus 25:14). Rabbi Elazar's and Rabbi Shmuel bar Nahmani's points are well-taken: Hurt feelings are not so easily remedied as a hurt pocketbook. Note, again, the "waltz": three comments and then the text moves on to a new topic.

In line 6 we are introduced to the idea of "whitening the face," the sages' way of saying "shaming someone." When people are publicly embarrassed, the blood drains from their faces and it appears as if they are actually losing blood. So the sages equate public shaming with murder. Indeed, according to the Halakhah, public shaming is considered a grave sin.

How could you repent for publicly shaming someone? It's hard! You must apologize to the person in the presence of all those who heard the insult, because your relationship with the listeners is damaged along with your relationship with the person you insulted. Therefore, unless you're willing to go to extraordinary lengths to reassemble the group, you must apologize almost immediately. A private apology for a public insult is not sufficient because your relationship with everyone who was present is damaged, and will remain so until the apology is accomplished in their eyes.

We can see how Talmud was created in this interchange (lines 6–7): the *tanna* (a kind of living CD-ROM who mentally stores information and can recite it when called upon) recites a tradition and the sage comments on it. This is one of the Gemara's most typical sequences: a tannaitic source is commented upon by a sage.

Sages
Resh Lakish

Rabbi Shimon ben Lakish, commonly known as Resh Lakish, was one of the greatest of the Palestinian *amoraim*. He was a student, colleague, and brother-in-law of Rabbi Yohanan.

As a youth, Resh Lakish studied Torah and showed great talent. However, apparently constrained by dire poverty, he sold himself as a gladiator in the Roman arena. Many stories are told of his exceptional courage and physical strength. In time, following a meeting with Rabbi Yohanan, he returned to the world of Torah, beginning as Rabbi Yohanan's student and then becoming his colleague and marrying his sister.

Rabbi Yohanan and Resh Lakish had many halakhic differences of opinion. However, in great measure Resh Lakish's intention was not to disagree with Rabbi Yohanan, but rather to clarify and elucidate matters by means of dialectical argumentation. Rabbi Yohanan regarded him with great respect and used to say, "My equal disagrees with me."

Resh Lakish was famous for his piety and rigor, and it was said that one could lend money without witnesses to a person with whom Resh Lakish spoke in public, for he spoke only to people of unblemished character. When he died he left a son who was notable for his talents and genius.

—Rabbi Steinsaltz

Rabbi Shmuel bar Nahmani.

A Palestinian *amora* of the second and third generations. Rabbi Shmuel bar Nahmani was an important teacher of Aggadah. He was a disciple of Rabbi Yonatan and transmitted many teachings in his name. He also studied with Rabbi Yehoshua ben Levi. He lived in Lydda in central Palestine.

—Rabbi Steinsaltz

Rabbi Elazar.

In the Talmud, citations of Rabbi Elazar with no patronymic refer to Rabbi Elazar ben Pedat, an *amora* of the second generation. He was born in Babylonia and immigrated to Eretz Israel and came to inherit Rabbi Yohanan's position as head of the Tiberias Yeshivah. In Babylonia he was a student of both Rav and Shmuel; his teacher in Eretz Israel was Rabbi Hanina bar Hama. He also studied with Rabbi Oshaya, but his main teacher was Rabbi Yohanan, and in time he came to be considered his colleague. He was given the honorific title of "master" of Eretz Israel. Many sages transmit teachings in his name, especially Rabbi Abbahu. He did not live long after Rabbi Yohanan. We know that he was a priest and that he had sons who died during his lifetime. The only one to survive was

Rabbi Pedat, who was the *amora* (translator) in Rabbi Assi's yeshivah.

—Rabbi Steinsaltz

Rabbi Yohanan.

This is Rabbi Yohanan bar Nappaha, one of the greatest *amoraim*, whose teachings are of primary importance in both the Babylonian and Jerusalem Talmuds. He lived in Tiberias to a great age.

Almost nothing is known of his family origins, but he became an orphan at an early age, and, although he inherited considerable property, he spent most of his wealth in his strong desire to study Torah constantly, so that he actually became poor. He was just old enough to study under Rabbi Yehudah HaNasi, the editor of the Mishnah, but most of his Torah knowledge was derived from Rabbi Yehudah HaNasi's students, from Hizkiyah ben Hiyya and from Rabbi Oshaya, and from his outstanding teacher Rabbi Yannai, who greatly praised him. In time he became the head of a yeshivah in Tiberias, marking the beginning of a period during which his fame and influence constantly increased. For a long time Rabbi Yohanan was the leading rabbinical scholar of the entire Jewish world, not only in Eretz Israel but also in Babylonia, whose sages respected him greatly. Many of them came to Eretz Israel to become his outstanding students.

He was a master of both Halakhah and Aggadah. His teachings in both areas are found very widely, and serve as the basis for both of the Talmuds. In recognition of his intellectual and spiritual greatness the Halakhah is decided according to his opinion in almost every case, even when Rav or Shmuel, the greatest *amoraim* of Babylonia (whom he regarded as greater than himself), disagree with him. Only when he disagrees with his teachers in Eretz Israel (such as Rabbi Yannai and Rabbi Yehoshua ben Levi) does the Halakhah not follow his opinion.

We know little about his life, and only certain details are recorded. Rabbi Yohanan was famous for being handsome, and much was said in praise of his comeliness. By nature he was excitable, so that occasionally he was too severe with his friends and students, and immediately afterwards was stricken with remorse. We know that his life was full of suffering. Ten of his sons died in his lifetime, although he also had daughters. There is a Geonic tradition that one of his sons remained alive—Rabbi Matena, who was an *amora* of Babylonia. The death of his student, friend, and brother-in-law, Resh Lakish, for which he considered himself responsible, brought his own death closer.

Rabbi Yohanan had many students. In fact all succeeding generations of *amoraim* in Eretz Israel were his students and imbibed his teachings—so much so that he is said to be the author of the Jerusalem Talmud. His greatest students were his brother-in-law Resh Lakish, Rabbi Elazar, Rabbi Hiyya bar Abba, Rabbi Abbahu, Rabbi Yose bar Hanina, Rabbi Ammi, and Rabbi Assi.

—Rabbi Steinsaltz

Rav Nahman bar Yitzhak.

One of the leading Babylonian *amoraim* of the fourth generation. Rav Nahman bar Yitzhak was born in Sura. His mother was the sister of Rav Aha bar Yosef. His principal teacher was Rav Nahman bar Ya'akov, but he also studied under Rav Hisda. After the death of Rava, Rav Nahman bar Yitzhak was appointed head of the Pumbedita Yeshivah.

—Rabbi Steinsaltz

Public Humiliation

As a little death,
public humiliation.
Think before you speak.

Thus our tanna taught:
Public humiliation
is a little death.

Like bloodshed it is
to cause her public shaming.
Thus our tanna taught.

—Naomi Hyman

A Tanna taught before Rav Nachman bar Yitzhak: Anyone who whitens the face of his fellow in public is as if he sheds blood.

Our faces are filled with color.

Shaming someone publicly so his face turns white is like shedding blood. Disappointing someone who then feels blue is like abandoning a promise. Embarrassing someone so her face turns red as a result of words or deeds is hurtful. Acting jealously toward someone, being green with envy, is childish. Speaking to someone until we are blue in the face shows stubbornness. Responding to someone while red with anger is harmful.

Our faces are filled with light.

Connecting with a special person casts a warm glow in her eyes. Complimenting another reflects joy on his face. Comforting each other kindles compassion. Studying

Torah shines new light on how to live. Reaching out to one in need brightens the day. Causing a friend to smile brings light to the world.

Barcheinu Avinu kulanu k'echad b'or panecha. Bless us all, Our Parent, with the Divine Light shining on us from Your face.

—*Mark Frydenberg*

Fragile Egos.

Putting others to shame in public underscores the Talmudic awareness of the fragility of the human ego. One's public identity takes time to construct, yet it is so easily damaged or destroyed. Such humiliation renders us helpless or dangerous in reaction.

—*Robert E. Reichlin*

NOTES

NOTES

TRANSLATION AND COMMENTARY

אָמַר לֵיהּ [1]**Abaye said to Rav Dimi: About what are people** especially **careful in Eretz Israel?**

אָמַר לֵיהּ [2]**Rav Dimi said to** Abaye: **About putting people to shame.** [3]**For Rabbi Ḥanina said: All descend to Gehinnom** (hell) after death in punishment for their sins, **except for three** categories of people.

הַכֹּל סָלְקָא דַּעְתָּךְ [4]**At first glance, this statement seems** incredible, and the Gemara immediately objects: **Can it enter your mind** to think that **"all descend"?** Is it conceivable that all people, except for those falling into one of the three categories about to be specified, deserve to be punished in Gehinnom?

אֶלָּא אֵימָא [5]**Rather,** Rabbi Ḥanina's statement needs to be amended as follows: **Say: Everyone who** is punished and **descends to Gehinnom** will eventually, after due time for atonement, **ascend** and leave Gehinnom, **except for three** types of sinners who **descend** to Gehinnom **and do not ascend,** because their crimes are so heinous. [6]**The following are the** three sins: (1) **Someone who cohabits with a married woman.** (2) **Someone who puts another person to shame in public.** (3) **Someone who calls another person by a derogatory name.**

מְכַנֶּה הַיְינוּ מַלְבִּין [7]The Gemara objects: **Calling a person by a derogatory name is the same as shaming** him. Why then are they considered distinct categories?

אַף עַל גַּב [8]The Gemara answers: There are cases in which calling a person by a derogatory name does not put him to shame. Rabbi Ḥanina listed this sin separately to teach us that it is an exceedingly grave offense to call a person by a derogatory name **even if he was used to** this derogatory name being used in place of **his name,** and is no longer embarrassed by it. For the *intent* of the person who uses the derogatory name is to degrade another human being, and that intention is a crime in its own right, even if no one is actually hurt by it.

אָמַר רַבָּה בַּר בַּר חָנָה [9]The Gemara cites additional Rabbinic teachings which stress the gravity of putting other people to shame: **Rabbah bar Bar Ḥanah said in the name of Rabbi Yoḥanan:**

LITERAL TRANSLATION

[1]Abaye said to Rav Dimi: About what are [people] careful in Eretz Israel (lit., "the west")?

[2]He said to him: About putting [people] to shame.

[3]For Rabbi Ḥanina said: All descend to Gehinnom, except for three.

[4]Can it enter your mind [that] "all [descend]"?

[5]Rather, say: All who descend to Gehinnom ascend, except for three who descend and do not ascend. [6]And they are these: Someone who cohabits with a married woman, someone who shames his fellow in public, and someone who calls his fellow by a bad name.

[7]Calling [a person by a bad name] is the same as shaming!

[8]Even though he is used to it as his name.

[9]Rabbah bar Bar Ḥanah said in the name of Rabbi Yoḥanan:

Hebrew text

[1]אָמַר לֵיהּ אַבַּיֵי לְרַב דִּימִי: בְּמַעַרְבָא בְּמַאי זְהִירֵי? [2]אָמַר לֵיהּ: בְּאַחְוּוּרֵי אַפֵּי. [3]דְּאָמַר רַבִּי חֲנִינָא: הַכֹּל יוֹרְדִין לַגֵּיהִנָּם, חוּץ מִשְּׁלֹשָׁה. [4]הַכֹּל סָלְקָא דַּעְתָּךְ? [5]אֶלָּא אֵימָא: כָּל הַיּוֹרְדִין לַגֵּיהִנָּם עוֹלִים, חוּץ מִשְּׁלֹשָׁה שֶׁיּוֹרְדִין וְאֵין עוֹלִין. [6]וְאֵלּוּ הֵן: הַבָּא עַל אֵשֶׁת אִישׁ, וְהַמַּלְבִּין פְּנֵי חֲבֵירוֹ בָּרַבִּים, וְהַמְכַנֶּה שֵׁם רַע לַחֲבֵירוֹ. [7]מְכַנֶּה הַיְינוּ מַלְבִּין! [8]אַף עַל גַּב דִּדָשׁ בֵּיהּ בִּשְׁמֵיהּ. [9]אָמַר רַבָּה בַּר בַּר חָנָה אָמַר רַבִּי יוֹחָנָן:

RASHI

הכל סלקא דעתך — וכי הכל יורדין. הכי גרסינן: כל היורדין לגיהנם עולין.

דדש ביה — כבר הורגל בכך שמכנים אותו כן, ואין פניו מתלבנות ומכל מקום — זה להכלימו מתכוין.

BACKGROUND

All who descend to Gehinnom. Elsewhere (*Rosh HaShanah* 17a) the Gemara states that "the wicked are judged in Gehinnom for twelve months," after which their sins are atoned for. However, certain sins are so heinous that they can never be expiated, and of such sinners we read in Isaiah (66:24): "Their worm shall not die, neither shall their fire be quenched."

Someone who cohabits with a married woman. The sin of adultery is extremely grave, and it is forbidden by the Ten Commandments. In other sources (see *Ḥagigah* 9b) the gravity of this prohibition is discussed. In addition to violating a severe prohibition and offending God, the adulterer also causes anguish and suffering to the woman's husband. Moreover, if the adultery comes to light, the woman is forbidden to her husband forever, so she too suffers not only for her sin but also by being separated from her husband.

NOTES

בְּמַעַרְבָא בְּמַאי זְהִירֵי **About what are people careful in the West?** The Gemara assumes that the residents of the "West" (i.e., Eretz Israel) were especially careful not to put others to shame, because doing so is tantamount to shedding blood, and the Torah explicitly exhorts us to avoid "defiling the land" (i.e., Eretz Israel) by committing murder (see Numbers 35:33 f; *Iyyun Ya'akov*).

חוּץ מִשְּׁלֹשָׁה שֶׁיּוֹרְדִין **Except for three who descend.** *Meiri* (following *Ramban*) explains that the penalty for these offenses is so severe because people who commit them generally do not realize that what they did is wrong, and hence do not repent.

HALAKHAH

הַמְכַנֶּה שֵׁם רַע לַחֲבֵירוֹ **Someone who calls his fellow by a bad name.** "It is forbidden to call other people by derogatory names in order to humiliate them, even if they are used to such names." (*Shulḥan Arukh, Ḥoshen Mishpat* 228:8.)

"And others say . . ."

p. 227 Commentary

This page begins with Abaye's question to Rav Dimi. Rav Dimi would often travel from the Land of Israel to Babylonia to fill them in, as it were, on customs of the Holy Land. The Note, on the bottom of this page, is particularly helpful in understanding Rav Dimi's answer.

What we have next is quite interesting. Rav Dimi cites a *baraita* but he appears to cite an incorrect version. It's not possible that everyone goes to Gehinnom (the Jewish version of Hell) except for three kinds of sinners, so the Gemara fixes the text so that it makes sense. This is not at all unusual. The Gemara often corrects erroneously reported traditions. All sinners, according to the amended version, eventually leave Gehinnom, except for three kinds whose sins are so heinous that they are never allowed out: one who "whitens the face," i.e., shames another person in public (thus the link with Rav Nahman's teaching on p. 226), as well as one who sleeps with a married woman and one who calls another by a derogatory name. What do these actions have in common? They each betray Judaism's commitment to honor God's image in every human being.

Now, what about this concept of Gehinnom? Many Jews hold the erroneous notion that Judaism does not postulate a Heaven or Hell. This is manifestly untrue. We do believe in an afterlife. However, we do not emphasize how one enters it or its machinations as much as some other religions do. In fact, this passage is one of a very few that outline what happens

once one has entered Gehinnom.

The Gemara then asks in lines 7–8 what is the difference between shaming a person in public and calling them a derogatory name. The answer is that even if the person's self-esteem is such that he or she does not mind being called by an offensive name, each of us is still bound to observe the mitzvah of treating each human being as created in God's image. We may not defile that Divine image in people even if they don't care whether we do.

Since Rabbi Steinsaltz mentions the passage on B. Hagigah 9b in his Background comment ("Someone who cohabits with a married woman"), we might do well to explore it. It is a mishnah and then some commentary:

> Rabbi Shimon ben M'nasya says: Who is [described by the phrase] "That which is crooked cannot be repaired" (Ecclesiastes 1:15)? This [describes] the one who has sexual relations with one prohibited [to him by the laws of adultery and incest] and begets from that relationship a bastard. If you would say [that this verse from Ecclesiastes] applies to a thief or a robber [you would be incorrect for] he can make restitution and [thereby] repair the damage he caused. Rabbi Shimon ben Yohai says, "We don't call [anyone] crooked unless he was straight at first and then became crooked. And who might this be? This is a student of a sage who becomes estranged from the Torah. (M. Hagigah 1:7)

This mishnah discusses what it means to have a situation that is beyond repair, i.e., someone is crooked and can't be made straight. The text offers three opinions: (1) a man who sleeps with a woman forbidden to him and produces a child from this union, (2) one who steals (although this option is rejected since this person can make restitution and pay damages), and (3) a sage who forsakes Torah. It is noted in the Gemara to this mishnah (B. Hagigah 9b) that even if no bastard is produced from an adulterous union the act still causes irreparable harm. Since men could have more than one wife in this era, sleeping with an unmarried woman was not the same sort of sin as sleeping with a married one. Only the latter was considered adultery. According to this opinion, even if no child results from this adulterous union it is a sin beyond repair because the woman is forbidden to her husband and the hurt feelings that result are irreparable. It is significant that impaired fertility and defective preservation of Torah are linked in this mishnah. The sages believed that one's students were one's spiritual children. Should such a "spiritual child" walk away from Torah one would have wasted one's spiritual fertility, as it were, and lost one's posterity.

—JZA

Sages
Rav Dimi.

An *amora* of the third and fourth generations, Rav Dimi lived in both Babylonia and Eretz Israel. He seems to have been a Babylonian who moved to Eretz Israel in his youth. He returned to Babylonia several times, bringing with him the teachings of Eretz Israel. Rav Dimi was responsible for the transmission of these teachings, and in the Jerusalem Talmud he is called Rav Avdimi (or Avduma) Nehuta. He was one of the sages who were given the

title "the emigrant Rabbis" because they carried the teachings of Eretz Israel to Babylonia (mainly the teachings of Rabbi Yohanan, Resh Lakish, and Rabbi Elazar). Others who shared in this task were Rabbah bar Hanah and Ulla, and later Rabin, Rav Shmuel bar Yehudah, and others. The Talmud reports dozens of laws that Rav Dimi brought from one Torah center to the other, and he debated with the greatest sages of his generation about them. At the end of his life, he is believed to have returned to Babylonia, where he died.

—Rabbi Steinsaltz

Rabbi Hanina.

When the name of the *amora* Rabbi Hanina is used without a patronymic in the Talmud, the reference is to Rabbi Hanina bar Hama, a first-generation *amora* from Eretz Israel.

Rabbi Hanina originally came from Babylonia, although he immigrated to Eretz Israel at a relatively early age and studied there with Rabbi Yehudah HaNasi, who was very fond of him (and indeed remarked that Rabbi Hanina was "not a human being, but an angel"). Rabbi Hanina also studied with Rabbi Yehudah HaNasi's most distinguished students, in particular with Rabbi Hiyya. On his deathbed, Rabbi Yehudah HaNasi designated Rabbi Hanina as the new head of his yeshivah, although the latter, in his great modesty, refused to accept the position as long as his older colleague, Rabbi Efes, was still alive.

Rabbi Hanina lived in Sepphoris, where he became wealthy as a honey dealer and established a large academy. He was renowned for his acuity, as well as for his uprightness and piety. Numerous halakhic and aggadic dicta of Rabbi Hanina appear in the Babylonian and Jerusalem Talmuds. He lived to a great age and had many students over an extended period, among them Rabbi Yehoshua ben Levi, who was a student-colleague of his, and Rabbi Yohanan, who studied with him for many years. The *amora* Rabbi Hama the son of Rabbi Hanina was his son.

Shaming another in public.

Try this with your family, a group of friends, or in a classroom:

Have a sheet of paper for each person, with their names at the tops. Each person should have a pen or pencil. Pass the sheets around from person to person. Each person is to write a positive statement about the person whose name appears at the top. Give them a few examples like: "Thank you for making me smile," "You have a wonderful sense of humor," "That color of blue looks good on you." It is as simple as that. When the sheets have made it around to the original person, take turns qvelling over the nice things that have been said.

—Shirley Barish

NOTES

TRANSLATION AND COMMENTARY

[59A] [1]Putting another person to shame in public is so grievous a sin that **it would be** preferable **to cohabit with a woman whose marital status is unclear,** even though such relations carry the risk of committing the serious crime of adultery, rather than **shame anyone publicly.**

מְנָא לָן [2]The Gemara asks: **From where do we know this?** What is the Biblical source for this statement?

מִדְּדָרַשׁ רָבָא [3]The Gemara answers: Rabbi Yoḥanan's statement was based on an interpretation of a verse in Psalms (35:15), **as expounded by Rava.** According to Rava's interpretation, King David's critics publicly embarrassed David about his relationship with Bathsheba, the wife of Uriah the Hittite (II Samuel, Chapter 11), and their offense was more serious than the illicit relationship itself. **For Rava expounded** as follows: **What is the meaning of** the following verse (Psalms 35:15), in which King David declared: **"And when I stumbled** my enemies **rejoiced and gathered together...they tore me, and did not cease"**? In this verse, King David laments that his enemies are constantly seeking opportunities to persecute him, but Rava explains that it has a deeper meaning. The Hebrew word *tzal'i* (צַלְעִי) — literally "my stumbling" — can also mean "my rib," or metaphorically, "my wife," since Eve was created from Adam's rib. Furthermore, the Hebrew words *lo damu* (לֹא דָמוּ) — literally "did not cease" or "did not fall silent" — can also mean "there was no blood." According to Rava, the verse, which speaks of David's enemies in general, actually refers to one particular sort of persecutor — the rivals who publicly humiliated David after his adultery with Bathsheba became public knowledge. Thus, according to Rava's explanation, David's enemies "rejoiced and gathered together over the scandal involving my wife." [4]At this point **David said before the Holy One, Blessed be He: "Master of the Universe, it is revealed and known before You that** I have atoned for my sin. In fact, **if** my enemies **were to tear my flesh** to pieces, **my blood would not drip to the ground"** (translating "did not cease" as "there would be no blood"). David's enemies would not be able to draw any more blood from him, because it is as if he has already lost all his blood from fasting to atone for his sin. Thus we see that it is a great wrong to torment a repentant sinner — to tear his flesh and seek to draw his blood — by seeking to humiliate him over

[59A] [1]נוֹחַ לוֹ לְאָדָם שֶׁיָּבוֹא עַל סְפֵק אֵשֶׁת אִישׁ וְאַל יַלְבִּין פְּנֵי חֲבֵירוֹ בָּרַבִּים.

[2]מְנָא לָן?

[3]מִדְּדָרַשׁ רָבָא. דְּדָרַשׁ רָבָא: מַאי דִּכְתִיב: "וּבְצַלְעִי שָׂמְחוּ וְנֶאֱסָפוּ... קָרְעוּ וְלֹא דָמוּ". [4]אָמַר דָּוִד לִפְנֵי הַקָּדוֹשׁ בָּרוּךְ הוּא: "רִבּוֹנוֹ שֶׁל עוֹלָם, גָּלוּי וְיָדוּעַ לְפָנֶיךָ שֶׁאִם הָיוּ מְקָרְעִים בְּשָׂרִי, לֹא הָיָה דָּמִי שׁוֹתֵת לָאָרֶץ.

LITERAL TRANSLATION

[59A] [1]It is better (lit., "easier") for a man to cohabit with a woman about whom there is a doubt whether she is married and not to put his fellow to shame in public.

[2]From where do we [know this]?

[3]From what Rava expounded. For Rava expounded: What is [it] that is written: "And when I stumbled, they rejoiced and gathered themselves together...they tore me, and did not cease." [4]David said before the Holy One, blessed be He: "Master of the Universe, it is revealed and known before You that if they had torn my flesh, my blood would not have dripped to the ground.

RASHI

ובצלעי — בשביל אשתי זו, שמתחילה חטאתי בה, כמו (בראשית ב) "ויבן את הצלע", שמחו ונאספו. **קרעו ולא דמו** — אם קרעוני לא מצאו דם. **כדדרש רבא** — דטובה מעשה של דוד ובת שבע משלהם. **וספק אשת איש היא.** שהיוצא למלחמת בית דוד גט כריתות כותב לאשתו על מנת שאם ימות שתהא מגורשת מעכשיו, ולא תיזקק ליבם, וכל אותן הימים היא ספק מגורשת, אם מת — מגורשת מתחילה, ואם לא מת — לא נתגרשה.

NOTES

הַבָּא עַל סְפֵק אֵשֶׁת אִישׁ **Cohabitation with a woman about whom there is a doubt whether she is married.** The commentators (*Tosafot* and others) ask why the Gemara spoke of a woman whose marital status is doubtful rather than of one who is definitely married. Among the explanations offered is that of *Talmidei Rabbenu Yonah* (in *Berakhot*), who suggest that it is easier to atone for a sin which one has definitely committed than for an uncertain sin, since people tend to rationalize uncertain sins away, claiming that they never sinned in the first place.

Tosafot here explains that the reference is to David's sin with Bathsheba, the wife of Uriah the Hittite. According to a Rabbinic tradition, even at that early time it was common for soldiers to give their wives a conditional bill of divorce, so that if the soldiers did not return from battle the wives would be divorced from the date the bill of divorce was given. Accordingly, Bathsheba was merely a "doubtfully married woman" with respect to David.

HALAKHAH

אֵשֶׁת אִישׁ **Cohabitation with a married woman.** "One who wittingly has conjugal relations with a married woman other than his wife is subject to death by strangulation." (*Rambam, Sefer Kedushah, Hilkhot Issurei Bi'ah* 1:6.)

TRANSLATION AND COMMENTARY

his past misdeeds. [1]David continues: **"Not only** do my enemies rejoice over my stumbling, but also they constantly draw attention to the matter **even when they engage in** the study of areas of the Halakhah that have nothing to do with me or my sin, such as the study of **the laws of *Nega'im*** (ritual impurity conferred by leprosy; Leviticus, Chapter 13 ff.) **and** the laws of ***Ohalot*** (ritual impurity conferred by "tents" spread over a corpse; Numbers 19:14)." "For example," David continues, "they ask me a Halakhic question of law which sounds innocuous but is meant solely to humiliate me. [2]Thus **they will say to me: 'David, what is the death penalty for someone who cohabits with a married woman?'** — a transparent reference to Bathsheba." [3]David, however, replied to them in kind: **"And I say to them:** 'Someone who cohabits with a married woman is subject to **death by strangulation, but** despite the gravity of his sin, **he** still **has a share in the world to come.** [4]On the other hand, **someone** — like you — **who puts another person to shame in public, does not have a share in the world to come."** Thus, says Rava, it was on the basis of this Midrashic interpretation of the verse from Psalms that Rabbi Yoḥanan said that it is worse to put a repentant sinner to shame, than to cohabit with a woman whose marital status is in doubt. Bathsheba had received a bill of divorce from her husband before he went off to war, and the bill of divorce was to take effect retroactively in the event that he did not return alive. While her husband was away at war, Bathsheba was considered a woman who might be divorced but might also still be married. For if her husband died, she would be divorced retroactively, but if he returned from the war, she would still be married to him.

וְאָמַר מָר זוּטְרָא בַּר טוֹבִיָּה [5]The Gemara now cites additional Rabbinic statements about the gravity of putting a person to shame in public. **Mar Zutra bar Toviyyah said in the name of Rav, and some say: [6]Rav Ḥana bar Bizna said in the name of Rabbi Shimon Ḥasida, and some say: Rabbi Yoḥanan said in the name of Rabbi Shimon ben Yoḥai: [7]It is better for a man to cast himself into a fiery furnace than to put another person to shame in public.**

[1]וְלֹא עוֹד, אֶלָּא אֲפִילּוּ בְּשָׁעָה שֶׁעוֹסְקִין בִּנְגָעִים וְאֳהָלוֹת אוֹמְרִים לִי: [2]׳דָּוִד, הַבָּא עַל אֵשֶׁת אִישׁ מִיתָתוֹ בַּמֶּה׳? [3]וַאֲנִי אוֹמֵר לָהֶם: ׳מִיתָתוֹ בְּחֶנֶק, וְיֵשׁ לוֹ חֵלֶק לָעוֹלָם הַבָּא. [4]אֲבָל הַמַּלְבִּין אֶת פְּנֵי חֲבֵירוֹ בָּרַבִּים אֵין לוֹ חֵלֶק לָעוֹלָם הַבָּא׳״. [5]וְאָמַר מָר זוּטְרָא בַּר טוֹבִיָּה אָמַר רַב; [6]וְאָמְרִי לַהּ: אָמַר רַב חָנָא בַּר בִּיזְנָא אָמַר רַבִּי שִׁמְעוֹן חֲסִידָא; וְאָמְרִי לַהּ אָמַר רַבִּי יוֹחָנָן מִשּׁוּם רַבִּי שִׁמְעוֹן בֶּן יוֹחַאי: [7]נוֹחַ לוֹ לְאָדָם שֶׁיַּפִּיל עַצְמוֹ לְכִבְשַׁן הָאֵשׁ וְאַל יַלְבִּין פְּנֵי חֲבֵירוֹ בָּרַבִּים.

LITERAL TRANSLATION

[1]And not only [this], but even when they engage in [the laws of] *Nega'im* ("Leprosies") and *Ohalot* ("Tents") they say to me: [2]'David, what is the death [penalty] for someone who cohabits with a married woman?' [3]And I say to them: 'His death is by strangulation, but he has a share in the world to come. [4]But someone who puts his fellow to shame in public does not have a share in the world to come.'"

[5]And Mar Zutra bar Toviyyah said in the name of Rav; [6]and some say: Rav Ḥana bar Bizna said in the name of Rabbi Shimon Ḥasida; and some say: Rabbi Yoḥanan said in the name of Rabbi Shimon ben Yoḥai: [7]It is better for a man to cast himself into a fiery furnace and not to put his fellow to shame in public.

NOTES

נְגָעִים וְאֳהָלוֹת The laws of *Neg'aim* and *Ohalot*. The commentators attempt to explain why David's opponents were studying these particular laws. *Tosafot* says that even though the laws of *Nega'im* and *Ohalot* have no connection with the laws of adultery, David's opponents nevertheless saw fit to digress from studying these Halakhot in order to discuss his sin.

Others suggest that these examples were given because the Sages said (*Pesaḥim* 50a) that, even though these laws are considered extremely complex in this world, they will be easy to master in the world to come. By contrast, putting other people to shame is generally considered a minor sin in this world, whereas it will be considered a major transgression in the world to come (*Iyyun Ya'akov*). Others explain that the Gemara spoke of *Nega'im* and *Ohalot* because leprous diseases befall people who speak ill of others — even if what they say is true, as in the case of King David. Thus the Gemara implies that David's opponents slandered him even though they should have known better, since they were studying the laws of *Nega'im* (*Riaf*).

מִיתָתוֹ בְּחֶנֶק, וְיֵשׁ לוֹ חֵלֶק לָעוֹלָם הַבָּא His death is by strangulation, but he has a share in the world to come. This statement seems to contradict the Gemara's previous statement (above, 58b), that adulterers "descend and do not ascend." *Rid* explains that the discussion here refers to a case in which the adulterer repented, in which case he indeed has a share in the world to come. *Ritva*, however, suggests that the death penalty atones for the adulterer's transgression, and he offers yet another explanation: An adulterer "descends and does not ascend" only if a *mamzer* was born from the illicit union. In such cases it is impossible to repent fully, since a palpable manifestation of the sin still exists (cf. Mishnah *Ḥagigah* 1:7).

SAGES

מָר זוּטְרָא בַּר טוֹבִיָּה Mar Zutra bar Toviyyah. A second-generation Babylonian Amora, Mar (or Rav) Zutra bar Toviyyah was an outstanding disciple of Rav, and in many Talmudic passages he transmits Rav's Halakhic and Aggadic teachings. After Rav's death, Mar Zutra studied in the yeshivah of Rav Yehudah, where he became a student-colleague of that scholar. His own teachings are also cited in a number of places.

רַב חָנָא בַּר בִּיזְנָא Rav Ḥana bar Bizna. A Babylonian Amora of the second and third generations, Rav Ḥana bar Bizna, who was a Rabbinical judge in Pumbedita, often transmitted the teachings of Rabbi Shimon Ḥasida. He was renowned among the scholars of his time both as an expert on Aggadah and as a Halakhic authority.

רַבִּי שִׁמְעוֹן חֲסִידָא Rabbi Shimon Ḥasida. A Palestinian Amora of the first and second generations, Rabbi Shimon Ḥasida must be distinguished from Rabbi Shimon HeḤasid, who was a Tanna and appears in several Baraitot.

BACKGROUND

בְּשָׁעָה שֶׁעוֹסְקִין בִּנְגָעִים וְאֳהָלוֹת When they engage in the laws of *Nega'im* and *Ohalot*. Many Aggadic passages depict King David as the head of a yeshivah engaged in intensive Torah study, much like the Mishnaic and Talmudic Sages. Such anachronistic descriptions did not disturb the Talmudic Sages, since their main interest was to illustrate moral lessons in a manner which their listeners would find meaningful, and anachronistic depictions of Biblical personalities certainly served this goal.

נוֹחַ לוֹ לְאָדָם שֶׁיַּפִּיל עַצְמוֹ לְכִבְשַׁן הָאֵשׁ It is better for a man to cast himself into a fiery furnace. *Tosafot* and *Rabbenu Yonah* seem to take this statement literally, and thus it follows that one should submit to death, if necessary, rather than put others to shame. Indeed, the Gemara relates elsewhere (*Ketubot* 67b) that the Amora Mar

NOTES

"And others say . . ."

pp. 228–229 Commentary

The Gemara is now proceeding to discuss the important teaching about the three kinds of people consigned to Gehinnom for shaming others (p. 227, lines 2–6). The assertion, there, that it is better to sleep with a woman whose marital status is in doubt rather than to insult someone in public causes the sages a bit of surprise. The proof of this comes from a complicated, two-part midrash on Psalm 35:15. (Warning: If this is too hard, go through it and try to understand it, but if you're becoming too frustrated, put it by for later. Do not get stuck on a passage that's genuinely difficult, even though Rabbi Steinsaltz's commentary helps by explaining the punning in the text.)

Here is an example of when looking up parallel passages can really help. The parallel is from tractate B. Sanhedrin, where the episode of David and Bathsheba is cast as a test of King David by God. King David wanted his name included in the first part of the Amidah in which we call on "The God of Abraham, the God of Isaac, and the God of Jacob." God tells David that if he can pass a test he can have his name added to the prayer. David fails with Bathsheba and we then have many expositions of verses from Psalms (which are attributed to David) relating to his sin with Bathsheba. Here is how this particular passage looks in B. Sanhedrin:

> Rava made [the following] interpretation [of a Scriptural verse]. What is meant by the verse, "They got together and rejoiced at my stumbling. Unknown crip-

ples gather around me and tear at me incessantly." (Psalm 35:15) Said David before the Holy One, blessed be He, "Master of the Universe, it is revealed and known before You that if they would have torn my flesh, my blood would not have flowed. And not only that, but at the hour when they were studying the four [kinds of] death sentences [handed down by] a Jewish court, they would stop their recitation of the laws and say to me, 'David, what is the death penalty for one who has sexual relations with a married woman?' I said to them, 'The death penalty for one who has sexual relations with a married woman is by strangulation, but at least [this man would have] a portion in the World to Come. But the one who embarrasses his fellow in public [literally, "whitens the face of his fellow"] does not have [a portion] in the World to Come.' " (B. Sanhedrin 107a)

In this version, everything seems more logical. Those taunting David have "whitened his face"—drawn blood, so to speak, with their jibes. During a discussion of the four modes of execution available to a Jewish court, they taunt him but he is able to retort that even though he might be liable to execution, he will still merit life in the World to Come whereas they will not.

This exposition (and the one in our primary passage) proves the point that one who sleeps with a woman whose marital status is unclear (see Rabbi Steinsaltz's note on p. 228) is better off than one who shames another in public. You can see, by comparing the passage from B. Sanhedrin to the one in Bava

Metzia, how much easier to understand the former is than the latter. This is one of the ways that using parallel texts can help you understand difficult passages. In fact, you might enjoy looking at the passage from Sanhedrin at more length since it is an engaging discussion of David's sin with Bathsheba.

How hard are Nega'im and Ohalot to study? Judge for yourself from these brief samples:

A house that is closed up [because of leprosy] communicates uncleanness from the inner side [by contact]. And a definitively [diagnosed house conveys ritual impurity through contact with] its inner side and its outer side. Both [sorts of houses] convey ritual impurity when one enters [them]. (M. Nega'im 13:4)

[If] an oven stands within the house [where a corpse lies], but its arched chimney is outside [the house], and pallbearers carried [the corpse] over [this chimney] the School of Shammai says: All [things in the house] are impure. But the School of Hillel say: The oven becomes impure but [the rest of] the house remains ritually pure. Rabbi Akiba says: Even the oven is ritually pure. (M. Ohalot 5:1)

These passages have to do with different kinds of impurities and how they are communicated. They are, indeed, rather difficult when compared with the mishnah we are studying now.

—JZA

Sages
Rav.

This is Rav Abba bar Aivo, the greatest of the first generation of Babylonian *amoraim*. Rav was born in Babylonia to a prominent family that had produced many Jewish sages and was descended from King David. He immigrated to Eretz Israel with the family of his uncle, Rabbi Hiyya, and studied Torah there, mainly with Rabbi Yehudah HaNasi. Rav was appointed to Rabbi Yehudah's court and remained in Eretz Israel for some time before returning to Babylonia, where he settled. Though there had been Torah centers in Babylonia before his time (in Hutzal and in Neharde'a), Rav founded the great yeshivah in Sura, raising the level of Torah study in Babylonia to that of Eretz Israel. After some time he was acknowledged as the chief Torah sage in Eretz Israel as well.

Since Rav discussed halakhic questions with the last of the *tannaim*, a principle was stated in the Talmud according to which Rav's authority is equal to that of the *tannaim*: a *baraita* cannot be used to challenge his teachings, since he too is a *tanna*. Indeed, according to a Geonic tradition, when Rav (or Rabbi) Abba is quoted in a *baraita*, the reference is to Rav. Three places in the Talmud refer to Rabbi Abba, the *tanna*. Rav's closest friend and his opponent in halakhic discussions was Shmuel, and their controversies are recorded throughout the Talmud. In matters of ritual law the Halakhah follows Rav, and in civil matters it follows Shmuel.

Rav lived to a ripe old age, and had many disciples. In fact, all the sages of the following generations were his students, and teachings cited in his name comprise a significant part of the Babylonian Talmud. The most famous of his students were Rav Huna, Rav Yehudah, Rav Hisda, and Rav Hamnuna. Rav had at least two sons, Aivo and Hiyya. Hiyya bar Rav was a sage, and Rav's grandson, Shimi bar Hiyya, was also an important sage who had the opportunity of studying with his grandfather.

Rav married into the family of the Exilarch, and Rabbana Nehemyah and Rabbana Ukva, sages descended from the Exilarch, were Rav's grandsons by his daughter.

—Rabbi Steinsaltz

Rava.

A great Babylonian *amora* of the fourth generation, Rava was a colleague of Abaye. His father, Rav Yosef bar Hama, was also a famous sage. Rava's outstanding teacher was Rav Nahman bar Ya'akov, and he was also a student of Rav Hisda, with whom he studied together with his colleague Rami bar Hama. Rav Hisda's daughter married Rami bar Hama, and when Rami bar Hama died, she married Rava. Rava also studied with Rav Yosef. He founded a yeshivah in Mehoza. In all the many halakhic controversies between him and Abaye, the Halakhah follows him, except for six cases. After Abaye's death, Rav was appointed head of the Pumbedita Yeshivah, which he transferred to his home city of Mehoza. Among his students were Rav Pappa and Rav Huna, the son of Rav Yehoshua. A great number of sages transmit teachings in his name: Rav Zevid Mar the son of Rav Yosef, Rav Mesharshiya, Rav Pappi, Ravina, and others. After his death the yeshivah of Mehoza split in two, and Rav Nahman bar Yitzhak filled his place as the head of the Pumbedita Yeshivah, while Rav Pappa established a yeshivah of his own in Neresh.

—Rabbi Steinsaltz

Shaming.

A quotation from Andre Malraux's *Man's Fate* (New York: Vintage/Random House, 1990, p. 281): ". . . a deep humiliation calls for a violent negation of the world." Hence, verbal *ona'ah* sets forth the conditions for destruction. (This same quote could be applied to Rabbi Akiva's statement about the impact of insult to Rabbi Eliezer, page 237–238, 59b, line 7, bottom of the page.)

—Robert E. Reichlin

NOTES

TRANSLATION AND COMMENTARY

מְנָא לָן ¹The Gemara asks: **From where** in the Bible do we know this?

מִתָּמָר ²It answers: **From** the case of **Tamar** (Genesis, Chapter 38). Tamar had been married to two of Judah's sons, each of whom had died without issue. Under the law of levirate marriage, she was required to marry another member of Judah's family. Judah seemed reluctant to allow her to marry his only remaining son, so Tamar disguised herself as a prostitute, seduced Judah himself, and persuaded him to give her his signet, cord, and staff. She became pregnant, and Judah accused her of adultery while already betrothed under the levirate-marriage law. The punishment for that crime was death by burning. Tamar's response **is written** in verse 25: **"When she was brought forth** to be executed, **she sent to her father-in-law** saying, I am pregnant by the man to whom this signet, cord, and staff belong." Tamar made no effort to clear herself by publicly declaring that Judah himself was the father of her unborn child. She waited until the last moment and left the matter to Judah's own conscience. Thus we see that she was willing to be burned to death, rather than publicly humiliate her father-in-law. Accordingly, we may infer that it is better to be cast into a fiery furnace than to put another person to shame in public.

אָמַר רַב חִנָּנָא בְּרֵיהּ דְּרַב אִידִי ³Continuing its discussion of the laws of verbal ona'ah, the Gemara notes: **Rav Ḥinena the son of Rav Idi said: What is the meaning of** the verse (Leviticus 25:17): **"And you shall not wrong each man his neighbor"?** Who is the "neighbor" to whom the verse refers? Rav Ḥinena the son of Rav Idi answers: [4]The verse means: **"Do not wrong a people that is with you in observance of the Torah and the commandments."** According to Rav Ḥinena, the word *amito* (עֲמִיתוֹ) — "his neighbor" — should be interpreted as if it were two words, *am ito* (עַם אִתוֹ), meaning "the people with him," i.e., people who are "together with him" in that they are religiously observant. Accordingly, he infers that the prohibition against verbal ona'ah applies specifically among people who are themselves observant of the Torah and its commandments.

אָמַר רַב [5]The Gemara now considers another Rabbinic statement about the gravity of causing anguish to other people. **Rav said: A person should always be careful about distressing his wife.** Rav explains: There is a reason why it is an especially grave sin for a husband to hurt his wife. [6]**Since a wife's tears are close at hand** — she is apt to shed tears if her husband insults her — Divine **punishment for distressing her is** also **near** at hand and ready to befall her husband as soon as he insults her. For while it is reprehensible to cause people anguish, it is even more serious to drive them to tears.

Hebrew Text (center column)

מְנָא לָן? [1]

מִתָּמָר, דִּכְתִיב: "הִיא מוּצֵאת, וְהִיא שָׁלְחָה אֶל חָמִיהָ". [2]

אָמַר רַב חִנָּנָא בְּרֵיהּ דְּרַב אִידִי: [3] מַאי דִכְתִיב: "וְלֹא תוֹנוּ אִישׁ אֶת עֲמִיתוֹ"? [4]"עַם שֶׁאִתְּךָ בְּתוֹרָה וּבְמִצְוֹת אַל תּוֹנֵיהוּ.

אָמַר רַב: לְעוֹלָם יְהֵא אָדָם זָהִיר בְּאוֹנָאַת אִשְׁתּוֹ, [5] [6]שֶׁמִּתּוֹךְ שֶׁדִּמְעָתָהּ מְצוּיָה, אוֹנָאָתָהּ קְרוֹבָה.

RASHI

היא מוצאת והיא שלחה — אף על פי שהיו מוציאין אותה לשריפה לא אמרה להם: ליהודה נבעלתי, ואם יודה הוא מעצמו — למי שאלה לו אנכי הרה, אלא שלח שלחה לו: למי שאלה לו אנכי הרה, ואם יודה הוא מעצמו, לגעריה. **עמיתו** — עם אתו. **באונאת אשתו** — באונאת דברים, לגעריה. אונאתה **קרובה לבא** — פורענות אונאתה ממהר לבא.

Left margin (Background / Sages)

Ukva entered a fiery furnace together with his wife in order to avoid putting someone to shame. However, *Rambam* and *Meiri* seem to maintain that Mar Zutra's statement was meant figuratively, and was only intended to emphasize the severity of the prohibition against publicly shaming others.

SAGES

רַב חִנָּנָא בְּרֵיהּ דְּרַב אִידִי **Rav Ḥinena the son of Rav Idi.** A Babylonian Amora of the third generation, Rav Ḥinena the son of Rav Idi was apparently a student of Rav Adda bar Ahavah (the first), and various teachings (primarily Aggadic) are cited in his name.

BACKGROUND

עַם שֶׁאִתְּךָ בְּתוֹרָה וּבְמִצְוֹת **A people that is with you in observance of the Torah and the commandments.** This Halakhah, which applies to the laws of verbal ona'ah, has parallels among other Halakhot governing honorable behavior with others. The basic assumption in all these cases is that one only honors those who are worthy of honor. A father or a leader is worthy of honor by virtue of his elevated position, and one may not disgrace, curse, or embarrass a fellow-Jew even if he is not conspicuously worthy of honor. However, someone who deviates from Jewish laws and commits sins in public brings dishonor upon himself by his deeds, thus depriving himself of the right to be honored by others. Therefore, until he repents, the rules about honoring other people do not apply to him.

לְעוֹלָם יְהֵא אָדָם זָהִיר בְּאוֹנָאַת אִשְׁתּוֹ **A man should always be careful about distressing his wife.** Even though God punishes all sinners, He answers immediately the cries of those who demand Divine redress, such as women who are more sensitive to insult than men (see Exodus 22:21-22). In addition, people are more likely to quarrel with their wives than with other women. It should also be noted that people are more apt to treat their wives disrespectfully

---

LITERAL TRANSLATION

[1]From where do we [know this]?

[2]From Tamar, for it is written: "When she was brought forth, she sent to her father-in-law."

[3]Rav Ḥinena the son of Rav Idi said: What is [it] that is written: "And you shall not wrong each man his neighbor"?

[4]Do not wrong a people that is with you in [observance of] the Torah and the commandments.

[5]Rav said: A man should always be careful about distressing his wife, [6]for since her tears are close at hand, [the punishment for] distressing her is near.

NOTES

עַם שֶׁאִתְּךָ עֲמִיתוֹ **"His neighbor" — one who is with you.** *Ritva* explains that this refers to a man's wife (rather than "a people that is with you," as explained in our commentary), since a man's wife is especially close to him (and hence "with him"). This explanation also accounts for the Gemara's association of the two seemingly independent themes of distressing people who are not observant and distressing one's wife.

אוֹנָאַת אִשְׁתּוֹ **Distressing one's wife.** Distressing any woman is a very serious offense, but the Gemara spoke specifically of distressing one's wife, because a man is required to honor his wife more than himself (*Iyyun Ya'akov*).

HALAKHAH

אוֹנָאַת אִשְׁתּוֹ **Wronging one's wife.** "A man must be especially careful not to hurt his wife's feelings, since she is easily hurt and liable to cry." (*Shulḥan Arukh, Ḥoshen Mishpat* 228:3.)

"And others say . . ."

p. 230 Commentary

We continue through the 1-2-3 waltz rhythm of our passage. The Gemara here is commenting on the *baraita* that outlines the three kinds of sinners who go to Gehinnom and never rise up from it. We had one midrashic example of this concept (King David's story) and now, on p. 230, we'll have two more midrashic examples of the gravity of shaming others. The first one is about how Tamar tried to avoid shaming Judah, to the point that she was on the verge of being burned to death along with the twins she was carrying.

Because Judah rescued Tamar and her two sons from the fire, Judah's descendants, Hananiah, Mishael, and Azariah, will be saved from a fire. To read the story, see Daniel chapter 3. You may also want to read all of Genesis chapter 38 to more fully appreciate the story of Judah and Tamar as well as look at B. Sotah 10a–b for a lovely, sustained midrashic exploration of this Torah story. The themes of fire and fertility, conflict and confession, repercussions and reciprocity are all featured in the story of the Akhnai oven that will soon be presented in the Bavli.

At this point you may object, saying to yourself, "If I take the time to read Daniel and Genesis and look up that Sotah passage it'll take me a week to study this one page!" So? What's your hurry? The goal isn't to finish quickly. The goal is to luxuriate in the richness of Torah and Talmud and learn to follow where your interest leads you; to listen to your intuitive, curious side. Who cares whether you finish this week

or next week? In some ways, Talmud is the first Hypertext, such as those currently found on the internet: one text leads to another connected one, and yet another, and so on.

The third midrashic comment about shaming another in public brings us back to the *baraita*/midrash that began this section (see p. 224, lines 5–6). It relies on a pun, as did the one about David. This one (lines 3–4) may upset you because it contends that the laws about shaming someone in public apply only to those who observe the Torah and *mitzvot*. In other words, this midrash seems to say, if people bring shame on themselves by failing to do *mitzvot*, then under Jewish law they've forfeited their right to protection against being shamed by others. How can we understand this ruling? Should there be equal protection regardless of a person's behavior? Or should people forfeit their rights when they bring shame upon themselves? There are no easy answers to these questions.

In lines 5 and 6 the Gemara moves on to a new topic: hurting one's wife's feelings. This theme will be intertwined with our primary motif of hurting people with words. At first, one might interpret lines 5 and 6 as sexist. In fact, they are quite kind and urge men to be sensitive to their wives' feelings. It will help us to understand Rav's statements about wives (here and on p. 231, line 5) if we know that he had a wretched married life (B. Yebamot 37b and 63a). Rav's mention of *ona'ah* and tears lead naturally to a teaching that foreshadows the denouement of the long and important story presented shortly in the Gemara.

—*JZA*

Shaming in Public

Tamar, daughter-in-law to Judah, used deceitful means to lure Judah into have sexual intercourse with her to become pregnant. Despite Tamar's conduct, she understood the substance of the laws of verbal *ona'ah* by refusing to publicly shame Judah even if it meant the loss of her life by execution as an adulteress. Tamar's courageous act in not publicly shaming Judah was apparently recognized by God, who allowed her to live. Tamar would have accepted death over committing verbal *ona'ah* and publicly shaming Judah: a true act of courage.

—H.J. Stern

Verbal *Ona'ah* to a Spouse

A fiduciary relationship is established by law between a husband and a wife. This is a relationship of utmost confidence and trust. If the trust is alleged to have been broken, the spouse who has broken the trust must demonstrate that he or she acted fairly.

Rav's comment, "A person should always be careful about distressing his wife," seems consistent with the modern day notion of a fiduciary relationship. However, the ancients seem to believe that causing one's wife anguish leads to swift divine punishment against the husband whereas the reverse was not true.

Equality of the sexes, especially on the issue of education, knowledge, and intellect, was not recognized by the rabbis. Rav states that "whoever follows his wife's counsel will eventually fall into Gehinnom" as his wife is liable to persuade him to commit a transgression. Although a contrary view to taking the wife's advice is expressed by Rav Pappa, the Gemara proclaims that the wife's counsel as to "religious matters" is invalid.

The ancients apparently viewed women either as less intelligent than men or in need of protection like a small child. It is a great achievement of modern America to recognize by law and by culture the equality of men and women in areas of the professions, business, legal relationships, and other intellectual pursuits. The rabbis may have been motivated by good intentions but they clearly did not understand the capabilities of women.

—H.J. Stern

NOTES

NOTES

TRANSLATION AND COMMENTARY

אָמַר רַבִּי אֶלְעָזָר [1]The Gemara now introduces another Rabbinic statement regarding the power of tears. **Rabbi Elazar said: From the day the Temple was destroyed the gates of prayer have been locked.** Nowadays, prayers are not accepted as readily as they were before the destruction, [2]**as the verse** (Lamentations 3:8), describing the situation after the destruction, **says: "Also when I cry and shout, He shuts out my prayer."** [3]**But,** Rabbi Elazar continues, **even though the gates of prayer have been locked, the gates of tears are not locked.** Even today, anyone who cries for divine intervention can still expect to be answered, [4]**as the verse** (Psalms 39:13) **says: "Hear my prayer, Lord, and give ear to my cry. You will not hold your peace at my tears."** The Psalmist *asks* that his prayers be heard, but states unequivocally that God will not hold His peace at his tears." Thus it follows that one who sheds tears before God is guaranteed divine assistance, even when ordinary prayers might not suffice.

וְאָמַר רַב [5]**And Rav** further **said** that, although a husband must take care not to hurt his wife's feelings, he should not follow her advice — for **whoever follows his wife's counsel will** eventually **fall into Gehinnom,** as his wife is liable to persuade him to commit a transgression. Rav illustrates his point by citing the case of Ahab, the most wicked of the Kings of Israel. Ahab committed his most serious sins at his wife's instigation, [6]**as the verse says** (I Kings 21:25): **"But there was none like Ahab,** who gave himself over to do what was evil in the sight of the Lord, as Jezebel his wife had incited him." Thus we see that a person who follows his wife's advice is liable to be condemned to Gehinnom.

אֲמַר לֵיהּ רַב פַּפָּא לְאַבַּיֵי [7]**Rav Pappa** challenged Rav's directive to shun the advice offered by one's wife and **said to Abaye: But surely people say: "If your wife is short, bend down and whisper to her,"** which shows that a husband should seek his wife's counsel!

לָא קַשְׁיָא [8]The Gemara resolves the contradiction: **There is** really **no difficulty.** Rav's recommendation to avoid seeking one's wife's counsel **applies to general matters** which a woman would be unlikely to understand. Following her advice in such matters could be disastrous. The popular proverb, on the other hand, which urges husbands to go to extremes to seek their wives' counsel, applies **to domestic matters,** which are a woman's domain. [9]**Another version** of the Gemara's resolution of the contradiction was also suggested: According to this version, Rav's statement **applies** specifically **to religious matters.** The popular proverb, on the other hand, applies **to general matters**, to anything that is not religious in nature, whether it is domestic

[1]אָמַר רַבִּי אֶלְעָזָר: מִיּוֹם שֶׁנֶּחֱרַב בֵּית הַמִּקְדָּשׁ נִנְעֲלוּ שַׁעֲרֵי תְפִילָּה, [2]שֶׁנֶּאֱמַר: ״גַּם כִּי אֶזְעַק וַאֲשַׁוֵּעַ, שָׂתַם תְּפִילָּתִי״. [3]וְאַף עַל פִּי שֶׁשַּׁעֲרֵי תְפִילָּה נִנְעֲלוּ, שַׁעֲרֵי דְמָעוֹת לֹא נִנְעֲלוּ, [4]שֶׁנֶּאֱמַר: ״שִׁמְעָה תְפִלָּתִי ה׳, וְשַׁוְעָתִי הַאֲזִינָה. אֶל דִּמְעָתִי אַל תֶּחֱרַשׁ״.

[5]וְאָמַר רַב: כָּל הַהוֹלֵךְ בַּעֲצַת אִשְׁתּוֹ נוֹפֵל בַּגֵּיהִנָּם, [6]שֶׁנֶּאֱמַר: ״רַק לֹא הָיָה כְאַחְאָב, וגו׳״. [7]אֲמַר לֵיהּ רַב פַּפָּא לְאַבַּיֵי: וְהָא אָמְרִי אֱינָשֵׁי: ״אִיתְּתָךְ גּוּצָא, גְּחֵין וְתִלְחוּשׁ לָהּ״! [8]לָא קַשְׁיָא. הָא בְּמִילֵּי דְעָלְמָא, וְהָא בְּמִילֵּי דְבֵיתָא. [9]לִישָּׁנָא אַחֲרִינָא: הָא בְּמִילֵּי דִשְׁמַיָּא, וְהָא בְּמִילֵּי דְעָלְמָא.

LITERAL TRANSLATION

[1]Rabbi Elazar said: From the day the Temple was destroyed the gates of prayer have been locked, [2]as it is said: "Also when I cry and shout, He shuts out my prayer." [3]But even though the gates of prayer have been locked, the gates of tears have not been locked, [4]as it is said: "Hear my prayer, Lord, and give ear to my cry. You will not hold Your peace at my tears."

[5]And Rav said: Whoever follows his wife's counsel falls into Gehinnom, [6]as it is said: "But there was none like Ahab, etc." [7]Rav Pappa said to Abaye: But surely people say: "[If] your wife is short, bend down and whisper to her"! [8]There is no difficulty. This [applies] to worldly matters, and this to domestic matters. [9]Another version: This [applies] to heavenly matters, and this to worldly matters.

RASHI

שמעה תפלתי — אין לשונו מלשון בקשה, שמבקש מאת הקדוש ברוך הוא שישמע תפלתו. אבל ״אל תחרש״ יש לשונו מלשון בקשה, ולומר: בזו אני בוטח שאין דרכך לשתוק ולא להחריש. ״אל תחרש״, אל תעשה, אל תתן, משמשין לשון בקשה ומשמשין לשון עתיד. כגון (תהלים קכא) ״אל יתן למוט״, הרי לשון בקשה, ״ויאמר יעקב לא תתן לי מאומה״ (בראשית ל), הוא לשון עתיד. **רק לא היה כאחאב** — סיפיה דקרא ״אשר הסתה אותו איזבל אשתו״. [**אתתך גוצא** = אשתך קטנה — כפוף עצמך ושמע דבריה].

than they would other women.

BACKGROUND

מִיּוֹם שֶׁנֶּחֱרַב בֵּית הַמִּקְדָּשׁ נִנְעֲלוּ שַׁעֲרֵי תְפִילָּה From the day the Temple was destroyed, the gates of prayer have been locked. Jewish philosophers explain that an especially close relationship obtained between God and the Jews as long as the Temple was standing, and hence prayer and repentance brought an immediate, tangible divine response during this period. By contrast, the destruction of the Temple brought an era of divine wrath in its wake; therefore, God's providence is not always fully manifest, and prayer is not as readily accepted.

שַׁעֲרֵי דְמָעוֹת לֹא נִנְעֲלוּ The gates of tears have not been locked. Even though divine providence is not always manifest since the destruction of the Temple, God nevertheless answers the prayers of sufferers on an individual basis; hence the Gemara's statement that "the gates of tears" are never locked. It is worth noting that numerous liturgical poems, some of which are recited during the closing service (*Ne'ilah*) on Yom Kippur, focus on this theme.

NOTES

מִיּוֹם שֶׁנֶּחֱרַב בֵּית הַמִּקְדָּשׁ From the day the Temple was destroyed. As long as the Temple was standing, people's prayers ascended to Heaven through the Temple gates (cf. I Kings 8:48 and *Rashi* on Genesis 28:17). Thus, after the Temple was destroyed, the gates of prayer were "locked" (*Maharsha*).

"And others say . . ."

p. 231 Commentary

The Talmud is such a beautiful literary creation! Even if it had nothing to tell us about Judaism, faith, history, religious symbolism, or anthropology (which it does, of course—and much more beyond that), we could delight in studying the Talmud for its literary qualities alone. Skip forward here and you'll see that lines 5–7 are parts two and three of the "waltz" on hurting wives' feelings, which began on p. 230, lines 5–6. However, the Talmud sets it up with some beautiful foreshadowing by including a "dip" in the waltz with lines 1–4. In this teaching we learn that tears unlock the gates of heaven. It's no accident that it is placed here, before a dramatic story in which a wife will quote almost those very words to her husband after he has caused her great anguish.

Lines 1–4 show how important tears are in communicating with God. Indeed, this is one method Jews have used throughout the centuries to ascend toward God's presence. If you want to know God's will for your life, one way to find it is to fast, pray, and cry. The Talmud's teaching has a less mystical meaning, too: One should be careful about causing hurt feelings, for they have true and terrible consequences.

The Gemara now returns to the material about wives and records two conflicting opinions. On the one hand, Rav says that whoever follows his wife's advice will eventually find himself in Gehinnom. But Rav Pappa gives the opposite advice: you should make an effort to seek your wife's advice. Rav and Rav Pappa were not sitting together having an argument in person. (Rav was an *amora* of the first generation (220–250 C.E.) and Rav Pappa was of the fifth generation (350–375 C.E.). Rather, these sages represent two opposing views likely to be found in every generation. While these two statements are arranged in chronological order, they may also reflect the values of the Gemara, which tends to put the statement that is most widely accepted last in a passage. The *stamma* in lines 8 and 9 attempts to elucidate the true difference between these two points of view. There is, in fact, probably no way to resolve them, nor should we try to do so: they accurately reflect the experiences of different groups of people and should be allowed to stand as they are.

—JZA

Sages
Rav Pappa.

One of the leading Babylonian *amoraim* of the fifth generation, Rav Pappa was a student of Abaye and of Rava, and was a colleague of Rav Huna the son of Rav Yehoshua. After Rava's death his yeshivah was divided: part went to Pumbedita with Rav Nahman bar Yitzhak, and the other part went to Neresh with Rav Pappa. Rav Pappa's yeshivah was famous and had many students, and among his disciples were Rav Ashi and Ravina. He served as head of his yeshivah for nineteen years.

—Rabbi Steinsaltz

Distressing one's spouse.

How about distressing the husband? I think it is just as bad to hurt or cause distress to one's husband as to one's wife. It took my husband and me a number of years to learn to respect each other's feelings. It doesn't happen overnight. We worked at it.

I will never forget when, many years ago, with an eight-month-old baby, I decided I didn't have time to fool with long hair and had it cut off. Well, I had no idea that my husband would react the way he did: the silent treatment for one whole week! Sure we made up, delightfully, and talked it out. He promised never to give me the silent treatment again and I promised never to make drastic changes (even to my hair) without first discussing it with him. And here we are almost forty-nine years later!

My husband and I were discussing this section of the Talmud. I made the statement that these sages seemed to really care for the welfare of the woman. My husband's response: "That's

because they knew the welfare of the man depended on the woman!" And we hadn't even gotten to discuss where it says "Honor your wives so that you become wealthy."

—*Shirley Barish*

Keep one's home well stocked with food.

How is your temperament when you are hungry? Try this experiment: With your spouse, friend, partner, etc., make a commitment for two days to eat a minimal amount of food. For example, breakfast: coffee, tea, juice; lunch: one cup of rice; dinner: one cup of pasta—no sauce! Important! Keep a journal for the two days. Pay special attention to your temperament and make journal entries of how you react to stress when you are hungry. At the end of the two-day period, break your fast and share your journal entries. Then make a donation of money, food, and time to your local Food Bank program.

—*Shirley Barish*

NOTES

NOTES

TRANSLATION AND COMMENTARY

or not. In all such questions, the wife's opinion is at least as good as the husband's, and her advice is invaluable.

אָמַר רַב חִסְדָּא [1]The Gemara now cites three additional Rabbinic statements dealing with the dire consequences of *ona'ah* — wronging one's fellow man — whether by fraud ("monetary *ona'ah*"; אוֹנָאַת מָמוֹן) or by causing him anguish ("verbal *ona'ah*"; אוֹנָאַת דְּבָרִים). All three statements make the same point, using different metaphors: that God takes a special interest in avenging the sins of fraud and verbal cruelty. The first metaphor is based on the image of prayers passing through the gates of Heaven on their way to God. On their way, they tend to be delayed or intercepted by the angels who guard the gates. **Rav Ḥisda said: All the** heavenly **gates are locked except for the gates** through which pass claims of redress for ***ona'ah*.** While other prayers may be intercepted and may not necessarily be answered, the prayers of a person who has been wronged and seeks divine intervention pass through the heavenly gates and go directly to God, who promptly answers them. In support of his statement, Rav Ḥisda quotes a verse which will also form the basis of the other two metaphors brought below. [2]**As the verse says** (Amos 7:7): **"Behold, the Lord stands by a wall** made by **a plumbline, and in His hand is a plumbline."** A plumbline is an instrument of measurement used to determine whether walls are vertical. From the image that God is holding a plumbline in His hand, we learn that He is particular about any deviation from correct measure. In other words, God pays direct attention to matters of *ona'ah* and does not allow them to be intercepted at the "gate in the wall."

אָמַר רַבִּי אֶלְעָזָר [3]The second metaphor is based on the idea that God normally punishes sin through messengers. In other words, God has built various mechanisms into the structure of the world, which right wrongs and punish evildoers. **Rabbi Elazar said: Every** sin **is punished by the hand of a messenger,** and not directly by the hand of God, **except for** the sin of *ona'ah*, for which God Himself exacts immediate punishment. [4]**As the verse says: "And in His hand is a plumbline."** The "plumbline" which determines whether *ona'ah* has been committed is held by God himself, implying that He personally attends to punishing those guilty of *ona'ah*.

אָמַר רַבִּי אַבָּהוּ [5]The third metaphor is based on the image of a heavenly curtain drawn between the Divine Presence and the rest of the world. In this image, God does not pay direct attention to events on the other side of the curtain, leaving them to be dealt with by His angels and messengers. **Rabbi Abbahu said: There are three sins before which the** heavenly **curtain is not closed.** Three offences remain within God's view and are

[1]אָמַר רַב חִסְדָּא: כָּל הַשְּׁעָרִים נִנְעָלִים חוּץ מִשַּׁעֲרֵי אוֹנָאָה, [2]שֶׁנֶּאֱמַר: "הִנֵּה ה׳ נִצָּב עַל חוֹמַת אֲנָךְ, וּבְיָדוֹ אֲנָךְ". [3]אָמַר רַבִּי אֶלְעָזָר: הַכֹּל נִפְרָע בִּידֵי שָׁלִיחַ חוּץ מֵאוֹנָאָה, [4]שֶׁנֶּאֱמַר: "וּבְיָדוֹ אֲנָךְ". [5]אָמַר רַבִּי אַבָּהוּ: שְׁלֹשָׁה אֵין הַפַּרְגּוֹד נִנְעָל בִּפְנֵיהֶם:

LITERAL TRANSLATION

[1]Rav Ḥisda said: All the gates are locked except for the gates of *ona'ah*, [2]as it is said: "Behold, the Lord stands by the wall of a plumbline, and in His hand is a plumbline."

[3]Rabbi Elazar said: Everything is punished by the hand of a messenger except for *ona'ah*, [4]as it is said: "And in His hand is a plumbline."

[5]Rabbi Abbahu said: [There are] three [sins] before which the curtain is not closed:

RASHI

כל השערים – של תפלה ננעלו. **חוץ משערי אונאה** – הצועק על אונאת דברים אין השער ננעל בפניו. **הכל על ידי שליח** – נפרעים על כל עבירות על ידי שליח. **ובידו** – לא מסרה לשליח. **פרגוד** – מחיצה שבין שכינה לצבא מרום. **אינו ננעל** – להפסיק ראייתן מן המקום, אלא תמיד רואה אותם עד שיפרע.

NOTES

מִשַּׁעֲרֵי אוֹנָאָה **The gates of *ona'ah*.** This does not mean that other prayers are not answered. Rather, people who offer other petitions must wait longer to have their requests fulfilled. By contrast, the prayers of those who have been wronged are answered immediately (*Torat Ḥayyim*).

שֶׁנֶּאֱמַר הִנֵּה ה׳ נִצָּב עַל חוֹמַת אֲנָךְ **As it is said: "Behold, the Lord stands by a wall of a plumbline."** *Maharsha* explains the inference from the verse somewhat differently from our commentary. According to him, one who stands inside a city whose gates are locked cannot see what is happening outside the city, whereas God, who (as it were) "stands by the wall of a plumbline," can see what is happening outside. Thus the verse implies that God perceives all wrongdoing, and no wall can separate Him from those who are wronged.

בִּידֵי שָׁלִיחַ **By the hand of a messenger.** *Rabbenu Yehonatan* explains the difference between sins punished directly by God and those punished by messengers as follows: Since messengers — meaning divine messengers as well as the structure of causality in the natural world — are not always available, people who commit ordinary sins are not always punished immediately. By contrast, offenses punished directly by God receive immediate redress, since God is everywhere.

HALAKHAH

שַׁעֲרֵי אוֹנָאָה לֹא נִנְעֲלוּ **The gates of *ona'ah* are not locked.** "The prayers of a person who was the object of verbal *ona'ah* are answered immediately." (*Shulḥan Arukh, Ḥoshen Mishpat* 228:1.)

[1]אוֹנָאָה, וְגֵזֶל, וַעֲבוֹדָה זָרָה. [2]אוֹנָאָה, דִּכְתִיב: ״וּבְיָדוֹ אֲנָךְ״. [3]גֵּזֶל, דִּכְתִיב: ״חָמָס וָשֹׁד יִשָּׁמַע בָּהּ עַל פָּנַי תָּמִיד״. [4]עֲבוֹדָה זָרָה, דִּכְתִיב: ״הָעָם הַמַּכְעִיסִים אֹתִי עַל פָּנַי תָּמִיד וגו׳״.
[5]אָמַר רַב יְהוּדָה: לְעוֹלָם יְהֵא אָדָם זָהִיר בִּתְבוּאָה בְּתוֹךְ בֵּיתוֹ, [6]שֶׁאֵין מְרִיבָה מְצוּיָה בְּתוֹךְ בֵּיתוֹ שֶׁל אָדָם אֶלָּא עַל עִסְקֵי תְבוּאָה, [7]שֶׁנֶּאֱמַר: ״הַשָּׂם גְּבוּלֵךְ שָׁלוֹם, חֵלֶב חִטִּים יַשְׂבִּיעֵךְ״.
[8]אֲמַר רַב פַּפָּא: הַיְינוּ דְּאָמְרִי אֱינָשֵׁי: ״כְּמִשְׁלַם שַׂעֲרֵי מִכַּדָּא, נָקֵישׁ וְאָתֵי תִּגְרָא בְּבֵיתָא״.
[9]וְאָמַר רַב חִינְנָא בַּר פַּפָּא: לְעוֹלָם יְהֵא אָדָם זָהִיר בִּתְבוּאָה בְּתוֹךְ בֵּיתוֹ, שֶׁלֹּא נִקְרְאוּ יִשְׂרָאֵל דַּלִּים אֶלָּא עַל עִסְקֵי תְבוּאָה, [10]שֶׁנֶּאֱמַר: ״וְהָיָה אִם זָרַע יִשְׂרָאֵל וגו׳״, [11]וּכְתִיב: ״וַיַּחֲנוּ

LITERAL TRANSLATION

[1]*Ona'ah*, and robbery, and idolatry. [2]*Ona'ah*, as it is written: "And in His hand is a plumbline." [3]Robbery, as it is written: "Violence and robbery is heard in her before Me continually." [4]Idolatry, as it is written: "The people that provoke Me to My face continually, etc."

[5]Rav Yehudah said: A man should always be careful that there is grain in his house, [6]for strife is found in a man's house only because of matters of grain, [7]as it is said: "He makes peace in your borders, and fills you with the finest of the wheat."

[8]Rav Pappa said: This is what people say: "When the barley is gone from the jar, strife knocks and comes into the house."

[9]And Rav Ḥinena bar Pappa said: A man should always be careful that there is grain in his house, for Israel were called poor only because of matters of grain, [10]as it is said: "And it was when Israel had sown, etc.," [11]and it is written: "And they encamped

TRANSLATION AND COMMENTARY

immediately redressed: [1]***Ona'ah*, robbery, and idolatry.** [2]We know that *ona'ah* receives direct divine attention, **as the verse** (ibid.) **says: "And in His hand is a plumbline."** The "plumbline" is readily available in God's hand, and the "curtain" does not interfere with His punishment. [3]The same applies to **robbery, as the verse** (Jeremiah 6:7) **says: "Violence and robbery is heard in** Jerusalem; **they are before Me constantly."** Here, too, robbery is said to be constantly before God, implying that He is always available to attend to its retribution, and it does not remain on the other side of the "curtain" as do other sins. [4]The same applies to **idolatry, as the verse** (Isaiah 65:3) **says: "The people that provoke Me to My face continually,** that sacrifice in gardens, and burn incense upon altars of brick." These are idolatrous rites, and Rabbi Abbahu infers that, since idoltrous "provocations" are constantly before "God's face," idolatry receives God's immediate personal attention, without obstruction from the "curtain."

אָמַר רַב יְהוּדָה [5]The Gemara now returns to the question of how a husband should behave toward his wife. Since a husband must not cause his wife anguish, it is wise to avert the domestic problems that often lead to quarrels. **Rav Yehudah said: A man should always be careful to have** enough **grain in his house.** [6]**For strife only besets a man's house because of matters related to grain** — when there is not enough food to eat. [7]**As the verse says** (Psalms 147:14): **"He who makes peace in your borders** does so by **satisfying you with the finest of the wheat,"** implying that people who do not have "the finest of the wheat" (i.e., sufficient food to eat) will not have "peace in their borders."

אָמַר רַב פַּפָּא [8]**Rav Pappa said: This is what people say.** Rav Yehudah's Scriptural exposition corresponds to the following proverb: **"When barley is gone from the jar, strife knocks** at the door **and comes into the house."**

וְאָמַר רַב חִינְנָא בַּר פַּפָּא [9]**Rav Ḥinena bar Pappa** suggested a further reason for keeping one's house well stocked with food, and **said: A person should always be careful to have** enough **grain in his house, for Israel were only called "poor" because of matters related to grain,** when their food was destroyed. In other words, a person is not really poor until he has no food. [10]**As the verse says** (Judges 6:3): **"And so it was when Israel had sown** that the Midianites came up, and the Amalekites, and the children of the East came up against them." [11]**And it is written** in the next verse (ibid. 6:4), **"And they encamped against** the Israelites, and destroyed the

RASHI

ובידו אנך — משמע שהיא תמיד אצלו ומשמש בה. **על פני** — לפני, ואין מחיצה בינו לבין העבירה. **אימתי גבולך שלום** — כש״חלב חטים ישביעך״ הקדוש ברוך הוא. **מכדא** — כד שנותנים בו שעורים. **נקיש ואתי תגרא** — התגר מקשקש ובא. ואני שמעתי: הכד מקשקש, כדרך כלי ריקם שנשמע בו קול הברה כשמקשקשין עליו.

אָמְרִי אֱינָשֵׁי People say. A term used that introduces a popular proverb or saying.

כְּמִשְׁלַם שַׂעֲרֵי מִכַּדָּא When the barley is gone from the jar. This proverb comes to illustrate the Gemara's statement that financial problems are a principal cause of domestic strife. Indeed, poverty is likely to bring out and enhance other, family-related problems of a non-economic nature, which might not otherwise arise. The Gemara apparently stressed this point to discourage people from making investments which could cause severe financial difficulties in the short run, even though they might be potentially lucrative in the long run.

NOTES

כְּמִשְׁלַם שַׂעֲרֵי מִכַּדָּא When the barley is gone from the jar. Barley was generally used as animal fodder in Talmudic times. Thus the maxim cited here implies that strife only befalls a house if its occupants have become so poor that they do not even have barley to eat (*Ein Ya'akov*).

NOTES

"And others say . . ."

pp. 232–233 Commentary

The Gemara continues with three more ideas about *ona'ah* (and the last one even has a triplet within it). According to this passage there are three metaphorical images that portray the way that God reacts quickly to hurt feelings: through a gate, through God's direct intervention, and through the drawing aside of a curtain before God.

In the Translation and Commentary of line 1 on page 232, you may be surprised to learn that angels guard the gates of heaven. You might not have thought that Jews believe in angels. However, some sages in the rabbinic era clearly did believe in angels and many lay persons certainly did. God's retinue was thought to resemble a Babylonian monarch's court. There were angels representing the seventy nations of the world and ministering angels who served God as advisors.

The image of the plumbline here (p. 232, lines 1–2) is a bit difficult. Again, if you can't quite grasp it, jsut go on and don't feel bad about it. If you'd like to understand it more fully, it will help you to read the whole passage in Amos:

> Thus my Lord Yahweh showed me: Indeed he was forming locusts, just when the latter growth was beginning to appear, that is, the latter growth after the king's mowings. When they were about to devour the vegetation of the land entirely, I said, "My Lord Yahweh, please forgive! How can Jacob survive, as he is so small?"
>
> Yahweh repented of this. "It shall not happen," Yahweh said. Thus my Lord Yahweh showed me: Indeed my Lord Yahweh was summoning showers of fire. When it had consumed the Great Deep, and was consuming the allotted land, "I said, "My Lord Yahweh, please desist! How can Jacob survive, as he is so small?" Yahweh repented of this. "This also shall not happen," my Lord Yahweh said. Thus he showed me: Indeed my Lord was standing beside a plastered wall [wall of *anak*], with a lump of tin (*anak*) in his hand. Yahweh said to me, "What do you see, Amos?" I said, "A lump of tin (*anak*)." My Lord said, "Soon I will put grief (*anak*) in the midst of my people Israel. I shall not spare them again. The high places of Isaac will be devastated, and Israel's sanctuaries will be laid waste; and I shall attack the house of Jeroboam with my sword." (Amos 7:1–9, Frances L. Andersen and David Noel Freedman, translators, *Amos: The Anchor Bible* (New York: Doubleday, 1989), pp. xxxvii–xxxviii)

It could be that God, dropping the plumbline directly from Heaven down to earth, circumvents all the normal intermediaries and that we can pick up the end of the line and talk to God directly as if it were a "telephone." In addition, God can move the plumbline around until it is placed where it is needed. Furthermore, the plumbline represents a straight line, i.e., the shortest distance between two points.

The word for plumbline, *anach* (aleph-nun-chaf), has two letters in common with *ona'ah*: aleph and nun. According to the

Anchor Bible, "There is . . . probably [a play on words] . . . though we are handicapped by not knowing what an *anach* actually is, or what the other meaning might be if a play on words were involved, which to us at least seems likely" (p. 616). Could the sages be making yet another play on words, as they have done so often in this passage? Could they be punning with this word, giving the verse the meaning, "Behold God stands on a wall of your hurt feelings and in His hand are your hurt feelings"? Thus, *ona'ah* would be directly in God's hand. This is another possible way of reading this difficult verse. This interpretation would be consistent with the second metaphor on this page (lines 3–4). It could mean that your hurt feelings (*anach*) aren't in the hand of a messenger but in God's very hand.

The third idea in this section equates *ona'ah*, robbery, and idolatry. These are the sins that come directly before God. You might ask, why do these three make the list and murder does not? On the one hand, as we've already learned, shaming someone is like shedding their blood (p. 226). On the other hand, the verses cited here (Jeremiah 6:7 and Isaiah 65:3) are the only times the words *al panai*, i.e., "before God's face," are used in this way in Hebrew Scriptures. There are many other times when this phrase is used in the *Tanach* but none of them refer to God. This may help explain some seemingly arbitrary connections made by the sages as they weave prooftexts together. The points the sages are trying to elucidate are crucial ones: What sins are so terrible that they go directly to God for judgment? What does it mean for something to be in God's hand, before God's face, or before the curtain that shield's God's presence? These questions deserve reflection.

On p. 233, line 5, we return to the material about creating harmony between husband and wife. These three sayings are about having enough grain in the house. Indeed, economic strife can be a major strain in a marriage. At this point, a pattern is discernible: woven in, among the material about *ona'ah*, is a subset of materials about being considerate of one's wife's feelings. (The Talmud was written by men and so this is how they saw the issue. If women had written it, it would doubtless have turned out differently.)

Why is this material here? There are many possible reasons, among them are three candidates: (1) The relationship between husband and wife is the model of the relationship of God and Israel. (2) The sin of *ona'ah* was related to adultery (p. 227, line 6) and to idolatry (p. 233, line 1), which is the theological equivalent of adultery. (3) The marital relationship may be the one wherein *ona'ah* is most likely to take place and thus serves as the clearest example of this phenomenon for the sages.

Try reading this passage without the husband/wife material (p. 230, lines 3–6; p. 231, lines 5–9; and p. 233, line 5 through p. 234, line 4) and see how smoothly it flows. This material was intentionally placed here. It was not haphazardly thrown in with little thought. These teachings about husbands and wives foreshadow the very important story to come in which hurt feelings play a crucial role in a God-husband-wife triangle.

—JZA

NOTES

TRANSLATION AND COMMENTARY

increase of the earth." [1]**And it is written** at the end of the passage (ibid., 6:6): **"And Israel became very poor because of Midian."** Thus we see that the Bible calls the Israelites "poor" after their grain was destroyed by their enemies.

וְאָמַר רַבִּי חֶלְבּוֹ [2]The Gemara continues its discussion of how a husband should conduct himself towards his wife. **Rabbi Ḥelbo said: A man should always be careful about his wife's honor, for blessing** (prosperity) **is only found in a man's house on account of his wife,** [3]**as the verse says** (Genesis 12:16): **"And** Pharaoh **treated Abram well for** his wife's **sake,** and he had sheep and oxen, etc." Accordingly, Rabbi Ḥelbo argues, the Torah is teaching us that in general a man's prosperity comes from his wife. [4]**And this is what Rava said to** his fellow townspeople, **the people of Meḥoza: Honor your wives so that you may become wealthy.**

עֲלֵיהֶם וגו׳״, [1]וּכְתִיב: ״וַיִּדַּל יִשְׂרָאֵל מְאֹד מִפְּנֵי מִדְיָן״. [2]וְאָמַר רַבִּי חֶלְבּוֹ: לְעוֹלָם יְהֵא אָדָם זָהִיר בִּכְבוֹד אִשְׁתּוֹ, שֶׁאֵין בְּרָכָה מְצוּיָה בְּתוֹךְ בֵּיתוֹ שֶׁל אָדָם אֶלָּא בִּשְׁבִיל אִשְׁתּוֹ, [3]שֶׁנֶּאֱמַר: ״וּלְאַבְרָם הֵטִיב בַּעֲבוּרָהּ״. [4]וְהַיְינוּ דַּאֲמַר לְהוּ רָבָא לִבְנֵי מְחוֹזָא: ״אוֹקִירוּ לִנְשַׁיְיכוּ כִּי הֵיכִי דְּתִתְעַתְּרוּ״. [5]תְּנַן הָתָם: ״חֲתָכוֹ חוּלְיוֹת וְנָתַן חוֹל בֵּין חוּלְיָא לְחוּלְיָא,

תְּנַן הָתָם [5]The Gemara now relates a story connected with the issue of causing anguish to other people, although its theological significance far transcends this specific ethical concern. The story begins with a Mishnah from tractate *Kelim,* which deals with the susceptibility of utensils to ritual impurity. If a primary source of ritual impurity, such as a dead animal, comes into contact with a utensil, the utensil becomes ritually impure only if it is susceptible to ritual impurity. The susceptibility of a utensil to contracting ritual impurity depends on its construction and on the material from which it is made. **We learned in a Mishnah** taught **elsewhere** (*Kelim* 5:10) that there is a difference of opinion regarding an oven: **"If** someone **cut** an earthenware oven horizontally **into** ring-shaped **pieces, and** then reconstructed it and **put sand between the pieces,** afterwards spreading clay on the oven to join the pieces together,

LITERAL TRANSLATION

against them, etc.," [1]and it is written: "And Israel became very poor because of Midian."

[2]And Rabbi Ḥelbo said: A man should always be careful about his wife's honor, for blessing is found in a man's house only on account of his wife, [3]as it is said: "And he treated Abram well for her sake." [4]And this is what Rava said to the people of Meḥoza: "Honor your wives so that you may become wealthy."

[5]We have learned there: "[If] he cut it [into] segments and put sand between segment and segment,

RASHI

וידל ישראל — לעיל מיניה כתיב ״ויחנו עליהם וישחיתו את יבול הארץ״. **אוקירו נשייכו** = כבדו נשותיכם. **מחוזא** — עיר שהיה רבא דר בתוכה כך שמה. **חתכו חוליות** — תנור העשוי חוליות מצרפו בכבשן כדרך כלי חרס, ואחר כך צירף החוליות, ונתן חול בין חוליא לחוליא.

NOTES

חֲתָכוֹ חוּלְיוֹת וְנָתַן חוֹל If he cut it into segments and put sand. Various explanations of the dispute between Rabbi Eliezer and the Sages have been suggested by the commentators. Some authorities explain that they disagreed as to whether an oven that was initially manufactured by cementing separate pieces of ceramic together can become ritually impure (i.e., if it later comes in contact with a dead body, etc.; thus *Rambam, Ra'avad* and others). Rabbi Eliezer maintains that the oven cannot contract ritual impurity, because the pieces do not fit together well, and hence the oven is considered broken, and the law is that broken utensils cannot contract ritual impurity (*Ra'avad*).

Others explain that the "oven of Akhnai" was a normal oven which had become ritually impure, after which the owner cut it into separate pieces which he later cemented together (*Rash, Ritva,* and others). According to this explanation, Rabbi Eliezer maintained that the oven becomes ritually pure, because cutting it into pieces is tantamount to breaking it, and even though it was later cemented together the pieces do not fit together well, because the sections of the oven remain separated from each other by layers of sand.

HALAKHAH

כְּבוֹד אִשְׁתּוֹ Honoring one's wife. "The Sages said that a man should love his wife like himself, and honor her more than himself." (*Rambam, Sefer Nashim, Hilkhot Ishut* 15:19.)

תַּנּוּר שֶׁחֲתָכוֹ חוּלְיוֹת An oven cut into segments. "An earthenware oven which was cut into pieces horizontally can become ritually impure, if it was overlaid with clay and the clay fired, even if there are layers of sand between the pieces," following the view of the Sages. (Ibid., *Sefer Tohorah, Hilkhot Kelim* 16:5.)

SAGES

רַבִּי חֶלְבּוֹ Rabbi Ḥelbo. A third-generation Babylonian Amora, Rabbi Ḥelbo was one of Rav Huna's outstanding students, and transmitted many of Rav Huna's Halakhic teachings. Later, Rabbi Ḥelbo immigrated to Eretz Israel (during Rav Huna's lifetime), apparently settling in Tiberias. There he met Rabbi Yoḥanan and studied Aggadah with Rabbi Shmuel bar Naḥmani, and Halakhah with the outstanding disciples of Rabbi Yoḥanan.

Rabbi Ḥelbo's Halakhic and Aggadic teachings are found in both the Babylonian and Jerusalem Talmuds, and many Amoraim of the next generation in Eretz Israel cite his teachings. He left no children.

BACKGROUND

כְּבוֹד אִשְׁתּוֹ His wife's honor. The honor referred to here is not merely respectful behavior and speech. It also has practical implications. Since people often honor each other because of their attire and jewelry, a husband is obligated to make certain that his wife is dressed in a way that does honor to him in public, and he must be more scrupulous of his wife's honor than of his own in this matter. This ruling explains the connection between honoring one's wife and earning a blessing. Anyone who honors his wife and buys her possessions, even above his economic status, is worthy of a blessing for that reason.

וְהַיְינוּ דַּאֲמַר לְהוּ רָבָא לִבְנֵי מְחוֹזָא And this is what Rava said to the people of Meḥoza. Rava lived in Meḥoza, and eventually moved the Pumbedita Yeshivah to that city, which was a major commercial center. Most of the Jews who lived there were apparently merchants who supported themselves solely through commerce, as opposed to most other Jews during that period, who engaged in agriculture. Accordingly, Rava phrased his remarks in a manner appropriate to the Meḥozans, since the residents of that city were very concerned about financial matters and were

"And others say . . ."

p. 234 Commentary

The ideas about how one honors his wife, presented in lines 2–4, may seem controversial or condescending. However, not only would a great deal of jewelry be one way for a man to treat his wife with honor (see Rabbi Steinsaltz's Background Note), but it could be a way of giving her some financial independence through the bestowal of substantial gifts.

Now we come to the very heart of this passage. It begins with a seemingly extraneous, unimportant story about an oven. (Then, as now, when a terrible argument develops in a group about something that seems inconsequential, it is often the case that the relationships in question have already been strained.) This story is set around 80–110 C.E. when Rabban Gamliel was head of the Academy that was trying to develop a new kind of Judaism after the Temple's destruction. This process involved a great deal of conflict, as this story demonstrates.

Rabban Gamliel's sister, Imma Shalom, was married to a famous sage, Rabbi Eliezer, who had a phenomenal, authoritative memory regarding the teachings of previous sages. Rabbi Eliezer had frequent conflicts with both his brother-in-law, Rabban Gamliel, and Rabbi Yehoshua, a far gentler man. (Indeed, it was because of Rabbi Yehoshua's gentleness and scholarship and Rabban Gamliel's somewhat autocratic style that Rabban Gamliel himself was excommunicated from the Academy. See B. Berachot 27b.) All these characters play a part in this, one of the most dramatic tales in all of rabbinic literature.

To understand this fight about the oven of Akhnai (a picture is found on p. 235) we need to know that for an object to be susceptible to ritual impurity it must fit into the category of a "whole" object, in this case a whole oven. Likewise, for an object to by insusceptible to ritual purity it cannot fit into the category of a whole object. A modern analogy may help clarify this issue. Imagine you found that a small lizard had died in your oven. This would make your oven ritually impure. The question is, if you disassemble your oven so that it no longer fits our cultural category of "working oven," can you reassemble the parts and use the oven again? Rabbi Eliezer allows us to use this convenient and cost-efficient remedy to our problem, but none of the rest of the sages allow it. They say the oven is off-limits forever and that anything prepared in this oven is ritually impure. Because Rabbi Eliezer argues publicly over this issue and refuses to go along with the majority, he is excommunicated and the hurt feelings that result cause great destruction.

A student, hearing this story, told of her experience as a girl in Israel. She and her mother had put a pizza into their oven to bake. When they took the pizza out of the oven, they found that two cockroaches had fallen onto the pizza and been baked into it! To purify the oven, the mother turned the heat in the oven up to its highest temperature for an hour. (No, they did not eat the pizza.)

—JZA

Sages
Rabban Gamliel II (of Yavneh).

Rabban Gamliel was president of the Sanhedrin and one of the most important *tannaim* in the period following the destruction of the Second Temple. His father, Rabban Shimon ben Gamliel (the Elder), had also been president of the Sanhedrin, and one of the leaders of the nation during the rebellion against Rome. Rabban Gamliel was brought to Yavneh by Rabban Yohanan ben Zakkai after the destruction of the Temple, so that he became known as Rabban Gamliel of Yavneh. After Rabban Yohanan ben Zakkai's death, Rabban Gamliel presided over the Sanhedrin.

During Rabban Gamliel's presidency, Yavneh became an important spiritual center. The greatest sages gathered around Rabban Gamliel: Rabbi Eliezer (Rabban Gamliel's brother-in-law), Rabbi Yehoshua, Rabbi Akiva, Rabbi Elazar ben Azaryah, and others. Rabban Gamliel wished to create a spiritual center for the Jews that would unite the entire people, as the Temple had done up until that time. For this reason he strove to enhance the honor and the central authority of the Sanhedrin and its president. His strict and vigorous leadership eventually led his colleagues to remove him from his post for a short period, replacing him with Rabbi Elazar ben Azaryah. However, since all knew that his motives and actions were for the good of the people and were not based on personal ambition, they soon restored him to his position.

We do not possess many halakhic rulings explicitly given in the name of Rabban Gamliel. However, in his time and under his influence some of the most important decisions in the history of Jewish spiritual life were made. These included the decision to follow the School of Hillel, rejection of the halakhic system of Rabbi Eliezer, and the establishment of fixed formulae of prayers. In those halakhic decisions attributed to Rabban Gamliel, we find an uncompromising approach to the Halakhah; in reaching his conclusions, he was faithful to his principles.

We know that two of his sons were sages: Rabban Shimon ben Gamliel, who served as president of the Sanhedrin after him, and Rabbi Hanina ben Gamliel.

—*Rabbi Steinsaltz*

Rabbi Yehoshua.

This is Rabbi Yehoshua ben Hananyah the Levite, one of the leading sages of the generation following the destruction of the Second Temple. Rabbi Yehoshua had served in the Temple as a singer and, after the destruction, was one of the students who went to Yavneh with their outstanding teacher, Rabban Yohanan ben Zakkai. Unlike his colleague Rabbi Eliezer, Rabbi Yehoshua maintained the system of his teacher and of Bet Hillel. Although Rabbi Yehoshua played an important part in the leadership of the people (for he was apparently a senior judge), he earned a meager living from hard and unremunerative work. After renewing his close ties with the house of the Nasi (the president of the Sanhedrin), he was apparently supported by Rabban Gamliel, who used to give him the tithe belonging to the Levites.

Rabbi Yehoshua was famous among both Jews and non-Jews as an extraordinary scholar, possessing wide knowledge not only of Torah but of secular studies. He was a celebrated preacher.

Continuing the method of his teacher, Rabban Yohanan ben Zakkai, Rabbi Yehoshua was a moderate person and tried to deter the people from rebellion against the Roman regime. For a while he had close relations with the emperor's house and was highly regarded there, as he had been sent to Rome with several national delegations. While Rabbi Yehoshua was modest and humble, he was very firm in his views and principles, and did not make concessions even when difficult personal controversies developed. However, in other matters he accepted authority, and in general he had a humorous, realistic temperament.

All the sages of the following generations were his students, and in most of the controversies with the sages of his own generation, the Halakhah followed his view. His system became the path taken by the Hala-khah. Hananyah, his nephew, was his outstanding student.

—Rabbi Steinsaltz

Honoring One's Wife

Today many men shower their wives with jewelry in an attempt to have the luster of the stones radiate upon them, thus enhancing their own reputations. Perhaps it would serve Jewish men well to have each man sing *Eishet Chayil* at the Shabbat table. This expression of appreciation of a wife's talents and strengths from the Book of Proverbs (chapter 31) would be "more precious than coral [or rubies]." (Proverbs 31:10)

—Steffie Odle

NOTES

TRANSLATION AND COMMENTARY

[1] **Rabbi Eliezer declares** the resulting oven **ritually pure** — i.e., not susceptible to ritual impurity — because in his opinion the oven is no longer regarded as a complete utensil and is therefore no longer susceptible to ritual impurity. While the pieces have indeed been joined together once more, the oven is nevertheless regarded as built of broken fragments, and such a structure is not susceptible to ritual impurity. **The Sages,** on the other hand, **declared it** to be sufficiently reconstructed to be **ritually impure** — i.e., subject to ritual impurity. In their opinion, although the oven was reconstructed from separate pieces, it is to be viewed as a repaired and whole vessel, because of the clay that has been spread over it on the outside. Notwithstanding the sand that separates its pieces, it is a single, whole unit, and is susceptible to ritual impurity like any other oven. [59B] And such an oven was called **'the oven of Akhnai.'"** (*Akhnai* means a type of snake.)

מַאי עַכְנַאי [2]The Gemara asks: **What is "Akhnai"?** Why was the oven named after a snake?

אָמַר רַב יְהוּדָה [3]The Gemara replies: **Rav Yehudah said in the name of Shmuel:** The Mishnah is hinting at the fierce argument between Rabbi Eliezer and the Sages, described in the Baraita below. The Rabbis who disputed Rabbi Eliezer's view **entwined** Rabbi Eliezer **with words, like a snake** wrapping itself around its prey, **and they** succeeded in having the oven **declared ritually impure.**

תָּנָא [4]The details of the dispute **were taught in** the following Baraita: **"On that day, Rabbi Eliezer used all the arguments in the world.** He produced powerful arguments to justify his position that the oven should be considered unreconstructed and not susceptible to ritual impurity. **But** the Sages **did not accept his** arguments, and insisted that the oven was susceptible to ritual impurity. [5]After Rabbi Eliezer saw that he was not able to persuade his colleagues with logical arguments, **he said to them: 'If the Halakhah is in accordance with me, let this carob tree prove it.'** [6]**The carob tree** immediately **uprooted** itself and moved **one hundred cubits — and some say four hundred cubits — from its** original **place.** [7]The Sages **said to him: 'Proof cannot be brought from a carob tree.'** [8]Rabbi Eliezer **then said to** the Sages: **'If the Halakhah is in accordance with me, let the channel of water prove it.' The channel of water** immediately **flowed backward,** against the direction in which it usually

[1]רַבִּי אֱלִיעֶזֶר מְטַהֵר וַחֲכָמִים מְטַמְּאִין. [59B] וְזֶה הוּא תַּנּוּר שֶׁל עַכְנַאי״.

[2]מַאי עַכְנַאי?

[3]אָמַר רַב יְהוּדָה אָמַר שְׁמוּאֵל: שֶׁהִקִּיפוּ דְּבָרִים כְּעַכְנָא זוֹ, וְטִמְּאוּהוּ.

[4]תָּנָא: ״בְּאוֹתוֹ הַיּוֹם הֵשִׁיב רַבִּי אֱלִיעֶזֶר כָּל תְּשׁוּבוֹת שֶׁבָּעוֹלָם וְלֹא קִיבְּלוּ הֵימֶנּוּ. [5]אָמַר לָהֶם: ׳אִם הֲלָכָה כְּמוֹתִי, חָרוּב זֶה יוֹכִיחַ׳. [6]נֶעֱקַר חָרוּב מִמְּקוֹמוֹ מֵאָה אַמָּה — וְאָמְרִי לַהּ אַרְבַּע מֵאוֹת אַמָּה. [7]אָמְרוּ לוֹ: ׳אֵין מְבִיאִין רְאָיָה מִן הֶחָרוּב׳. [8]חָזַר וְאָמַר לָהֶם: ׳אִם הֲלָכָה כְּמוֹתִי, אַמַּת הַמַּיִם יוֹכִיחוּ׳. חָזְרוּ אַמַּת

LITERAL TRANSLATION

[1]Rabbi Eliezer declares it ritually pure and the Sages declare it ritually impure. [59B] And this is the oven of Akhnai."

[2]What is Akhnai?

[3]Rav Yehudah said in the name of Shmuel: Because they encircled [him with] words like this snake, and declared it ritually impure.

[4]It has been taught: "On that day, Rabbi Eliezer used (lit., 'replied') all the arguments (lit., 'replies') in the world, but they did not accept [them] from him. [5]He said to them: 'If the Halakhah is in accordance with me, let this carob tree prove [it].' [6]The carob tree was uprooted from its place one hundred cubits — and some say four hundred cubits. [7]They said to him: 'One does not bring proof from a carob tree.' [8]He then said to them: 'If the Halakhah is in accordance with me, let the channel of water prove [it].' The channel of water turned

RASHI

רבי אליעזר מטהר — שאין זה כלי חרס אלא בנין, כעין כלי גללים וכלי אדמה שאין מקבלין טומאה. **וחכמים מטמאין** — דאזלי בתר סוליות. שאר תנורים שלהם היו עשוים כעין קדירות גדולות ופיו למעלה, וצורף בכבשן כשאר קדירות ומטלטלים. אלא שהיה מושיבו על הארץ או על הדף, ומדביק את טפילות הטיט סביב על כולו לעשותו עב שיקלוט ויחזיק את חומו. **עכנאי** — נחש. דרכו לעשות בעגולה להכניס זנבו אצל פיו.

therefore interested in any advice that might make them rich.

REALIA

תַּנּוּר שֶׁל עַכְנַאי **The oven of Akhnai.** An oven of Akhnai (based on an oven found in Masada). According to Rabbi Eliezer, if such an oven was cut into pieces horizontally (cf. the lines in the illustration), it could not become susceptible to ritual impurity even if the pieces were later cemented together.

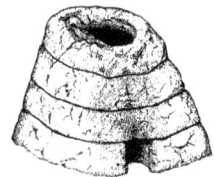

LANGUAGE

עַכְנָא **Snake.** This is the Aramaic form of the Greek word ἔχις, or ἔχιδνα, *echis* or *echidna*, meaning "snake," "viper." Some authorities believe that Akhnai was the name of the man who made the oven (*Tosafot* and others). Several people mentioned in the sources bear this name, especially in the form current in Eretz Israel, Ḥakhinai (חֲכִינַאי). According to this interpretation, the words of the Gemara here are a homiletic addition, indicating that the name of the oven was appropriate.

NOTES

שֶׁהִקִּיפוּ דְּבָרִים כְּעַכְנָא **Because they entwined him with words like a snake.** Just as a snake winds itself round its prey and does not permit it to escape, so too the Sages offered such cogent proof of their viewpoint that Rabbi Eliezer was unable to refute their objections (*Rabbenu Nissim Gaon*).

חָרוּב וְאַמַּת הַמַּיִם **The carob tree and the channel of water.** The commentators explain that God performs miracles for

"And others say . . ."

p. 235 Commentary

How are we to understand this story? We can certainly understand it on the level of metaphor. The tree and water are both symbols of Torah and Rabbi Eliezer is uprooting and reversing the Torah, as it were. Perhaps the argument between Rabbi Eliezer and the sages was so fierce that it seemed to threaten the very existence of the Academy, seeming to make its walls fall in.

While we can understand the story on the level of metaphor, we should also allow it to speak to us on the level of legend or myth. This is a dramatic tale, told with dramatic flair. In short, it has elements of truth, of morality, and of entertainment all together at the same time. We can get the most out of this story, and others like it, when we understand it on many levels rather than trying to view it in just one way.

One of the most basic rules in the Mishnah is that the anonymous majority wins. Perhaps it was this fight, and ones like it, that caused this principle to be established.

—JZA

Concepts
The Halakhah follows an anonymous mishnah.

Some *amoraim*, such as Rabbi Yohanan, took this principle as a consistent basis for their decisions. It derives from the assumption that the anonymous presentation of a certain opinion in the mishnah proves that Rabbi Yehudah HaNasi and his court decided that this was the halakhah, and there was no court greater or more important than that of Rabbi Yehudah HaNasi in the following generations. This principle has a number of refinements. In some cases we find both an anonymous mishnah and a difference of opinion between *tannaim.* If the difference of opinion precedes the anonymous mishnah, then the Halakhah agrees with the anonymous mishnah. But if the anonymous mishnah is followed by the difference of opinion, the Halakhah does not necessarily agree with the anonymous mishnah. These principles regarding anonymous statements in the Mishnah are complicated by the fact that anonymous statements cited in various places occasionally disagree with each other, or a difference of opinion in connection with an anonymous statement may appear elsewhere in the Mishnah. The details of these matters are a matter of controversy among rabbinical authorities.

—Rabbi Steinsaltz

On Akhnai's oven: To what may this be compared?

Once a group of employees sat in a meeting room debating the readiness of a new product for introduction into the market. The employees agreed that the product was not ready for release, but one manager said, "It is ready for release." And, he said to them, "If my opinion is right, let my BMW be moved to a reserved parking place." And the Beemer moved. But the employees said, "This is not the right way to decide these things." The manager said to them, "If I am right, let all of the traffic on the expressway prove it." And suddenly all of the cars began traveling in the opposite direction. But the employees said, "This is not the right way to decide these things." The manager said to them, "If I am right, let the executive suite issue a statement to that effect." Immediately, all of the cell phones and beepers beeped and rang, and when they were answered, a voice said, "Why do you argue with the manager? The product IS ready for release!" Immediately, the team leader rose to her feet and said, "The matter is not to be decided in the executive suite. We are the ones that know the product best, and you have given us the responsibility for its release!" And the product was not released. Later, one of the employees asked how the president and chief operating officer had reacted to these events. The response? "My employees have defeated me! My employees have defeated me!"

Perhaps the Talmud includes the tale of Akhnai's oven in a tractate concerning business matters so that we might draw from it lessons not just about transactions, but also about organizations. The rabbis have portrayed God as One who surrenders control so that we might grow into our fullness, as One who celebrates our independence. I would like to suggest that there is a lesson to be learned about the way we organize ourselves for the purpose of accomplishing goals. Just as God surrenders control over the interpretation of the Torah—even though the results may not have been what God wanted—to the rabbis grappling with the reality of applying the Torah here on Earth, so the leaders of organizations will best achieve their goals by surrendering a certain amount of control to the employees who are closest to the clients, customers, or processes. Just as the rabbis—and not God—were best suited to determine the application of Torah in their world, so are the people who work closest to the process—and not those in the executive suite—best suited to manage those processes. In this way, the organizations and the people who comprise them can grow into their fullness.

—Naomi Hyman

NOTES

NOTES

SAGES

רַבִּי אֱלִיעֶזֶר **Rabbi Eliezer.** When the name "Rabbi Eliezer" occurs in the Talmud without a patronymic, it refers to Rabbi Eliezer ben Hyrcanus (also known as Rabbi Eliezer the Great), who was one of the leading scholars in the period after the destruction of the Second Temple.

Rabbi Eliezer was born to a wealthy family of Levites, which traced its descent back to Moses. Rabbi Eliezer began studying Torah late in life, but quickly became an outstanding and beloved disciple of Rabban Yohanan ben Zakkai. Indeed, Rabban Yohanan remarked that "if all the Sages of Israel were on one side of the scale and Eliezer ben Hyrcanus on the other, he would outweigh them all."

Rabbi Eliezer was known for his remarkable memory, and was famed for faithfully reporting and following the traditions of others without altering them. He himself leaned towards the views of Bet Shammai, even though he studied with Rabban Yohanan ben Zakkai, who was a follower of Bet Hillel. Rabbi Eliezer's principal opponent, Rabbi Yehoshua ben Hananyah, generally followed the views of Bet Hillel, and many basic Halakhic disputes between these scholars are reported in the Mishnah.

Because of his staunch and unflinching adherence to tradition, Rabbi Eliezer was unwilling to accede to the majority view where his own views were based on tradition. Indeed, Rabbi Eliezer's conduct generated so much tension among the Sages that his own brother-in-law, Rabban Gamliel, eventually excommunicated him, to prevent controversy from proliferating. This ban was lifted only after Rabbi Eliezer's death.

All the Sages of the next generation were Rabbi Eliezer's students. Most prominent among them was Rabbi Akiva. Rabbi Eliezer's son, Hyrcanus, was also a Sage.

TRANSLATION AND COMMENTARY

flowed. [1] The Sages **said to him: 'Proof cannot be brought from a channel of water** either.' [2] Rabbi Eliezer **then said** to the Sages: **'If the Halakhah is in accordance with me, let the walls of the House of Study prove it.' The walls of the House of Study** then **leaned** and were about to **fall.** [3] **Rabbi Yehoshua,** one of Rabbi Eliezer's chief opponents among the Sages, **rebuked** the falling walls, **saying to them: 'If Talmudic scholars argue with one another** in their discussions **about the Halakhah, what affair is it of yours?'** [4] **The walls did not fall** down, **out of respect for Rabbi Yehoshua, nor** did they **straighten, out of respect for Rabbi Eliezer, and** indeed those walls **still remain leaning** to this day. [5] **Rabbi Eliezer then said** to the Sages: **'If the Halakhah is in accordance with me, let it be proved** directly **from Heaven.'** [6] **Suddenly a heavenly voice went forth and said** to the Sages: **'Why are you disputing with Rabbi Eliezer? The Halakhah is in accordance with him in all cir-**cumstances!' [7] **Rabbi Yehoshua rose to his feet and** quoted a portion of a verse (Deuteronomy 30:12), **saying: 'The Torah is not in heaven!'''**

LITERAL TRANSLATION

backward. [1] They said to him: 'One does not bring proof from a channel of water.' [2] He then said to them: 'If the Halakhah is in accordance with me, let the walls of the House of Study prove [it].' The walls of the House of Study leaned to fall. [3] Rabbi Yehoshua rebuked them, [and] said to them: 'If Talmudic Sages argue with one another about the Halakhah, what affair is it of yours (lit., "what is your nature")?' [4] They did not fall, out of respect for Rabbi Yehoshua; but they did not straighten, out of respect for Rabbi Eliezer, and they still remain leaning. [5] He then said to them: 'If the Halakhah is in accordance with me, let it be proved from Heaven.' [6] A [heavenly] voice went forth and said: 'Why are you [disputing] with Rabbi Eliezer, for the Halakhah is in accordance with him everywhere?' [7] Rabbi Yehoshua rose to his feet and said: 'It is not in heaven.''

הַמַּיִם לַאֲחוֹרֵיהֶם. ¹אָמְרוּ לוֹ: 'אֵין מְבִיאִין רְאָיָה מֵאַמַּת הַמַּיִם'. ²חָזַר וְאָמַר לָהֶם: 'אִם הֲלָכָה כְּמוֹתִי, כּוֹתְלֵי בֵּית הַמִּדְרָשׁ יוֹכִיחוּ'. הִטּוּ כּוֹתְלֵי בֵּית הַמִּדְרָשׁ לִיפּוֹל. ³גָּעַר בָּהֶם רַבִּי יְהוֹשֻׁעַ, אָמַר לָהֶם: 'אִם תַּלְמִידֵי חֲכָמִים מְנַצְּחִים זֶה אֶת זֶה בַּהֲלָכָה, אַתֶּם מַה טִּיבְכֶם'? ⁴לֹא נָפְלוּ, מִפְּנֵי כְּבוֹדוֹ שֶׁל רַבִּי יְהוֹשֻׁעַ, וְלֹא זָקְפוּ, מִפְּנֵי כְּבוֹדוֹ שֶׁל רַבִּי אֱלִיעֶזֶר, וַעֲדַיִן מַטִּין וְעוֹמְדִין. ⁵חָזַר וְאָמַר לָהֶם: 'אִם הֲלָכָה כְּמוֹתִי, מִן הַשָּׁמַיִם יוֹכִיחוּ'. ⁶יָצְאָתָה בַּת קוֹל וְאָמְרָה: 'מַה לָּכֶם אֵצֶל רַבִּי אֱלִיעֶזֶר שֶׁהֲלָכָה כְּמוֹתוֹ בְּכָל מָקוֹם'? ⁷עָמַד רַבִּי יְהוֹשֻׁעַ עַל רַגְלָיו וְאָמַר: 'לֹא בַשָּׁמַיִם הִיא''.

NOTES

the righteous in every generation, just as He did in Biblical times for the Prophets. Accordingly, God demonstrated His agreement with Rabbi Eliezer's view by performing these wonders (see *Rabbenu Hananel* and *Rabbenu Nissim Gaon*). *Rabbenu Hananel,* however, maintains that these miracles did not actually occur. Rather, they took place in a dream witnessed by one of Rabbi Eliezer's contemporaries (which was nevertheless taken seriously by the Rabbis).

The commentators suggest various explanations as to why Rabbi Eliezer appealed to a carob tree, to a stream of water, and to the walls of the House of Study to prove that he was correct (see *Maharsha* and others). *Rabbi Shlomo Molkho* explains that these items symbolized the various elements of which the world is composed.

יָצְאָתָה בַּת קוֹל **A heavenly voice went forth.** The commentators attempt to explain how the heavenly voice could be wrong (as shown by the fact that the Rabbis refused to accept it). *Rabbenu Nissim Gaon* suggests that, since the heavenly voice declared that "the Halakhah is in accordance with Rabbi Eliezer *everywhere,*" without specifically mentioning the case of the "oven of Akhnai," the Sages felt that this case might be an exception. Moreover, the heavenly voice might have been a divine attempt to test the Rabbis, to see whether they could be induced to deviate from their original decision, which was binding (because it was arrived at by majority rule).

Rabbi Shlomo Molkho claims that the disputed oven was indeed ritually pure, as Rabbi Eliezer had said. But the Rabbis declared it impure, so as to prevent confusion with other types of ovens, which are susceptible to ritual impurity according to all opinions. The Sages' ruling thus constituted a "protective measure" intended to prevent inadvertent violation of the law.

HALAKHAH

לֹא בַשָּׁמַיִם הִיא **It is not in heaven.** "The Torah states of itself: 'It is not in heaven,' and from here we learn that a prophet is not authorized to introduce new laws which do not appear in the Torah. Even if a prophet performed signs and wonders, declaring that God sent him to introduce new laws or cancel existing ones, or to suggest novel Halakhic interpretations, he is a false prophet." (*Rambam, Sefer HaMada, Hilkhot Yesodei HaTorah* 9:1.)

"And others say . . ."

p. 236 Commentary

What happens when a community is in crisis—when the paradigm by which it had been organized is dying and a new paradigm is emerging? There is competition between the old and new paradigms and occasionally this manifests itself as one faction standing steadfastly by the older paradigm and attacking another faction for following a new one. That's another possible explanation of what is happening here. Rabbi Eliezer represents the old way and Rabbi Yehoshua represents the new. (Read Thomas S. Kuhn's classic book, *The Structure of Scientific Revolutions, Second Edition, Enlarged*, University of Chicago, 1970, to learn how this dynamic works.)

What happens in a community when an intense conflict breaks out in public? It becomes a touchstone for the community, crystallizing peoples' positions. They may recall and retell the roles they played in the conflict for years afterward. On a deeper, spiritual level, this story could lead each of us to ask, "How do I know God is talking to me? How do I hear God? Through physical signs? Voices? Through the voice of a brave new majority?"

This story also demands that we think about where Jewish law comes from. Is it an authoritative tradition? Or is it the majority? Or is it in heaven? What role does God play in the determination of Jewish law? Is law the point of Judaism? Or does law simply become a way of identifying the goal of one's spiritual development?

On a more practical level, we could understand the wall-falling part of the story as a retrospective explanation of why walls that were on the verge of falling did not do so. In other words, the walls were shaky and people wondered why they never fell in. If you ever have a chance to visit Israel and see archeological remains there you won't wonder why the issue of falling walls was a big topic of discussion in the Talmud! For example, take a look at B. Taanit 20b–21a (which Rabbi Steinsaltz has translated: Volume 14, Taanit Part II, pp. 83–94) for some great shaky wall stories.

What is a *bat kol*? It is translated as "a heavenly voice" but that doesn't quite give the whole picture. The sages envisioned heaven as a royal court. today, we are used to seeing the "king's" (or president's, or prime minister's) face and hearing the "king's" voice all the time on television. This was not the case in ancient times. How did the king make his decrees known? By sending out messengers to announce his will. The *bat kol* is the heavenly equivalent of those earthly messengers. So when the *bat kol* makes its announcement, it is taken as a direct pronouncement from God utilizing the technology of the day.

—JZA

The Torah Is Not in Heaven

If we no longer pay attention to the Heavenly voice we may also lose the ability to hear each other.

—*Steffie Odle*

The Voice From Heaven

So it seems that these four rabbis had a series of theological arguments, and three were always in accord against the fourth. One day, the odd rabbi out, after the usual "3 to 1, majority rules" statement that signified that he had lost again, decided to appeal to a higher authority.

"Oh, God!" he cried. "I know in my heart that I am right and they are wrong! Please give me a sign to prove it to them!"

It was a beautiful, sunny day. As soon as the rabbi finished his prayer, a storm cloud moved across the sky above the four. It rumbled once and dissolved. "A sign from God! See, I'm right, I knew it!" But the other three disagreed, pointing out that storm clouds form on hot days.

So the rabbi prayed again: "Oh, God, I need a bigger sign to show that I am right and they are wrong. So please, God, a bigger sign!"

This time four storm clouds appeared, rushed toward each other to form one big cloud, and a bolt of lightning slammed into a tree on a nearby hill.

"I told you I was right!" cried the rabbi, but his friends insisted that nothing had happened that could not be explained by natural causes.

The rabbi was getting ready to ask for a very big sign, but just as he said, "Oh God . . .," the sky turned pitch black, the earth shook, and a deep booming voice intoned, "HEEEEEEEE'S RIIIIIIIIGHT!"

The rabbi put his hands on his hips, turned to the other three, and said, "Well?"

"So," shrugged one of the other rabbis, "now it's 3 to 2."

—*From The Jewish Humor Internet List*

NOTES

N O T E S

[1]מַאי ״לֹא בַּשָּׁמַיִם הִיא״?
[2]אָמַר רַבִּי יִרְמְיָה: שֶׁכְּבָר נִתְּנָה תּוֹרָה מֵהַר סִינַי, אֵין אָנוּ מַשְׁגִּיחִין בְּבַת קוֹל, שֶׁכְּבָר כָּתַבְתָּ בְּהַר סִינַי בַּתּוֹרָה: ״אַחֲרֵי רַבִּים לְהַטֹּת״.
[3]אַשְׁכְּחֵיהּ רַבִּי נָתָן לְאֵלִיָּהוּ, אֲמַר לֵיהּ: ״מַאי עָבֵיד קוּדְשָׁא בְּרִיךְ הוּא בְּהַהִיא שַׁעְתָּא״? [4]אֲמַר לֵיהּ: ״קָא חָיֵיךְ וְאָמַר: ׳נִצְּחוּנִי בָּנַי, נִצְּחוּנִי בָּנַי׳״.
[5]אָמְרוּ: ״אוֹתוֹ הַיּוֹם הֵבִיאוּ כָּל טְהָרוֹת שֶׁטִּיהֵר רַבִּי אֱלִיעֶזֶר וּשְׂרָפוּם בָּאֵשׁ, וְנִמְנוּ עָלָיו וּבֵרְכוּהוּ. [6]וְאָמְרוּ: ׳מִי יֵלֵךְ וְיוֹדִיעוֹ׳? [7]אָמַר לָהֶם רַבִּי עֲקִיבָא: ׳אֲנִי אֵלֵךְ, שֶׁמָּא

LITERAL TRANSLATION

[1]What does "it is not in heaven" [mean]?
[2]Rabbi Yirmeyah said: That the Torah was already given on Mount Sinai, [and] we do not pay attention to a [heavenly] voice, for You already wrote in the Torah at Mount Sinai: "After the majority to incline."
[3]Rabbi Natan met Elijah [and] said to him: "What did the Holy One, blessed be He, do at that time?" [4]He said to him: "He smiled and said: 'My sons have defeated Me, My sons have defeated Me.'"
[5]They said: "That day they brought all the objects that Rabbi Eliezer had declared ritually pure and burned them in a fire, and they voted (lit., 'were counted') about him and they excommunicated (lit., 'blessed') him. [6]And they said: 'Who will go and inform him?' [7]Rabbi Akiva said to them: 'I will go, lest

RASHI

כל טהרות שטיהר רבי אליעזר – על ידי מעשה שאירע נשאלה הלכה זו בבית המדרש, שנפלה טומאה לאויר תנור זה, וחזרו ועשאו על גביו טהרות, וטיהרם רבי אליעזר. והביאום ושרפום לפניו.

TRANSLATION AND COMMENTARY

מַאי לֹא בַּשָּׁמַיִם הִיא [1]The Gemara interrupts the Baraita and asks for a clarification: **What** did Rabbi Yehoshua mean when he quoted the Scriptural verse that "the Torah **is not in heaven**"?

אָמַר רַבִּי יִרְמְיָה [2]**Rabbi Yirmeyah said** in reply: Since God **already gave the Torah** to the Jewish people **on Mount Sinai, we no** longer **pay attention to heavenly voices** that attempt to intervene in matters of Halakhah. **For You,** God, **already wrote in the Torah at Mount Sinai** (Exodus 23:2), **"After the majority to incline."** From this verse we learn that Halakhic disputes must be resolved by majority vote of the Rabbis. God could not contradict His own decision to allow Torah questions to be decided by free debate and majority vote.

אַשְׁכְּחֵיהּ רַבִּי נָתָן לְאֵלִיָּהוּ [3]The Gemara relates that generations later **Rabbi Natan met** the Prophet **Elijah.** (Several of the Talmudic Sages had visions of Elijah the Prophet, and discussed Halakhic questions with him.) Rabbi Natan asked Elijah about the debate between Rabbi Eliezer and Rabbi Yehoshua. **He said to him: "What did the Holy One, blessed be He, do at that time** when Rabbi Yehoshua refused to heed the heavenly voice?" [4]In reply, **Elijah said to** Rabbi Natan: "God **smiled and said: 'My sons have defeated Me, My sons have defeated Me!'"** God's sons "defeated Him" with their arguments. Rabbi Yehoshua was correct in his contention that a view confirmed by majority vote must be accepted, even where God Himself holds the opposite view.

אָמְרוּ [5]The Rabbis who related this story in the Baraita continued and **said: "That day,** Rabbi Eliezer would not accept the Sages' decision. They, therefore, decided to make a public demonstration of their decision. **They brought all the foodstuffs** that had been prepared in an Akhnai oven and **which Rabbi Eliezer had declared ritually pure, and burned them in a fire,** to show that Rabbi Eliezer's position was rejected by the Halakhah. Afterwards **they** met **and took a vote and excommunicated** Rabbi Eliezer ('blessed' here is a euphemism for 'excommunicated') for refusing to accept the majority view." The Baraita continues to describe the consequences of this momentous act. Even though the Sages thought they were justified, they could expect Rabbi Eliezer to be sorely offended. They wished to mitigate the anguish he would feel as much as possible, in view of the gravity of hurting the feelings of another person. (It is because of this section of the Baraita that this story is related here.) [6]"The Sages **said: 'Who will go and inform** Rabbi Eliezer that he has been excommunicated? [7]**Rabbi Akiva said to them: 'I will go,** since I am his student and I will inform him in the most tactful

BACKGROUND

בַּת קוֹל A heavenly voice. The Hebrew expression employed here (בַּת קוֹל) has two different meanings: (1) An echo (literally, בַּת קוֹל means "daughter of a voice"), and (2) a heavenly voice, i.e., a quasi-prophetic voice which a person hears within himself, although he perceives it as coming from outside himself. Hearing such a "heavenly voice" was regarded as a type of revelation, albeit of lesser clarity and force than actual prophecy. Hence the expression בַּת קוֹל, because such a voice is an "echo" of true prophecy.

לֹא בַּשָּׁמַיִם הִיא It is not in heaven. Even though it is explicitly forbidden to deviate from Torah law (and indeed, a prophet who advocates the abrogation of Torah law is punishable by death), the Torah itself recognized the outstanding Torah scholars of each generation as the authoritative interpreters of the law, and hence the Gemara's statement that the Torah is "not in heaven."

NOTES

נִצְּחוּנִי בָּנַי My sons have defeated Me. The commentators attempt to explain why God smiled when "His sons defeated Him." Some authorities explain that God was happy because the Sages, by refusing to accept the heavenly voice, affirmed their belief in the eternity of the Torah, demonstrating that even a prophet is not authorized to alter Torah laws (see *Rambam*'s introduction to *Mishneh Torah*).

וּבֵרְכוּהוּ They excommunicated him. *Rashi* explains that a ban of *niddui* — "ostracism" — was pronounced against Rabbi Eliezer, such ostracism being the standard penalty for people who treated other scholars disrespectfully. A person ostracized in this manner was not permitted to wear leather shoes or cut his hair, and other people were required to keep at least four cubits away from him.

Ramban and other commentators, however, explain that a more severe type of ban, *ḥerem* — "excommunication" — was pronounced against Rabbi Eliezer. Unlike *niddui*, *ḥerem* entails a prohibition against doing business with the

"And others say . . ."

p. 237 Commentary

How can the assertion "It's not in heaven" be understood? The Gemara offers a few possible answers. In line 2, a prooftext is offered. This is the standard text that supports the sages' assertion that one follows the majority. One is straightforward explication in line 2. The other, in lines 3–4, is missing in the Yerushalmi's version of this story, and shows God's delight at being overcome. Note, too, that the material in lines 3 and 4 is in Aramaic while the story up to now has been in Hebrew, a probable indication that these insights are a later addition to the story. So, in the Bavli, God is happy when people claim power while the Yerushalmi is silent on the matter of God's laughter at such a moment.

In the Bavli, God doesn't want mindless obedience. What delights God? When we make the tradition our own. When we debate, when we take part, when we have enough confidence in the process in which we are engaged to say that we don't need supernatural help.

Among the many wonderful interpretations of these words, "It is not in heaven!" (Deuteronomy 30:11), is this one:

Rabbi Hanina said: "It [the Torah] and all [the] instruments of its art [i.e., those things one needs to learn Torah] were given: its humility, its righteousness, its uprightness, and the giving of its reward. (Deuteronomy Rabbah 8:6)

It's not just that the Torah isn't in heaven, but that all the gifts one needs to study Torah, and that come with Torah study, aren't laid by in heaven, either. They're immediately available. We don't have to wait till we die or till the messiah comes to gain the benefits of Torah study. Torah (and Talmud) study should have a real, palpable impact on our lives almost as soon as we begin a regular regimen of study. It is no accident, then, that Rabbi Eliezer loses the ability to teach Torah because he fails to manifest the humility of a vessel of Torah. Torah study should have given him more of the heavenly qualities listed by Rabbi Hanina. Instead, Rabbi Eliezer seems to have fewer and fewer of these qualities as he continues on his path.

In line 5, we learn that Rabbi Eliezer was excommunicated. The text says literally, "blessed." However, we, too, may say "blessed" when we mean "cursed" as, for example, when we trip on something and say, "I tripped over that blessed coffee table!" (Or we may say, "That blankety-blank urn!") Since Rabbi Eliezer's temper was so fierce, no one was anxious to be the one to notify him that the very institution to which he had devoted so much of his life had utterly rejected him. Only Rabbi Akiva, whose bravery is portrayed graphically in other parts of the Talmud (e.g., B. Berachot 61b), would take up the challenge.

—JZA

My Children Have Defeated Me. . . .

Rabbi Natan met Elijah and said to him, "What did the Holy Blessed One do at that time? He said to him, 'God smiled and said, My children have defeated Me. My children have defeated Me.'"

The Talmud explains that Rabbi Yehoshua refuses to heed the call of the *bat kol*/heavenly voice regarding an issue of Halakhah; God smiles and then twice announces defeat.

Why does God smile if God is being defeated? Why does God announce this defeat twice?

Psalm 81, the psalm recited each Thursday morning, inspires an answer. The themes of this psalm expand upon Elijah's response and perhaps provide a context for the remark, 'God smiled and said, My children have defeated Me. My children have defeated Me.' (quoted text is from Psalm 81)

"Sing joyfully to Adonai our Strength. Shout gladly to the God of Jacob."
"It is the Law for the People Israel."

The People Israel rejoices in learning the Way of Torah. God smiled.

"I tested your faith in the wilderness. Heed this warning, My People Israel. If you would only listen . . ."

Remember the golden calf the children of Israel formed in the desert. My children have defeated Me.

"I gave them to their stubbornness. I let them follow their own devices. If only my people would listen to Me."

"Recall the tablets of stone that Moses threw down in anger." My children have defeated Me.

"I heard a voice I never knew," says the psalmist. Though he didn't listen to the Voice he heard from the heavens, Rabbi Yehoshua followed the Word given from the heavens describing how we should live on earth.

Perhaps God realized that God was not losing control, but rather sharing control with those created in the Divine Image. Perhaps God was not defeated, but rather, the people were following God's Word. God's cries of despair turned into words of blessing and abundance:

"Yisrael bidrachai y'haleichu" . . ."that the People Israel will walk in my ways." In order that they learn Halakhah/the Way, and the promise to be fulfilled:

"I will feed you with richest wheat; I will satisfy you with honey from the rock."

—*Mark Frydenberg*

NOTES

NOTES

יֵלֵךְ אָדָם שֶׁאֵינוֹ הָגוּן וְיוֹדִיעוֹ, וְנִמְצָא מַחֲרִיב אֶת כָּל הָעוֹלָם כּוּלּוֹ׳. [1]מֶה עָשָׂה רַבִּי עֲקִיבָא? [2]לָבַשׁ שְׁחוֹרִים, וְנִתְעַטֵּף שְׁחוֹרִים, וְיָשַׁב לְפָנָיו בְּרִיחוּק אַרְבַּע אַמּוֹת. [3]אָמַר לוֹ רַבִּי אֱלִיעֶזֶר: ׳עֲקִיבָא, מַה יּוֹם מִיּוֹמַיִם׳? [4]אָמַר לוֹ: ׳רַבִּי, כִּמְדוּמֶּה לִי שֶׁחֲבֵירִים בְּדֵילִים מִמְּךָ׳. [5]אַף הוּא קָרַע בְּגָדָיו וְחָלַץ מִנְעָלָיו, וְנִשְׁמַט וְיָשַׁב עַל גַּבֵּי קַרְקַע. [6]זָלְגוּ עֵינָיו דְּמָעוֹת. [7]לָקָה הָעוֹלָם: שְׁלִישׁ בְּזֵיתִים, וּשְׁלִישׁ בְּחִטִּים, וּשְׁלִישׁ בִּשְׂעוֹרִים. [8]וְיֵשׁ אוֹמְרִים: אַף בָּצֵק שֶׁבִּידֵי אִשָּׁה טָפַח״.

[9]תָּנָא: ״אַךְ גָּדוֹל הָיָה בְּאוֹתוֹ הַיּוֹם, שֶׁבְּכָל מָקוֹם שֶׁנָּתַן בּוֹ עֵינָיו רַבִּי אֱלִיעֶזֶר נִשְׂרַף. [10]וְאַף רַבָּן גַּמְלִיאֵל הָיָה בָּא בִּסְפִינָה, עָמַד עָלָיו נַחְשׁוֹל לְטַבְּעוֹ. [11]אָמַר: ׳כִּמְדוּמֶּה לִי שֶׁאֵין זֶה אֶלָּא בִּשְׁבִיל רַבִּי אֱלִיעֶזֶר בֶּן הוֹרְקָנוֹס׳. [12]עָמַד עַל רַגְלָיו

LITERAL TRANSLATION

someone who is unsuitable will go and inform him, and as a result he will destroy the entire world.' [1]What did Rabbi Akiva do? [2]He dressed in black [garments] and wrapped himself in black, and sat before him at a distance of four cubits. [3]Rabbi Eliezer said to him: 'Akiva, what is [the difference between] today and any other day (lit., 'what is one day from two days')?' [4]He said to him: 'Rabbi, it seems to me that [your] colleagues are staying away from you.' [5]He, too, rent his garments and took off his shoes, and he slipped down and sat on the ground. [6]His eyes streamed with tears. [7]The world was smitten: one-third of the olives, and one-third of the wheat, and one-third of the barley. [8]And some say [that] even the dough in a woman's hands swelled."

[9][A Tanna] taught: "There was a great calamity on that day, for every place upon which Rabbi Eliezer laid his eyes was burnt. [10]And Rabban Gamliel, too, was coming on a ship, [and] a wave rose up against him to drown him. [11]He said: 'It seems to me that this is only because of Rabbi Eliezer ben Hyrcanus.' [12]He rose to his feet

TRANSLATION AND COMMENTARY

manner possible, **lest someone** else **who is unsuitable will go and inform him** in a rude, insulting manner, **and as a result** Rabbi Eliezer **will** become so angry that he will cause **the entire world to be destroyed** in divine retribution for the anguish caused him.' [1]**What did Rabbi Akiva do** in order to inform Rabbi Eliezer? [2]**He dressed in black garments and wrapped himself in black, and sat before** Rabbi Eliezer **at a distance of four cubits,** since it is prohibited to stand or sit within four cubits of a person who has been excommunicated. [3]**Rabbi Eliezer said to** Rabbi Akiva: **'Akiva, what is the difference between today and yesterday?** Why are you acting so strangely today, dressing in black and sitting at a distance from me?' [4]Rabbi Akiva **said to** Rabbi Eliezer: **'My teacher, it seems to me that your colleagues are staying away from you.'** In this way Rabbi Akiva delicately informed Rabbi Eliezer that he had been excommunicated. [5]Rabbi Eliezer understood the message, so **he too rent his garments and took off his shoes** as a sign of mourning, **and he slipped down** from his chair **and sat on the ground** like a mourner. [6]Rabbi Eliezer's **eyes streamed with tears** of shame and anguish. [7]Rabbi Eliezer's anguish had immediate consequences. **The world was smitten: One-third of the olives, one-third of the wheat, and one-third of the barley** were destroyed. [8]Indeed, **some say that even the dough in women's hands swelled** and spoiled."

תָּנָא [9]The Gemara now quotes another Baraita that describes the consequences of Rabbi Eliezer's excommunication: **A Tanna taught: "There was great** divine wrath on **the day** Rabbi Eliezer was excommunicated and a great **calamity** befell the world, **for whatever Rabbi Eliezer laid his eyes upon was burnt.** [10]**Rabban Gamliel, too,** was affected; he **was traveling on a ship, and a** huge **wave rose over him to drown him.** As Nasi and head of the central yeshivah at Yavneh, Rabban Gamliel was the leading Sage of the period. Therefore he was personally responsible for the measures taken against Rabbi Eliezer. [11]When Rabban Gamliel realized that he was about to drown, **he said** to himself: **'It seems to me that this can only be** happening to me **because of** the anguish caused to **Rabbi Eliezer ben Hyrcanus.'** [12]Rabban Gamliel **rose to his feet**

RASHI

לבש שחורים – ענין צער ואבל. **אף הוא קרע בגדיו** – שהמנודה חייב בקריעה. **חלץ מנעליו** – שהמנודה אסור בנעילת הסנדל, במועד קטן (טו,ב). **ונשמט** – מן הכסא. **טפח** – נתקלקל. **אך גדול** = מכה גדולה. **רבן גמליאל** – נשיא היה, ועל פיו נעשה.

NOTES

excommunicated person. To be sure, people were ordinarily not put into *ḥerem* unless repeated *niddui* proved ineffective. But Rabbi Eliezer was treated especially strictly, since his defiant attitude bordered on outright rebellion against the Sages.

לָבַשׁ שְׁחוֹרִים He dressed in black garments. *Maharsha* explains that Rabbi Akiva did this out of respect for Rabbi Eliezer, acting as if he, Rabbi Akiva, had been excommunicated, rather than his teacher. For the same reason, Rabbi Akiva euphemistically said that "it seems to me that your colleagues are staying away from you," rather than "have excommunicated you."

"And others say . . ."

p. 238 Commentary

How might we tactfully tell someone really bad news? By showing that we understand their hurt feelings and that this news hurts us, too. This is what Rabbi Akiva, one of Rabbi Eliezer's most promising students, did for his teacher. Rabbi Akiva demonstrated that his teacher's excommunication was a source of pain for him by wearing black and coming as close to Rabbi Eliezer as he could.

However, even Rabbi Akiva's gentle breaking of such news could not forestall Rabbi Eliezer's powerful reaction. His tears bring on a strong reaction in the world. This is the reason this story is here, in the commentary to this mishnah: to show the power of hurt feelings. If we want to understand this phenomenon on a mystical level, we will take the story literally. If we want to look at it somewhat more politically, we could theorize that the burnings carried out by Rabbi Eliezer's followers were retaliatory actions against the sages. Since the items Rabbi Eliezer called clean were burned by the sages, perhaps his followers burnt things that the sages called clean in retribution.

Similarly, we can understand Rabban Gamliel's near drowning as a metaphor: the excommunication of Rabbi Eliezer threatened to bring down Rabban Gamliel's leadership.

We might also understand it as Rabban Gamliel's guilty conscience: anytime something bad happened to him his guilt over excommunicating his brother-in-law rose up to accuse him. Alternatively, we can understand the story in a straightforward way. God can speak to us through natural phenomena. God is constantly communicating with us in diverse ways. What varies is our ability and willingness to listen to the messages.

—JZA

Rent His Garments

As a final gift to me, my mother of blessed memory taught: When a person knows that she is dying she begins the process of separation. In a way she begins to snip the fabric of each relationship. Often the process begins with the strongest ties because this separation requires the most strength. The dying person usually leads the way because she must snip every strand of every relationship while we, the loved ones, are only snipping one. Further, after death occurs, we make the final snip in our garmet acknowledging that the last threads of the relationship are severed. As I pass on the wisdom of my mother to my children, my patients, and my friends, I believe that my mother fulfills the blessing of living to one hundred twenty years.

—Steffie Odle

TRANSLATION AND COMMENTARY

and said: 'Master of the Universe, You know full well that I did not excommunicate Rabbi Eliezer **for my own** personal **honor, nor for the honor of my father's house. Rather,** Rabbi Eliezer was excommunicated **for Your honor,** because it is essential that no individual, great as he may be, should reject a decision reached by the majority, **so that controversies will not multiply in Israel.'** [1]Swayed by Rabban Gamliel's explanation, **the sea** then **rested from its wrath.**

אִימָּא שָׁלוֹם [2]The Gemara continues with one final story in relation to Rabbi Eliezer's excommunication, which connects the incident to the prohibition against verbal *ona'ah*: **Imma Shalom, Rabbi Eliezer's wife, was** also **Rabban Gamliel's sister.** [3]**From this incident** — Rabbi Eliezer's excommunication — **onward, she would not let Rabbi Eliezer fall on his face** when he recited his prayers. On weekdays, it is customary to recite supplicatory prayers, called "falling on one's face." Imma Shalom did not allow her husband to recite these prayers, lest he pray for divine assistance to overcome the tragedy that had befallen him, and Rabban Gamliel, her brother, might be punished. [4]**One day,** Imma Shalom thought that **it was** the day of **the New Moon** (*Rosh Ḥodesh*), the first day of the month according to the lunar calendar, when these supplicatory prayers are not recited. Imma Shalom therefore assumed that her husband would not recite this prayer on that day, and did not take care to keep him from "falling on his face." But in fact Imma Shalom had erred in her calculations, and she mistook **a full month for a short one.** The moon takes about twenty-nine-and-a-half days to revolve around the earth. Accordingly, some months (called "short" or "defective" months) are twenty-nine days long, while others (called "full" months) are thirty days long. Imma Shalom thought that the preceding month had been short (i.e., only twenty-nine days long), when in fact it was "full" (thirty days long). Thus, the day that she thought was Rosh Ḥodesh was really the last day of the previous month, when it was customary to offer special supplications. [5]**Some say** that the incident happened in a slightly different manner: **A poor person came and stood at the door, and** Imma Shalom **brought out bread for him,** as a result of which she was temporarily distracted. [6]For whichever reason, she was distracted and **she found** Rabbi Eliezer **fallen on his face** in prayer. **She said to him: "Rise! You have killed my brother."** She was certain that Rabban Gamliel had died, since she assumed that Rabbi Eliezer had given expression to the pain he felt because of his excommunication, and that this had led to divine retribution against Rabban Gamliel. [7]**Meanwhile,** as Imma Shalom was talking to her husband, **the sound of a horn came from Rabban Gamliel's house** and an announcement was made confirming the fact **that he had died.** [8]Rabbi Eliezer **said to** Imma Shalom: **"How did you know** that Rabban Gamliel had died?" [9]**She said to him: "I have the following**

וְאָמַר: ׳רִבּוֹנוֹ שֶׁל עוֹלָם, גָּלוּי וְיָדוּעַ לְפָנֶיךָ שֶׁלֹּא לִכְבוֹדִי עָשִׂיתִי, וְלֹא לִכְבוֹד בֵּית אַבָּא עָשִׂיתִי, אֶלָּא לִכְבוֹדְךָ, שֶׁלֹּא יִרְבּוּ מַחֲלוֹקוֹת בְּיִשְׂרָאֵל׳. [1]נָח הַיָּם מִזַּעְפּוֹ״.

[2]אִימָּא שָׁלוֹם, דְּבֵיתְהוּ דְּרַבִּי אֱלִיעֶזֶר, אַחְתֵּיהּ דְּרַבָּן גַּמְלִיאֵל הֲוַאי. [3]מֵהַהוּא מַעֲשֶׂה וְאֵילָךְ לָא הֲוָה שָׁבְקָה לֵיהּ לְרַבִּי אֱלִיעֶזֶר לְמֵיפַּל עַל אַפֵּיהּ. [4]הַהוּא יוֹמָא רֵישׁ יַרְחָא הֲוָה, וְאִיחֲלַף לָהּ בֵּין מָלֵא לְחָסֵר. [5]אִיכָּא דְּאָמְרִי: אֲתָא עַנְיָא וְקָאֵי אַבָּבָא, אַפִּיקָא לֵיהּ רִיפְתָּא. [6]אַשְׁכַּחְתֵּיהּ דְּנָפַל עַל אַנְפֵּיהּ, אֲמַרָה לֵיהּ: ״קוּם! קְטַלִית לְאָחִי״. [7]אַדְּהָכִי, נְפַק שִׁיפּוּרָא מִבֵּית רַבָּן גַּמְלִיאֵל דִּשְׁכִיב. [8]אֲמַר לָהּ: ״מְנָא יָדַעַתְּ״? [9]אֲמַרָה לֵיהּ: ״כָּךְ

LITERAL TRANSLATION

and said: 'Master of the Universe, it is revealed and known before You that I did not do [this] for my [own] honor, nor did I do [it] for the honor of my father's house, but for Your honor, so that controversies will not multiply in Israel.' [1]The sea rested from its wrath."

[2]Imma Shalom, Rabbi Eliezer's wife, was Rabban Gamliel's sister. [3]From that incident onward she did not let Rabbi Eliezer fall on his face. [4]One day it was the New Moon, and she mistook a full [month] for a short one. [5]Some say: A poor person came and stood at the door, [and] she brought out bread for him. [6]She found him fallen on his face, [and] she said to him: "Rise! You have killed my brother." [7]Meanwhile the sound of a horn came from Rabban Gamliel's house that he had died. [8]He said to her: "From where did you know?" [9]She said to him: "I have

RASHI

שלא ירבו מחלוקות – שלא ירגיל היחיד לחלוק על המרובין. **אימא שלום** – כך שמה. **בין מלא לחסר** – סבורה היתה שיהא החדש חסר וקבוע ביום שלשים, ולא יפול ביום החדש על פניו. והיה מלא, ולא נקבע עד יום שלשים ואחד, ולא נזהרה בו ביום שלשים ונפל על פניו.

BACKGROUND

אִימָּא שָׁלוֹם Imma Shalom (lit., "Mother Shalom"). "Imma" is apparently an honorific title applied to distinguished women, either because of their age or their personal status. Like other women from important families, Imma Shalom was learned; and in other places as well she reports the teachings of her brother and traditions from her father's house.

לְמֵיפַּל עַל אַפֵּיהּ To fall on his face. "Falling on one's face" is an act of private prayer consisting of supplications and requests recited following the Eighteen Benedictions in the synagogue, and it is also part of the service on fast days. During Talmudic times people actually used to prostrate themselves — "to fall on their faces" — on the floor. Afterwards it became the practice to perform this action symbolically, by placing one's head on one's hand. Today this prayer is known as *Taḥanun* (תַּחֲנוּן — "supplication") and has a standard form, the main portion of which is a passage from Psalms.

נְפַק שִׁיפּוּרָא The sound of a horn came. In Talmudic times a person's death was announced by a blast of the shofar, so that everyone would be informed in advance of the funeral. It was particularly necessary to announce the death of the Nasi, because of the great honor with which he was regarded, and everyone had to take part in mourning for him.

"And others say . . ."

p. 239 Commentary

At this point, it might be interesting and productive to contrast the way this story is told here and in the Yerushalmi. Why now? Because the tannaitic teaching on p. 238, line 9 through p. 239, line 8 about Rabban Gamliel and Imma Shalom, which we're about to encounter, is missing in the Yerushalmi. There (Y. Moed Katan 3:1, Y. 81 c–d), Rabbi Eliezer's ecommunication is related to such bans ending, rather than the power of hurt feelings and excommunication beginning, as it is here. This is significant. The compositors of the Yerushalmi and the Bavli could have put the story of the Akhnai oven *anywhere*. Their placements were strategic. The Bavli wants to bring out the seriousness of hurt feelings and the story is shaped accordingly. The Yerushalmi apparently wants to underscore how people could get along well. Therefore, this story is placed in Moed Katan in the Yerushalmi, commenting on a mishnah that talks about the *end* of excommunication.

A factor that may aid our understanding of Talmudic story telling style is the realization that the action may be telescoped in terms of time. The story is being told as if Rabbi Eliezer's excommunication happened on the same day or within a month's time. One might more productively imagine that what is reported happened over a span of several years.

How does Rabban Gamliel avert the danger that is about to drown him (be it a wave, a guilty conscience, or his opposition in the Academy)? By pointing to the purity of his motives. He didn't excommunicate Rabbi Eliezer out of ego or spite but out of a sense of fair play. No person, no matter how powerful in intellect and feeling, may be allowed to overrule the decision of a majority. No single participant may violate group process and remain in the group if that group is to survive. All the group members must operate with integrity and try to reduce fights by not giving in to theatrics. In other words, "making waves" when you're upset is neither effective nor right in the Academy of this era.

The events that end Rabbi Eliezer's story may be quite upsetting. Imma Shalom controls her husband's temper by constantly monitoring him since she knows what will happen if he is allowed to approach heaven with his tears. In lines 4 and 5 the Gemara offers two options: either Imma Shalom miscalculated the day of a new moon or she gave bread to a poor person who came to her door. Which version do you prefer? What is truthful about each one? Why do you think both were recorded? These questions don't have any set answers but they can be enlightening to consider.

When Imma Shalom sees that Rabbi Eliezer has prayed with a strength that caused anything he looked at to be burnt she knows immediately that her brother has been killed. This is the moment when we look for a miracle in the story . . . but there is none. Rabbi Eliezer's hurt feelings kill Rabban Gamliel. It could be that Rabban Gamliel's leadership was "killed" by Rabbi Eliezer's supporters. Or it could be that the anguish Rabban Gamliel felt over excommunicating his brother-in-law corroded his health until he died. Or it could be that Rabbi Eliezer literally killed Rabban Gamliel with his prayers. Regardless of the way(s) in which we understand the story, there is no happy ending here as there is in the Yerushalmi. Rabbi Eliezer remains excommunicated and Rabban Gamliel is killed. Imma Shalom's feelings are never recorded. She merely sums up the whole episode by authoritatively quoting a teaching she learned in her father's house: Hurt feelings go directly to God. Imma Shalom is strong and rational, acting to deter Rabbi Eliezer's outbursts and quoting a teaching as authoritatively as her husband or brother could.

In the Talmud, as in the Bible, a story is arranged so that its crucial point is in the center. In this story we began with a point of emotional pain: Rabbi Eliezer's hurt and shame that his ruling about the oven of Akhnai is not accepted. We then have a dramatic interchange with supernatural forces being brought into play. At the center of the story, we have God's pleasure at the cleverness of the sages. This, then, is the point of this story as told in the Bavli: God treasures the ability of the sages to outwit, as it were, even God. Then, we have more supernatural events (the burnings and the wave; fire and water) and finally we have Imma Shalom's teaching about hurt feelings that was introduced on p. 231, line 3. So the story forms a pyramid:

1. A teaching involving hurt feelings
  2. Supernatural consequences
    3. God's delight
  2a. Supernatural consequences
1a. A teaching involving hurt feelings

The preservation of the sages' process and the affirmation that the process is more important than any one sage's objective "correctness" about tradition are what the Bavli underscores. In addition, the passage is about the importance of hurt feelings and this accounts for its placement in the commentary to this mishnah. The two points are complementary. A process that takes no account of feelings won't work, just as a system that only caters to feelings without some sense of limits and integrity won't function either.

—JZA

Niddah and Niddui

In the Bavli's retelling the story of Rabbi Eliezer's *niddui*, his anguish is described not only by the olives, wheat, and barley being destroyed, but also that "the dough in women's hands swelled (and was spoiled)." This comment connects *niddah* and *challah*: just as the dough now cannot be baked, his spiritual insights must remain uncooked (untransmitted, untaught). He is cut off from his spiritual children; neither does the dough reach its next generation. The loss of fruition in one arena causes the loss of fruition in the other.

—Ken Carr

"The gates of prayer have been locked, but the gates of tears are not locked."

The Temple in Jerusalem was the spiritual center of the Jewish people, and tradition teaches that the gates of prayer will remain closed until it is rebuilt. Yet we can take steps to open the gates of prayer in our own lives by continuously working to rebuild our own spiritual centers.

With each day one gate closes and another opens. I ask God to watch over me, as I walk life's path from one gate to another.

Help me reach the gate of understanding. Teach me to enter the gate of compassion. Open for me the gates of righteousness, that I may enter them to praise Yah. This is the gateway to Adonai, the righteous shall enter there. [Psalm 118:1–20]

—Mark Frydenberg

NOTES

מְקוּבְּלָנִי מִבֵּית אֲבִי אַבָּא: כָּל הַשְּׁעָרִים נִנְעָלִים חוּץ מִשַּׁעֲרֵי אוֹנָאָה״.

[1]תָּנוּ רַבָּנַן: ״הַמְאַנֶּה אֶת הַגֵּר עוֹבֵר בִּשְׁלֹשָׁה לָאוִין, וְהַלּוֹחֲצוֹ עוֹבֵר בִּשְׁנַיִם״.

[2]מַאי שְׁנָא מְאַנֶּה? [3]דִּכְתִיבִי שְׁלֹשָׁה לָאוִין: ״וְגֵר לֹא תוֹנֶה״, ״וְכִי יָגוּר אִתְּךָ גֵּר בְּאַרְצְכֶם, לֹא תוֹנוּ אֹתוֹ״, וְ״לֹא תוֹנוּ אִישׁ אֶת עֲמִיתוֹ״, [4]וְגֵר בִּכְלַל ״עֲמִיתוֹ״ הוּא? [5]לוֹחֲצוֹ נַמִּי, שְׁלֹשָׁה כְּתִיבִי: ״וְלֹא תִלְחָצֶנּוּ״, ״וְגֵר לֹא תִלְחָץ״, וְ״לֹא תִהְיֶה לוֹ כְּנֹשֶׁה״, [6]וְגֵר בִּכְלָל הוּא!

LITERAL TRANSLATION

this tradition from my grandfather's house: All the gates are locked except for the gates of *ona'ah*." [1]Our Rabbis taught: "Someone who wrongs a convert violates three prohibitions, and someone who oppresses him violates two." [2]Why is someone who wrongs [a convert] different? [3][Is it] because three prohibitions are written: "And a stranger you shall not wrong," "And if the stranger dwells with you in your land, you shall not wrong him," and "You shall not wrong each man his fellow," [4]and a convert is included in "his fellow." [5][If] he oppresses him, too, three [prohibitions] are written: "And you shall not oppress him," "And a stranger you shall not oppress," and "You shall not be to him as a usurer," [6]and a convert is included!

TRANSLATION AND COMMENTARY

tradition from my grandfather's house: All the heavenly **gates are locked except for the gates** through which prayers concerning ***ona'ah*** pass." And since Rabbi Eliezer had been the victim of verbal *ona'ah*, his wife was certain that his prayers would be answered.

תָּנוּ רַבָּנַן [1]The Gemara now presents another Baraita which elaborates on the prohibition against verbal *ona'ah*: **Our Rabbis taught: "Someone who wrongs a convert** by verbal *ona'ah* **violates three prohibitions, and someone who oppresses him** in financial matters **violates two** prohibitions."

מַאי שְׁנָא מְאַנֶּה [2]The Gemara challenges the distinction made in this Baraita: **Why is someone** who verbally **wrongs a convert** treated **differently** — more severely — than someone who oppresses him financially? [3]**Is it because three prohibitions were written** in connection with someone who verbally wrongs a stranger (understood in this context as a convert), namely: (1) **"And a stranger you shall not wrong"** (Exodus 2:2). (2) **"And if a stranger dwells with you in your land, you shall not wrong him"** (Leviticus 19:33). **And** (3) **"You shall not wrong, each man his fellow"** (Leviticus 25:17) — the verse quoted at the beginning of the discussion, above 58b, which prohibits causing anguish to any fellow Jew. [4]Now, **a convert is included in** the category of **a fellow** Jew, therefore, this verse also prohibits causing anguish to converts. [5]But, argues the Gemara, the same should also apply to a person who **oppresses** a convert financially! Here, too, **three prohibitions** are violated. For there **are also** three prohibitions **written** about oppressing a convert, namely: (1) **"And you shall not oppress him"** (Exodus 22:2), the continuation of the first verse cited above, which prohibits causing anguish. (2) **"And a stranger you shall not oppress"** (Exodus 23:9). **And** (3) **"You shall not be to him as a usurer"** (Exodus 22:24), which prohibits forcing a Jew to take desperate measures to repay a debt that he is not in a position to repay. [6]Now, **a convert is included** in this prohibition which, once again, applies to all Jews! Thus, it would appear that a person who oppresses a convert financially violates three prohibitions, and not just two, as stated in the Baraita!

RASHI

מבית אבי אבא — מבית אבי המשפחה, שבת נשיאים היתה, והם מבית דוד. **חוץ משערי אונאה** — לפי שצער הלב היא, וקרוב להוריד דמעות. **המאנה את הגר** — אונאת דברים. **הלוחצו** = דוחקו. **לא תהיה לו כנושה** — לחץ הוא, שדוחקו לתבוע חובו. **הכי גרסינן: מאי שנא מאנה דכתיב ביה תלתא: "וגר לא תונה", "לא תונו אותו", "ולא תונו איש את עמיתו"** — וגר בכלל עמיתו הוא. **לוחצו נמי תלתא כתיב ביה** — "וגר לא תלחץ", "ולא תלחצנו", ו"לא תהיה לו כנושה".

NOTES

מִבֵּית אֲבִי אַבָּא **From my grandfather's house.** *Rashi* and *Tosafot* explain that Imma Shalom was referring to her descent from the royal House of David. *Ritva* observes that the reference may be to Rabban Shimon ben Gamliel the first, whose teachings were not so well known as those of other members of the dynasty.

חוּץ מִשַּׁעֲרֵי אוֹנָאָה **Except for the gates of *ona'ah*.** Even though the Sages who excommunicated Rabbi Eliezer were apparently justified in doing so, they were punished because they hurt his feelings and caused him unnecessary distress (*Rabbi Ya'akov Emden*).

HALAKHAH

אוֹנָאַת הַגֵּר **Wronging a convert.** "One must be especially careful not to hurt a convert either by wounding him with unkind words or by defrauding him financially, since the Torah explicitly forbids this on many occasions." (*Shulḥan Arukh, Ḥoshen Mishpat* 228:2.)

BACKGROUND

הַמְאַנֶּה אֶת הַגֵּר **Someone who wrongs a convert.** As the Gemara indicates here, a special prohibition applies to wronging and oppressing converts (in addition to the more general prohibition against oppressing any Jew). Even though converts are considered full-fledged Jews, special laws apply to them: Since converts cannot look to their families for support (and are fully dependent upon God instead), they are more sensitive to insult, and hence they need special protection. Moreover, converts are entitled to special privileges since they willingly chose to leave their non-Jewish background to join the Jewish people.

TRANSLATION AND COMMENTARY

אֶלָּא [1]In the light of this objection, the Gemara amends the Baraita and concludes: **Rather, the law is the same** for a person who wrongs a convert verbally and one who oppresses him financially. In both cases, the offender **violates three prohibitions.**

תַּנְיָא [2]Continuing the discussion about wronging a convert, the Gemara notes: **It was taught in a Baraita: "Rabbi Eliezer the Great** (Rabbi Eliezer ben Hyrcanus) **says: Why did the Torah warn us about converts in thirty-six places — and some say in forty-six places?** Why did the Torah consider it necessary so frequently to stress the importance of protecting the interests of converts?" [3]Rabbi Eliezer answers: **"Because the inclination** of converts **is bad,** and insulting or mistreating them may cause them to return to their former ways."

מַאי דִּכְתִיב [4]The Gemara concludes its discussion about showing sensitivity to converts by commenting on the verse cited in the previous discussion: **What is the meaning of** the verse (Exodus 22:2): **"And a stranger you shall not wrong and you shall not oppress him, for you were strangers in the land of Egypt"?** Converts are similar to new immigrants in a strange land. Why does the fact that the Jewish people, too, were once strangers in Egypt give them greater insight into the prohibition against causing converts anguish?

תָּנֵינָא [5]The Gemara answers: **We have learned** in a Baraita: **"Rabbi Natan said:** This verse teaches us: **Do not point out your own defect in another person."** A Jew should not wrong a convert by reminding him that he is a newcomer living among a people that was not always his own, for the Jews themselves were once in the same situation. [6]**And this is what people say:** Rabbi Natan's exposition of the verse is corroborated by the following proverb: **Someone who had a relative who was hanged, should not say to another person, "Hang up this fish,"** because any mention of hanging recalls his family's shame.

MISHNAH אֵין מְעָרְבִין פֵּירוֹת [7]Having considered the monetary *ona'ah* involved in overcharging or underpaying, and the verbal *ona'ah* involved in putting other people to shame, the Mishnah now turns to another type of *ona'ah*. Certain business practices are forbidden because they involve deception, even though it is not possible to quantify the fraud in financial terms. In general, a merchant may not tell a customer that his product has some intangible advantage that it in fact does not have. For example, if a merchant claims that he is selling the produce of a particular field, he **may not mix produce** from another field

[1]אֶלָּא, אֶחָד זֶה וְאֶחָד זֶה בִּשְׁלֹשָׁה.

[2]תַּנְיָא: ״רַבִּי אֱלִיעֶזֶר הַגָּדוֹל אוֹמֵר: מִפְּנֵי מַה הִזְהִירָה תּוֹרָה בִּשְׁלֹשִׁים וְשִׁשָּׁה מְקוֹמוֹת — וְאָמְרִי לָהּ בְּאַרְבָּעִים וְשִׁשָּׁה מְקוֹמוֹת — בְּגֵר? [3]מִפְּנֵי שֶׁסּוּרוֹ רַע״.

[4]מַאי דִּכְתִיב: ״וְגֵר לֹא תוֹנֶה וְלֹא תִלְחָצֶנּוּ, כִּי גֵרִים הֱיִיתֶם בְּאֶרֶץ מִצְרָיִם״?

[5]תָּנֵינָא: ״רַבִּי נָתָן אוֹמֵר: מוּם שֶׁבְּךָ אַל תֹּאמַר לַחֲבֵרְךָ״.

[6]וְהַיְינוּ דְּאָמְרִי אֱינָשֵׁי: דִּזְקִיף לֵיהּ זְקִיפָא בִּדְיוֹתְקֵיהּ, לָא נֵימָא לֵיהּ לְחַבְרֵיהּ ״זְקֵיף בִּינִיתָא״.

משנה [7]אֵין מְעָרְבִין פֵּירוֹת

LITERAL TRANSLATION

[1]Rather, both in this case and in that [he violates] three [prohibitions].

[2]It has been taught: "Rabbi Eliezer the Great says: Why did the Torah warn [us] in thirty-six places — and some say in forty-six places — concerning a convert? [3]Because his inclination is bad.

[4]What is [the meaning of] that which is written: "And a stranger you shall not wrong and you shall not oppress him, for you were strangers in the land of Egypt?"

[5]We have learned: "Rabbi Natan said: A defect that is in you do not say to your fellow."

[6]And this is what people say: Someone who had a person who was hanged in his family, should not say to his fellow, "Hang a fish."

MISHNAH [7]One may not mix produce (lit., "fruit")

RASHI

מום שבך אל תאמר לחברך — כיון דגרים הייתם, גנאי הוא לכם להזכיר שם גירות. **מאן דאית ליה זקיפא בדיותקיה לא נימא לחבריה זקיף ביניתא** — מי שיש לו תלוי במשפחתו לא יאמר לעבדו או בן ביתו: תלה לי דג זה, שכל שם תלייה גנאי הוא לו.

משנה אין מערבין פירות בפירות — בעל הבית שאומר: פירות שדה פלוני אני מוכר לך כך וכך סאין, לא יערבנו בפירות שדה אחרת.

NOTES

שְׁלֹשִׁים וְשִׁשָּׁה — אַרְבָּעִים וְשִׁשָּׁה Thirty-six places … forty-six places. Midrash Tanḥuma states that there are fifty-eight such places. It would seem, therefore, that the thirty-six or forty-six "warnings" mentioned here include all the other Biblical verses that speak of strangers, e.g., "You were strangers in Egypt" (Exodus 22:20, etc.). *Ra'avad* explains that the difference of opinion regarding how many "warnings" there are depends on which verses are included — all verses which refer to strangers, or only those that do not mention strangers together with widows and orphans.

סוּרוֹ רַע Because his inclination is bad. *Rashi* (*Horayot* 13a, and see *Rashash,* ibid.) explains: Because his natural inclination is evil.

LANGUAGE

סוּרוֹ His inclination. According to some authorities this word derives from a Biblical word meaning something which has spoiled, as in Psalms, 14:3, where the related verb means "became filthy." Others claim that it is a short form of סֵיאוּר, something which has turned sour, in the figurative sense of moral corruption.

בִּדְיוֹתְקֵיהּ In his family. This word is derived from the Middle Persian *dutak*, which means "family."

BACKGROUND

סוּרוֹ רַע His inclination is bad. The phrase סוּרוֹ רַע mainly refers to bad habits. A convert, who did not grow up as a Jew, was educated and habituated to a different way of life, and if he is insulted he may easily return to his previous ways.

מוּם שֶׁבְּךָ אַל תֹּאמַר לַחֲבֵרְךָ A defect that is in you do not say to your fellow. As the Torah itself states, Jews must be sensitive to the suffering of strangers, since they too were strangers in Egypt, as it is written (Exodus 23:9): "For you know the heart of a stranger, since you were strangers in the land of Egypt." Rabbi Natan adds another dimension to the reasoning: Since the Jews themselves were strangers, they should not taunt others for this flaw. They, too, wandered through foreign countries, and did not always have a country of their own.

REALIA

בִּינִיתָא Fish.

A type of fish called *binita* in both Aramaic and Arabic. Approximately 200 types of fish from the carp family, which are found throughout the world, are considered *binita*. Some of these fish are small, while others are very large. Two types of *binita* are found in Eretz Israel (primarily in the Sea of Galilee), and to this day are considered exceptionally choice (among other things, because of their high nutritional value). The

NOTES

"And others say . . ."

p. 240–241 Commentary

The waltz begins again. The commentary to this first mishnah concludes with three more *baraitot* (p. 240, line 2 and p. 241, line 2 and line 5), all having to do with the *ger*, or stranger/convert, and the care that must be taken to safeguard this person's integrity. The Torah frequently states laws that protect the stranger and remind us to do things because we were strangers in Egypt. This emphasis on the *ger*, taken by the sages to also refer to a convert to Judaism, is the subject of a great deal of commentary. The as now, there were ambivalent feelings about converts to Judaism. On the one hand, we are to welcome them and not mention their previous faith. On the other hand, there are some negative feelings expressed about the *ger*, as we see on these two pages.

In the first *baraita*, we return to the distinction between verbal and monetary *ona'ah* as it applies to the *ger*. It's clear that there are a great number of prooftexts that forbid mistreating a *ger* in any way and the Gemara concludes that it is just as bad to harm a convert verbally as monetarily (p. 241, line 1). Likewise, on p. 241, line 2, there are two opinions as to how many times the Torah warns us about *ona'ah* involving a *ger*.

How do we understand line 3, which says that the convert's inclination is bad? One way we can grasp it is to contemplate the following real-life scenario. Imagine an interfaith marriage in which the Jewish partner asks the non-Jewish partner to convert so that they can have a Jewish household. If there is pressure on the non-Jew to convert and/or it becomes part of a family power play, the conversion wouldn't be as genuine as it could be otherwise and resentment and anger may build around this issue. It may become a sore point in the couple's fights. If the convert is not fully accepted by the Jewish community, or if the couple divorces, the convert may reject Judaism and revert to his or her former religion. Unfortunately, this scenario is played out all too often in our community today.

Rabbi Steinsaltz mentions B. Horayot 13a in his Note on p. 241. There, we have the relative ranking of persons in Israel according to the pedigree of their bloodline (or lack thereof):

> Mishnah: A Priest takes precedence over a Levite, a Levite over an Israelite, an Israelite over a bastard, and a bastard over a *Natin*, and a *Natin* over a convert, a convert over a freed slave. When [does this order of priorities apply? These rules apply when] everything else is equal. But if the bastard was a student of the sages and the High Priest was unobservant, a bastard [who was] a student of the sages takes precedence over the unobservant High Priest.

> Gemara: A *Natin* takes precedence over a convert [because] the one [the *Natin*] was brought up with us in holiness and the other was not brought up with us in holiness. (B. Horayot 13a)

A *Natin* is a Jew descended from the Gibeonites, who deceived Joshua (Joshua 9:3 ff) and were made into woodcutters and waterdrawers for the congregation because of their ancestors' misdeeds. However, they are still lifelong parts of the congregation, whereas converts were not brought up in a Jewish environment. This is why the *Natin* outranks the convert. However, note that the whole hierarchy is invalidated when the factor of learning is activated. Torah learning supersedes bloodlines and can elevate anyone to the level of a high priest. Indeed, many famous sages were converts or the children of converts.

This passage explores the idea that hurting the feelings of a *ger* might cause him or her to reject Judaism. However, in other places in the Talmud the sages affirm that converts are sometimes those who most scrupulously observe Judaism. For example, we learn elsewhere:

> We do not make up a group [of people eating of one Passover sacrifice during the seder] entirely of converts lest they be [too] exacting about it and nullify the rite. (B. Pesachim 91b)

Here, converts are portrayed as far more punctilious than born Jews about the observance of *mitzvot*. Even within the Jewish community we can see this phenomenon. When Jews become *ba'alei teshuvah* and take on a more observant lifestyle, they can be more eager to observe every stringent form of law than Jews who were raised in observant households. Both views, one portraying converts as more likely to return to their former religion and one viewing them as more likely to be punctilious in their observance, have validity. Thankfully, our tradition allows us to acknowledge the range of behaviors that converts (and born Jews) exhibit.

On the last line of p. 241 we begin the second of the three *mishnayot* we will study in this book. It is about deceptive trade practices that almost everyone has encountered at the gro-

cery store at one time or another. As you read this passage, you may be surprised at how little human nature and business practice have changed in fifteen hundred years.

—JZA

Concepts
Lav/A prohibition.

The name regularly given in the Talmud to a prohibition of the Torah. The punishment for violating a prohibition is greater than for omitting to perform a positive commandment for the transgressor is generally condemned to lashes. There are, however, many exceptions to this rule. When the observance of a positive commandment necessitates the violation of a prohibition, the obligation to fulfill the positive commandment generally takes precedence over avoiding transgressing the prohibition. Traditionally the Torah is said to contain 365 prohibitions. (*Talmud Reference Guide*, p. 207)

Don't say, "Hang a fish."

Is this good advice?

The Talmud explains that to spare oneself from recalling the shame of other members of one's family, someone with a relative who was hanged should not say to another person, "Hang a fish."

Some things are painful to talk about with others. My friend's son has a learning disability. Another friend married someone who isn't Jewish. A relative committed suicide. My cousins can't have children. My aunt died from cancer. My father had a heart attack. I had the opportunity to help another, but walked away.

The proverb suggests that I shouldn't discuss some of these issues for fear that the responses I hear will bring up shameful memories for me about members of my circle of loved ones.

Is the Talmud telling me that I should hide my problems and the problems of those closest to me—as though if I don't mention them, they will go away?

What is the boundary between trying to protect someone from shame and helping that person move beyond it?

Such conversations are difficult. Yet they can bring out the best memories of those whose situation may have caused one to feel shame. They open the door to mourn, to accept, and to grow. With the comfort of a close circle of loved ones, it is possible to move past the pain. It is possible to move beyond the hurt and overcome the shame.

Rabbi Nachman of Bratslav said, *Kol ha-olam kulo, gesher tsar m'od. V'hayikar lo l'fached klal.* "All the world is a narrow bridge. The most important thing is not to be afraid."

As you cross the bridge, try to catch a fish to hang proudly when you get home.

—*Mark Frydenberg*

Forbidden business practices

Intent to deceive, by omission or commission, of the nature or quality of goods or services in modern America is considered despicable. Courts and juries have awarded punitive damages to the injured parties in such cases. Punitive damages are a monetary award above and beyond the actual damages suffered. The degree of deception usually determines the amount of the punitive damages.

At times there is a fine line between a deceptive business practice and a usual business custom. We are told by the sages there are places where it is customary to permit merchants to add water to wine without disclosure to the customer. The sages seemed to allow the business practice of enhancing or otherwise improving the quality of a product, such as wine or grain, by mixing different sediments or new produce without prior disclosure to the buyer. Such practices were not allowed if the mixing caused the products to be inferior. The clearest way of avoiding a deceptive business practice, or the appearance of a deceptive business practice, is full disclosure to the consumer of the nature and quality of the goods or services. If, in all instances, the consumer is made aware of the nature and quality of the goods before the purchase, then no deception can arise.

—*H.J. Stern*

TRANSLATION AND COMMENTARY

with this produce, as the buyer may have a personal preference for produce from that particular field. **Even** where the quality of the produce of the two fields is the same — for example, where both fields have new produce — it is forbidden to mix **new** produce **with** other **new** produce. [60A] [1]**And it goes without saying** that it is prohibited to deceive the buyer by combining produce of different qualities, such as **new produce with old produce.** The word "produce" in this context refers primarily to grain. Since older grain makes a better flour, older produce is worth more. By adding inferior produce to it, the seller reduces the value of the merchandise, which the buyer mistakenly thinks consists entirely of old produce.

בֶּאֱמֶת אָמְרוּ [2]**In truth** the Sages **said** that even though it is ordinarily prohibited to combine different grades of produce, it is permitted to do so if the quality of the produce added is indisputably superior to that which the buyer intends to acquire. Thus, in the previous example, it would be permitted to add old grain to new grain; and **in the case of wine, it is permitted to mix strong wine with mild wine, since** the strong wine **improves** the taste of the mild one.

אֵין מְעָרְבִין [3]Similarly, a wine merchant **may not mix the wine sediment** found in one barrel of wine **with wine** from another barrel. Even though, as the Mishnah will explain, the merchant is entitled to include a certain percentage of sediment in the wine he sells, he may not add sediment from another barrel, if the wine in this barrel happens to be unusually clear, for the sediment from the other barrel may cause the wine to spoil. **But** when the seller transfers wine from his barrel into the buyer's container, **he may give** the buyer the wine with **its** own **sediment**, and he need not strain out the sediment that is already there.

מִי שֶׁנִּתְעָרֵב [4]If **someone's wine was** diluted by being **mixed with water, he may not sell it in a shop, unless he informs** the buyer that it has been diluted. The normal practice was to dilute wine with water immediately before serving it, but not beforehand. Thus, if the merchant sold diluted wine without informing his customer, he would be likely to deceive him as to its true value. [5]Moreover, the owner of the diluted wine may **not** sell it **to a** wine **merchant** at all, **even if he informed** the merchant that the wine was diluted. **Since it was** not customary to sell diluted wine in shops, the reason the merchant was willing to buy this unsalable wine could **only have been to deceive** potential customers by selling it as undiluted wine.

בְּפֵירוֹת, אֲפִילוּ חֲדָשִׁים בַּחֲדָשִׁים. [60A] [1]וְאֵין צָרִיךְ לוֹמַר חֲדָשִׁים בִּישָׁנִים.
[2]בֶּאֱמֶת אָמְרוּ: בַּיַּיִן, הִתִּירוּ לְעָרֵב קָשֶׁה בְּרַךְ, מִפְּנֵי שֶׁהוּא מַשְׁבִּיחוֹ.
[3]אֵין מְעָרְבִין שִׁמְרֵי יַיִן בְּיַיִן, אֲבָל נוֹתֵן לוֹ אֶת שְׁמָרָיו.
[4]מִי שֶׁנִּתְעָרֵב מַיִם בְּיֵינוֹ לֹא יִמְכְּרֶנּוּ בַּחֲנוּת אֶלָּא אִם כֵּן הוֹדִיעוֹ. [5]וְלֹא לְתַגָּר אַף עַל פִּי שֶׁהוֹדִיעוֹ, שֶׁאֵינוֹ אֶלָּא לְרַמּוֹת בּוֹ.

LITERAL TRANSLATION

with produce, [not] even new with new. [60A] [1]And it is not necessary to say new [produce] with old [produce].

[2]In truth they said: In [the case of] wine, they permitted to mix strong (lit., "hard") [wine] with mild [wine], since it improves it.

[3]One may not mix wine sediment with wine, but he may give him its sediment.

[4]Someone whose wine was mixed with water may not sell it in a shop unless he informed him. [5]And he may not [sell it] to a merchant even if he informed him, for he only [takes it] to defraud with it.

RASHI

ואין צריך לומר חדשים בישנים — פסק למכור לו ישנים לא יערב בהן חדשים, שהישנים יבשים ועושין קמח יותר מן החדשים. **מפני שמשביחו** — קשה משביח את הרך. לפיכך, פסק עמו רך — מערב בו קשה. ודוקא קתני קשה ברך ולא רך בקשה. פסק עמו קשה — לא יערב בו את הרך. וכן אין צריך לומר חדשים בישנים, דוקא, אבל ישנים בחדשים, שפיר דמי. **אין מערבין שמרי יין ביין** — בגמרא מפרש לה. **ימכרנו בחנות** — פרוטה פרוטה. **אלא אם כן הודיעו** — לכל אחד ואחד מהן שמים מעורבין בו. **ולא לתגר** — ימכרנו ביחד, ואף על פי שמודיעו. **לפי שאינו לוקחו אלא לרמות** — ולמכרו בחנות.

binita found in Syria and Babylonia are even larger. *Binita* were baked and cooked. From the reference in the Gemara to hanging such fish, we may infer that it was also customary to dry them.

TERMINOLOGY

בֶּאֱמֶת אָמְרוּ In truth they said. This expression usually introduces an authoritive and uncontested Halakhah — a Halakhah handed down to Moses on Mount Sinai (הֲלָכָה לְמֹשֶׁה מִסִּינַי).

BACKGROUND

לְעָרֵב קָשֶׁה בְּרַךְ To mix strong wine with mild wine. By "strong wine" the Mishnah means wine with a high alcohol content, whereas "mild wine" has a low alcohol concentration. Nowadays, too, grapes grown in different areas produce wines with different alcohol concentrations. The Mishnah assumes that buyers generally preferred wine with a higher alcohol content, both because it tasted better and because such wine lasted longer and was less likely to spoil.

NOTES

שֶׁאֵינוֹ אֶלָּא לְרַמּוֹת בּוֹ For he only takes it to defraud with it. It is forbidden to sell diluted wine to merchants because they are likely to resell it to shopkeepers without telling them that it has been diluted, particularly since they themselves did not dilute it (*Sma*).

HALAKHAH

בַּיַּיִן הִתִּירוּ לְעָרֵב In the case of wine they permitted to mix. "It is permitted to mix strong wine with milder wine (and vice versa [*Rema*]) if it is still in the winepresses, since doing so improves the taste of the mixture. However, if people ordinarily taste wine before they buy it, it is permitted to mix strong wine with milder wine (and vice versa), even if the wine has been removed from the winepresses, provided that the mixture tastes adulterated." (Ibid., 228:11.)

מִי שֶׁנִּתְעָרֵב מַיִם בְּיֵינוֹ Someone whose wine was mixed with water. "It is prohibited to dilute wine with water before selling it. However, if wine was accidentally mixed with water, the mixture may be sold in a shop, provided that the

TRANSLATION AND COMMENTARY

[1]On the other hand, **in places where it is customary** for merchants **to add water to wine** before selling it, **it is permitted** for them **to add** water and then sell the wine without warning their customers, for the customers naturally assume that the wine has been diluted.

הַתַּגָּר נוֹטֵל מֵחָמֵשׁ גְּרָנוֹת [2]The Mishnah concludes by noting that, even though a private person who claims he is selling the produce of a particular field may not mix produce from a different field with it, **a merchant may take grain from five** different **granaries and put it into one** single **container,** or wine **from five** different **winepresses and put it into one cask.** Even though a buyer who sees the merchant collecting grain at a particular granary may believe that he is selling grain from that field alone, it is still permitted, because this is normal business practice. [3]In general, the merchant is permitted to mix produce in the customary fashion, **as long as he does not intend to combine** produce of inferior quality with superior produce, and represent the mixture as produce of superior quality.

GEMARA תָּנוּ רַבָּנַן [4]The Mishnah ruled that it is forbidden to add inferior produce, but it is permitted to add superior produce. However, the added produce must be indisputably superior in every way. **Our Rabbis taught** the following Baraita: **"It goes without saying that** if new produce is cheaper than older produce — for example, **where the new** produce **sells for four** se'ahs of produce per sela, **and the old for three** se'ahs of produce per sela — then the old produce is indisputably superior to the new, and **it is not permitted to mix** the new produce with the older produce and then charge a higher price for the entire mixture, for this is outright deception. On the other hand, in such a case it would be permitted to add old produce to a supply of new produce. [5]**But** the prohibition against mixing applies **even** in less straightforward cases, such as **when** the new produce costs more than the older produce — for example, when the **new** produce **sells for three** se'ahs of produce per sela **and the older** produce **sells for four** se'ahs of produce per sela. Even though this

[1]מָקוֹם שֶׁנָּהֲגוּ לְהַטִּיל מַיִם בַּיַּיִן, יַטִּילוּ.

[2]הַתַּגָּר נוֹטֵל מֵחָמֵשׁ גְּרָנוֹת וְנוֹתֵן לְתוֹךְ מְגוּרָה אַחַת, מֵחָמֵשׁ גִּתּוֹת וְנוֹתֵן לְתוֹךְ פִּיטוֹם אֶחָד, [3]וּבִלְבַד שֶׁלֹּא יְהֵא מִתְכַּוֵּין לְעָרֵב.

גמרא [4]תָּנוּ רַבָּנַן: "אֵין צָרִיךְ לוֹמַר חֲדָשׁוֹת מֵאַרְבַּע וִישָׁנוֹת מִשָּׁלֹשׁ דְּאֵין מְעָרְבִין. [5]אֶלָּא אֲפִילּוּ חֲדָשׁוֹת מִשָּׁלֹשׁ וִישָׁנוֹת

LITERAL TRANSLATION

[1][In a] place where they are accustomed to add water to wine, they may add.

[2]A merchant may take [grain] from five granaries and put [it] into one container, [or] from five winepresses and put [it] into one cask, [3]as long as he does not intend to mix [them].

GEMARA [4]Our Rabbis taught: "It is not necessary to say that [where] new [sells] for four and old for three, one may not mix. [5]But even [where] new [sells] for three and old

RASHI

מקום שנהגו להטיל מים ביין יטילו — דכיון שנהגו — אין כאן טעות, שכל היינות בחזקת כן. **התגר נוטל מחמש גרנות וכו'** — שהכל יודעין בו שלא גדלו בשדותיו, ומבני אדם הרבה לוקח, ובחזקת כן לוקחין. **מגורה** — אוצר שאוצרין בו תבואה. **גורן** — הוא שדשין וזורין בו את התבואה, ודרך התגר לקנות מבעלי בתים בשעת הגורן, ולהכניס למגורה שלו. **שלא יתכוין לערב** — ולהוציא קול לקנות הרבה ממקום משובח, לערב בו ממקום אחר, ושכיניו סבורין שכל הפירות מאותו מקום.

גמרא תנו רבנן אין צריך לומר חדשות מארבע — סאין בסלע. **וישנות משלש** — סאין בסלע. **דאין מערבין** — חדשות בישנות, דהואיל ובחזקת ישנות מוכרן, נמצא מאנהו ומוכר לו זולות בתורת יקרות.

NOTES

הַעֲרוֹבֶת פֵּירוֹת Mixing produce. *Rashi* explains that it is prohibited to mix produce grown in different fields, because the buyer may want produce from a particular field. *Ra'avad* and *Rosh*, however, explain that it is only prohibited to mix inferior produce with superior produce.

HALAKHAH

buyer is informed that the wine is diluted. However, such a mixture may not be sold to a merchant (even if he is told that the wine is diluted), lest he deceive potential buyers by selling the mixture to them without informing them that it is diluted." (Ibid., 228:12.)

מָקוֹם שֶׁנָּהֲגוּ לְהַטִּיל מַיִם בַּיַּיִן In a place where they are accustomed to add water to wine. "In places where it is customary to dilute wine with water, this is permitted while the wine is still in the winepresses," following the Mishnah's ruling and Rav's explanation in the Gemara. (Ibid., 228:13.)

הַתַּגָּר מְעָרֵב מִכַּמָּה מְקוֹמוֹת Merchants may mix produce from different sources. "Merchants may buy wine prepared in different winepresses, or grain stored in different granaries, and mix them together, since everyone knows that such food was obtained from different sources, unless the merchant did so with the express intention of deceiving his customers," following the Mishnah. (Ibid., 228:16.)

עֵירוּב פֵּירוֹת בְּפֵירוֹת Mixing different kinds of produce. "It is forbidden to mix a small amount of inferior produce with a large quantity of superior produce and sell the mixture as if it were superior produce. It is even forbidden to mix new produce with other new produce, and it goes without saying that it is forbidden to mix old produce, which is worth more than new produce, with new produce. In addition, it is

BACKGROUND

מָקוֹם שֶׁנָּהֲגוּ לְהַטִּיל מַיִם בַּיַּיִן In a place where they are accustomed to add water to wine. Wine was almost always diluted before being drunk. Indeed, some of the Rabbis maintained that undiluted wine was unfit for consumption, and hence no blessing was to be recited over it. Precisely by how much wine was diluted varied from place to place, both because of variations in local drinking habits and because grapes cultivated in different areas produced vintages of different strengths. However, wine was usually diluted by mixing one part of wine with two parts of water. Nevertheless, wine was generally sold undiluted, and only mixed with water by the buyer (unless it was sold for immediate consumption).

LANGUAGE

פִּיטוֹם Cask. The Hebrew word should be read פִּיטוֹס, from the Greek πίθος, *pithos*, which means a large earthenware jar.

REALIA

פִּיטוֹם (more correctly פִּיטוֹס) **Cask.**

A פִּיטוֹס was a very large earthenware jar. Its height was the height of a man, and it contained hundreds of liters of liquid.

N O T E S

"And others say . . ."

p. 242–243 Commentary

This is a mishnah to study in the produce section of the grocery store. We have here easily recognizable forms of monetary *ona'ah* that everyone has come in contact with at one time or another. The issue of mixing one sort of produce with another, or one vintage of produce with another, is complicated. Sometimes you want only the fruit of a certain field or a specific product (e.g., single-malt whiskey). Sometimes you not only don't mind a combination of produce but actually prefer the improvement caused by a mixture (e.g., blended whiskey). So, for example, when we have single-malt versus blended whiskeys we are comparing different items and we may want the specific blend of whiskeys we are purchasing. The mishnah here shows two underlying principles: (1) A merchant's intent and honesty are primary. As long as the merchant does not mean to deceive or defraud by mixing produce then such actions are allowed. (2) Local custom is followed in transactions regarding produce (and much else). This imbues Jewish communities with the flexibility to adapt to their local business and legal environments while remaining true to the Jewish tradition.

Line 2 contains the phrase *be'emet amru*, "in truth they said." This is a superfluous phrase that stands out in the usually terse Mishnah. Therefore, this phrase is analyzed in the Gemara (p. 244).

You may ask, what is all this business about diluting? Wine in the sages' day was sold as a strong concentrate and diluted right before drinking, much the way concentrated orange juice is used in this country. When you read about diluted wine in lines 4 and 5, imagine how you would feel if you thought you were buying concentrated orange juice and it turned out you purchased juice that was already diluted. On the other hand, in reference to p. 243, lines 2–3, you would have no problem drinking milk that was a combination of the output of different cows and different dairies, as indeed we do today.

Of course, wine is not just another liquid. It symbolizes civilization (grapes are processed into something special). Wine is also used as a means of mystic union with God: when you drink wine you imbibe the very essence of your Creator. It is as if wine is the drinkable form of God's essence just as bread is the edible form of God's essence, incense God's essence we smell, Torah the essence we experience with our intellect, and so forth. Jews may feel uncomfortable with this imagery because it is now associated with Christianity. However, these Christian ideas came from a Judaism that had already incorporated these concepts into the standard Jewish liturgy. We should feel no hesitation at reclaiming the deep, mystical significance of these practices.

—JZA

Concepts
Conclusive law.

Used in the following ways: (1) A ruling at the end of a Talmudic dispute, usually in the form "The Halakhah follows the opinion of Rabbi X."

These rulings were generally inserted when the Talmud was finally edited. (2) Occasionally used in the sense of "a theoretical ruling" as opposed to "a practical ruling." If a decision was actually carried out in practice, it has far greater legal weight than a decision that was merely issued in theory. (3) In Talmudic language, the word halakhah is sometimes used as a short form of—"A law of Moses from Sinai," i.e., a law that has no Scriptural basis, but, according to tradition, was given by God to Moses orally at the same time as the written Torah. Such laws have the same authority as Scriptural laws.

—Rabbi Steinsaltz

Regional Custom

In many types of civil disputes, the rule is "everything follows the local custom." Specifically, we assume that buyer and seller, or employer and employee, are legally bound by the conditions of purchase or employment ordinarily followed in a given locality, unless they explicitly specified otherwise.

—Rabbi Steinsaltz

What's in the wine?

It's amazing! The first laws about truth in labeling! Think of it: today in the grocery we can't taste what we are about to buy, but as we shop a good deal of time is spent reading the labels for the contents. And, our government continues to insist that the labels contain the truth—no deception is allowed. If caught, a company is called to task for its deception. Wonder of wonders: our sages were so far ahead of their time!

—Shirley Barish

NOTES

N O T E S

עֲדָא אָמְרָה This says. This expression is Galilean Aramaic, the dialect spoken in Eretz Israel, as opposed to Babylonian Aramaic, the dialect used in the Babylonian Talmud. Indeed, this term appears frequently in the Jerusalem Talmud, where it is spelled הָדָא אָמְרָה, ע and ה interchanging because people did not distinguish between guttural letters at that time.

TRANSLATION AND COMMENTARY

particular supply of new produce is superior, the merchant **may** still **not mix** the new produce with the older produce and sell the mixture as old produce, even if he charges the lower price for the entire mixture. The reason is as follows: It is possible that **a person** may be willing to pay more for new produce **because he wants to age it** — i.e., to store it for a long time — and new produce stores better than old. But a customer who specifies that he wishes to purchase old produce is clearly not interested in storing it. Hence, for him, the new produce is inferior and the seller is guilty of deception if he sells it to him as old."

בֶּאֱמֶת אָמְרוּ [1]The Gemara now analyzes the next clause of the Mishnah: **"In truth** the Sages **said: In the case of wine, it is permitted to mix strong wine with mild wine, since this improves it, etc."** [2]Without reference to the ruling itself, the Gemara comments on an unusual expression it contains: **Rabbi Elazar said: This** Mishnah **implies** that **every** time we find the expression **"in truth they said"** in a Mishnah, the statement so introduced **is** accepted as an authoritative **Halakhic** ruling. Rabbi Elazar states that our Mishnah is the classic example of this phrase, since the ruling in question is clearly authoritative, because the reasoning behind it is explicit ("because doing so improves it") and indisputable. Accordingly, we may infer from here that wherever the expression "in truth they said" appears, the ruling so introduced is authoritative, even if the reasoning behind the ruling is not as obvious as it is here.

אָמַר רַב נַחְמָן [3]**Rav Naḥman said:** The Sages **taught this Mishnah** — that it is permitted to mix strong wine with milder wine — only when the wines are still **in the winepresses**. Only in the early stages of production, before the wines have completed the process of fermentation, does blending the different kinds improve the quality. However, after each type of wine has already acquired its own distinct flavor and aroma, blending may spoil the resulting mixture, and is prohibited.

וְהָאִידָּנָא [4]**But**, the Gemara asks, why do merchants **nowadays mix** different kinds of wine, even though **the wines are not in the winepresses** any more, and each type of wine has already acquired its distinctive flavor and aroma?

מֵאַרְבַּע אֵין מְעָרְבִין, מִפְּנֵי שֶׁאָדָם רוֹצֶה לְיַשְּׁנָן״. [1]״בֶּאֱמֶת אָמְרוּ: בַּיַּיִן, הִתִּירוּ לְעָרֵב קָשֶׁה בְּרַךְ מִפְּנֵי שֶׁהוּא מַשְׁבִּיחוֹ וכו׳״. [2]אָמַר רַבִּי אֶלְעָזָר: עֲדָא אָמְרָה: כָּל ״בֶּאֱמֶת אָמְרוּ״ הֲלָכָה הִיא. [3]אָמַר רַב נַחְמָן: וּבֵין הַגִּיתּוֹת שָׁנוּ. [4]וְהָאִידָּנָא דְּקָא מְעָרְבִי שֶׁלֹּא בֵּין הַגִּיתּוֹת?

LITERAL TRANSLATION

for four one may not mix, since a man may wish to age them."

[1]"In truth they said: In [the case of] wine, they permitted to mix strong [wine] with mild [wine], since it improves it, etc."

[2]Rabbi Elazar said: This says: Every "in truth they said" is the Halakhah.

[3]Rav Naḥman said: And they taught [this] in (lit., "between") the winepresses.

[4]And nowadays, when they mix [when the wine] is not in the winepresses?

RASHI

אלא אפילו חדשות משלש וישנות מארבע אין מערבין — ואף על פי שהחדשות יקרות מהן. **מפני שאדם רוצה לישנן** — מפני שעילוי דמיהן של חדשות אינן מפני שהן טובות כישנות, אלא שאדם רוצה לישנן. וזה שפסק עמו על הישנות, אינו רוצה לישנן, לפיכך אסור לערב בהו חדשות ואפילו מעולות בדמים. **עדא אמרה** = זאת אומרת. כל עדא כמו הדא. **באמת הלכה** — מדיהב טעם למילתיה "מפני שמשביחו", ואין לגמגם בדבר, ונקט בה למתניתין "באמת" — שמע מינה כל היכא דתני "באמת" הלכה, ואין לחסם ולגמגם בדבר. **ובין הגיתות שנו** — דמשביחו, שתוססין זה עם זה ונעשים טעם אחד, אבל לאחר הגיתות, שכבר קלט כל אחד ריחו וטעמו, אין משביחו אלא פוגמו.

NOTES

כָּל בֶּאֱמֶת אָמְרוּ Every "in truth they said." According to *Rashi*, followed by our commentary, since the Mishnah set forth the reasoning for its ruling, we may infer that this decision is binding, and thus the same presumably applies in all cases in which the expression "in truth they said" is used.

Rabbenu Yehonatan, however, maintains that "in truth they said" is tantamount to a formula used in an oath, and hence we may infer that any statement so introduced is binding. *Rav Hai Gaon* had a slightly different reading in the Gemara here, namely: "Every statement introduced by the expression 'in truth they said' is a Halakhah transmitted to Moses at Sinai," i.e., a law given orally to Moses by God. However, *Ri* (cited by *Rosh* in *Hilkhot Mikva'ot*) observes that certain laws introduced by the expression "in truth they said" are of Rabbinic origin. Thus the Gemara must mean that these rulings are as clear-cut and decisive as those transmitted to Moses at Sinai.

בֵּין הַגִּיתּוֹת In the winepresses. When different kinds of wine are mixed while still in the winepresses, the resulting mixture retains its flavor for a long time. However, if they are mixed later, the mixture retains its flavor for only a short time, after which it spoils. Hence this is forbidden, since the buyer will think that the mixture will retain its flavor for a long time (*Ḥiddushim HaMeyuḥasim LeRitva* and *Meiri*).

HALAKHAH

forbidden to mix new produce with old produce even if the old produce is worth more," following the Mishnah and the Gemara's interpretation. (*Shulḥan Arukh, Ḥoshen Mishpat* 228:10.)

"And others say . . ."

p. 244 Commentary

In what should now be a familiar rhythm to you, the Gemara immediately brings a *baraita* that enriches and deepens the mishnah's information. You can't mix produce even when you're improving the quality because it might not be what the customer wants. For example, when you buy avocados, you might be willing to pay more for some that are already soft. However, if you are buying them for a party to be held a week hence, you wouldn't want ones that are ripe today. Rather, you'd want some that are hard so that you can allow them to ripen.

In line 1 on p. 244 is the commentary on *be'emet amru*. This phrase is taken to mean that the ruling is completely authoritative even if the reason for the ruling isn't clear. (One Talmud student likened this to the way parents say to children, "Because I said so!" One is to obey out of respect for the source of the ruling.)

—JZA

NOTES

[1]אָמַר רַב פַּפָּא: דְּיָדְעִי וְקָא מָחְלִי.

[2]רַב אַחָא בְּרֵיהּ דְּרַב אִיקָא אָמַר: הָא מַנִּי? [3]רַבִּי אַחָא הִיא. דְּתַנְיָא: "רַבִּי אַחָא מַתִּיר בְּדָבָר הַנִּטְעָם".

[4]"וְאֵין מְעָרְבִין שִׁמְרֵי יַיִן בְּיַיִן, אֲבָל נוֹתֵן לוֹ אֶת שְׁמָרָיו וכו'". [5]וְהָא אָמְרַתְּ רֵישָׁא אֵין מְעָרְבִין כְּלָל! [6]וְכִי תֵּימָא: מַאי "נוֹתֵן לוֹ אֶת שְׁמָרָיו"? [7]דְּקָא מוֹדַע לֵיהּ? [8]הָא, מִדְּקָתָנֵי סֵיפָא: "לֹא יִמְכְּרֶנּוּ בַּחֲנוּת אֶלָּא אִם כֵּן מוֹדִיעוֹ, וְלֹא לַתַּגָּר אַף עַל פִּי שֶׁמּוֹדִיעוֹ", [9]מִכְּלָל דְּרֵישָׁא אַף עַל גַּב דְּלָא מוֹדַע לֵיהּ!

[10]אָמַר רַב יְהוּדָה: הָכִי קָאָמַר:

LITERAL TRANSLATION

[1]Rav Pappa said: Since [people] know and forgive.

[2]Rav Aḥa the son of Rav Ika said: Whose [opinion] is this? [3]It is [that of] Rabbi Aḥa. For it was taught: "Rabbi Aḥa permits in [the case of] something which is tasted."

[4]"And one may not mix wine sediment with wine, but he may give him its sediment, etc." [5]But surely you said [in] the first clause [that] one may not mix at all! [6]And if you say: What is "he may give him its sediment"? [7]That he informs him? [8]Surely, since the last clause teaches: "He may not sell it in a shop unless he informs him, and he may not [sell it] to a merchant even if he informs him," [9]this implies that the first clause [applies] even if he did not inform him!

[10]Rav Yehudah said: He says thus:

TRANSLATION AND COMMENTARY

אָמַר רַב פַּפָּא [1]In reply, **Rav Pappa said: Since people are aware** that the custom nowadays is to mix different kinds of wine, **and** they are nevertheless willing to **waive** their right to unadulterated wine, there is no objection to mixing different types of wine, even after the wines have left the winepresses.

רַב אַחָא בְּרֵיהּ דְּרַב אִיקָא [2]**Rav Aḥa the son of Rav Ika** suggested an alternative explanation for the common practice. He **said: Whose view does this** practice reflect? [3]**It is Rabbi Aḥa's, as was taught in** the following Baraita: **"Rabbi Aḥa permits** merchants to mix different kinds of food **in the case of something which is** ordinarily **tasted** before it is purchased." Thus, according to Rabbi Aḥa, it is permitted to mix different types of wine, because people ordinarily taste wine before they buy it, and can therefore easily detect that it has been mixed.

וְאֵין מְעָרְבִין שִׁמְרֵי יַיִן [4]The Gemara proceeds to analyze the next clause of the Mishnah: **"And he may not mix wine sediment with wine, but he may give him its sediment, etc."** [5]**But surely,** the Gemara argues, this clause is self-contradictory! How can the Mishnah state that "the merchant may give the buyer its sediment," when it **said in the first clause** of the statement **that "he may not mix"** wine sediment with wine **at all?** [6]**Now you may say** that this contradiction can be resolved by interpreting the second clause of the statement as follows: To **what** case **does** the Mishnah's permission **"to give** the buyer **its sediment"** apply? [7]Only **when** the seller **informed** the buyer that he was giving him wine containing sediment, and obtained the buyer's consent. Conversely, the Mishnah's prohibition against mixing sediment with wine applies only where he did not inform him. Thus the Mishnah would be referring to two different cases, and would not contradict itself. [8]But this interpretation is unacceptable, as the Gemara now explains: **Surely the latter clause of the Mishnah** explicitly mentions informing the buyer, as it **teaches: "He may not sell** diluted wine **in a shop unless he informs** the buyer that it was diluted; **nor** may he sell it **to a** wine **merchant, even if he informed him** that it was diluted." Thus we see that when the Mishnah wishes to make this point, it does so explicitly. [9]**This implies that the first clause**, which permits giving the buyer sediment and does not stipulate that the buyer should be informed, **applies even if** the seller **did not inform** the buyer that the wine contained sediment! Since the clause of the Mishnah which permits giving the buyer sediment does not specify that the buyer must be told that the wine contains sediment, it would appear that this is permitted even if the buyer was not told that the wine contains sediment! Thus the internal contradiction in the Mishnah stands: Is one allowed to mix sediment with the wine or not?

אָמַר רַב יְהוּדָה [10]**Rav Yehudah** suggested a solution, **saying:** In fact, the Mishnah does not contradict itself.

RASHI

דידעי – הכל יודעים שהוחזקו לערב. **בדבר הנטעם** – שאדם טועם קודם שלקחו, ויכול להבחין שנתערב בו. **והא מדקתני סיפא** – ומפליג בין הודיעו ללא הודיעו – מכלל דרישא דקתני "אבל נותן לו את שמריו" – אף על גב דלא אודעיה.

רַב אַחָא בְּרֵיהּ דְּרַב אִיקָא Rav Aḥa the son of Rav Ika. A fifth-generation Babylonian Amora, Rav Aḥa the son of Rav Ika was the nephew of Rav Aḥa bar Ya'akov (both scholars apparently lived in the same city, Papunya). Rav Aḥa the son of Rav Ika studied with many fourth- and fifth-generation Amoraim, and engaged in Halakhic discussions with Rav Pappa, and later with Rav Ashi. His teachings — some of which were transmitted by his student, Rav Huna bar Manoaḥ — are cited in various places in the Talmud.

רַבִּי אַחָא Rabbi Aḥa. A Tanna of the last generation. Rabbi Aḥa's teachings appear only in Baraitot, but not in the Mishnah. Rabbi Aḥa cites the dicta of other fifth-generation Tannaim; and many of the last Tannaim, in turn, cite his teachings.

HALAKHAH

עירוב בְּדָבָר הַנִּטְעָם Mixing foods where people taste the food first. "In places where it is customary to taste food before buying it, it is permitted to mix ingredients of varying quality, provided that everyone can ascertain this by tasting the mixture," following Rava and Rabbi Aḥa, whose views seem to be accepted by the Talmud. (Ibid., 228:14.)

אֵין מְעָרְבִין שְׁמָרִים שֶׁל אֶמֶשׁ בְּשֶׁל יוֹם, וְלֹא שֶׁל יוֹם בְּשֶׁל אֶמֶשׁ, [1]אֲבָל נוֹתֵן לוֹ אֶת שְׁמָרָיו. [2]תַּנְיָא נַמִי הָכִי: "רַבִּי יְהוּדָה אוֹמֵר: הַשּׁוֹפֶה יַיִן לַחֲבֵירוֹ, הֲרֵי זֶה לֹא יְעָרֵב שֶׁל אֶמֶשׁ בְּשֶׁל יוֹם, וְלֹא שֶׁל יוֹם בְּשֶׁל אֶמֶשׁ, [3]אֲבָל מְעָרֵב שֶׁל אֶמֶשׁ בְּשֶׁל אֶמֶשׁ, וְשֶׁל יוֹם בְּשֶׁל יוֹם".

[4]"מִי שֶׁנִּתְעָרֵב מַיִם בְּיֵינוֹ הֲרֵי זֶה לֹא יִמְכְּרֶנּוּ בַּחֲנוּת אֶלָּא אִם כֵּן מוֹדִיעוֹ וכו'". [5]רָבָא אַיְיתוּ לֵיהּ חַמְרָא מֵחֲנוּתָא, מְזַגֵּיהּ, טַעֲמֵיהּ, לָא הֲוָה בְּסִים. [6]שְׁדַרֵיהּ לַחֲנוּתָא.

[7]אֲמַר לֵיהּ אַבַּיֵי: וְהָא אֲנַן תְּנַן: "וְלֹא לַתַּגָּר אַף עַל פִּי שֶׁהוֹדִיעוֹ"!

[8]אֲמַר לֵיהּ: מִזְגָא דִּידִי מֵידַע

LITERAL TRANSLATION

One may not mix yesterday's sediment with today's, nor today's with yesterday's, [1]but he may give him its sediment.

[2]It was also taught thus: "Rabbi Yehudah says: Someone who pours off wine for his fellow, he should not mix yesterday's with today's, nor today's with yesterday's, [3]but he may mix yesterday's with yesterday's, or today's with today's."

[4]"Someone whose wine was mixed with water may not sell it in a shop, unless he informs him, etc." [5]Rava was brought wine from a shop, he mixed it [with water, and] tasted it, [and] it was not tasty. [6]He sent it [back] to the shop.

[7]Abaye said to him: But surely we have learned: "And he may not [sell it] to a merchant, even if he informed him"!

[8]He said to him: My mixing is

RASHI

של אמש — מיין ששפה אמש, ונשארו השמרים, אין מערבין אותו ביין ששפה היום, ששמרי יין זה מקלקלין יין אחר. **אבל נותן הוא לו את שמריו** — של יין עצמו. ויום ואמש לאו דוקא, והוא הדין ליום ויום משתי חביות, אלא אורחא דמילתא נקט, דסתם יום ואמש משתי חביות. **השופה יין** — כל דבר הצלול הנזרק בנחת מכלי אל כלי שלא יתערבו בו שמרים קרו לה שפייה. **מזגיה** — נתן בו מים שכן דרכו. **בסים** — מבוסם וטוב. **והא אנן תנן ולא לתגר שאינו אלא לרמות בו'** — וחנווני היינו תגר, ויחזור חנווני זה וימכרנו בחזקת יין בחנות. והרי המים מעורבין בו ואתה מכרת לו, ואיכא "לפני עור" (ויקרא יט). **מזיגא דידי מידע ידיע** — שאני נותן בו מים הרבה.

TRANSLATION AND COMMENTARY

This is what the Mishnah **is saying:** The merchant **may not mix** wine and sediment from two different barrels. For example, he may not take the **sediment** from **yesterday's** barrel of wine and mix it **with today's** wine, **nor** may he mix sediment from **today's** wine **with yesterday's** wine. (The Gemara's use of "yesterday" and "today" is merely an illustration. The same rule would apply to two barrels opened on the same day.) [1]**But he may give** the buyer the barrel of wine with **its own** sediment, and need not strain the wine before selling it.

תַּנְיָא נַמִי הָכִי [2]The Gemara now cites a Baraita which supports Rav Yehudah's interpretation of the Mishnah: The following Baraita **also taught this: "Rabbi Yehudah says:** When the seller **pours out wine for another person,** transferring the wine from his own barrel into the other person's container, **he may not mix** sediment from **yesterday's** barrel **with** wine from **today's** barrel, **nor** may he mix sediment from **today's** barrel **with** wine from **yesterday's** barrel, [3]**but he may mix yesterday's** sediment **with** wine from **yesterday's** barrel, **or today's** sediment **with** wine from **today's** barrel."

מִי שֶׁנִּתְעָרֵב [4]The Gemara proceeds to discuss the next clause of the Mishnah: "If **someone's wine was mixed with water, he may not sell it in a shop unless he informs** the buyer that it has been diluted, etc." [5]The Gemara relates that **Rava was** once **brought wine from a shop,** after which **he mixed it with water and tasted it.** [6]The wine Rava bought, however, **was not tasty,** so **he sent it back to the shop.**

אֲמַר לֵיהּ אַבַּיֵי [7]**Abaye** then **said to** Rava: **But surely we have learned** in our Mishnah: **"One may not** sell wine diluted with water **to a merchant, even if one informed him** that it was diluted." How, then, could Rava have sent diluted wine back to the shop? Why was he not concerned lest the merchant pass it off as undiluted wine?

אֲמַר לֵיהּ [8]In reply, Rava **said to** Abaye: **My mixture is** easily **recognizable,** for I add more water to my wine

BACKGROUND

שְׁמָרִים שֶׁל אֶמֶשׁ Yesterday's sediment. Wine sediment is used to expedite the fermentation of the grape juice, transforming it into wine. Such sediment was also used to produce wine at home. In addition, wine sediment was used as a food supplement for animals, since it is rich in protein. However, people generally avoided mixing sediment of different types, since they taste different from one another, and hence are apt to spoil the taste of the grapes used for wine production.

מִזְגָא דִּידִי מֵידַע יָדִיעַ My mixing is well known. Rava was of the opinion that each part of wine should be diluted with three parts of water (rather than two, as done by most people). Indeed, the Gemara relates elsewhere (see *Nedarim* 55a) that Rav Yosef, who was blind, was able to ascertain through taste that a particular mixture of wine had been prepared by Rava.

TERMINOLOGY

תַּנְיָא נַמִי הָכִי It was also taught thus. A term used to introduce a Baraita which supports the previous statement by the Gemara or by an individual Amora.

NOTES

מִזְגָא דִּידִי My mixing. Wine had to be diluted in Talmudic times because it was so strong. Rava's mixture was known to be especially weak: While most people diluted one part of wine with two parts of water, Rava diluted each part of wine with three parts of water.

HALAKHAH

תַּעֲרוֹבֶת שְׁמָרִים Mixing sediments. "It is forbidden to mix sediment from one container of wine with wine from another container. However, one may mix sediment from a particular container of wine when selling wine from that container (*Rosh*)." (*Shulḥan Arukh, Ḥoshen Mishpat* 228:15, and *Sma* ad loc.)

N O T E S

"And others say . . ."

pp. 245–246 Commentary

In lines 4–9 we have a classic bit of stammaitic material. It cites no named sources, it's in Aramaic (except where it's quoting the mishnah), and it's an (ultimately unsuccesful) attempt to harmonize all the teachings of the mishnah. Then we have two teachings by Rabbi Yehudah that make a bit more sense of the whole matter. His teachings underline the honesty demanded of the wine merchant. One is not allowed to continually transfer sediment from barrel to barrel. One may only sell the sediment that goes with a given barrel of wine.

In line 4, we move to the next clause of the mishnah about not reselling wine once it has been diluted (just as we wouldn't resell concentrated orange juice as such once we'd diluted it). Ordinarily, we would expect a great sage to follow the Mishnah punctiliously as if it was a law book. However, if it is a study book—a vision for living that has to be modified for application to everyday life— then we wouldn't necessarily imagine a sage would adhere to every word in his day-to-day affairs. This question of whether the Mishnah is a law book or a study book (or both) is one that has preoccupied scholars for decades and will, no doubt, continue to do so. However, here we have one small example that may point to an answer. Rava, one of the greatest sages that ever lived, returns his mixed wine to a store. This is clearly against the mishnah's ruling. It is a small example of the difference between the ideal of the Mishnah and the demands of real life expressed in the Gemara.

This is also a good example of how we can read the Talmud with many different problems in mind at the same time. This passage sheds light on at least three issues: diluting wine, honesty in business, and the nature of the document before us. Learning to keep one's mind open on many levels simultaneously is one of the best results of Talmud study. We learn to expand our consciousness and awareness—almost as if we were practicing meditation.

—JZA

NOTES

TRANSLATION AND COMMENTARY

than do most people. Therefore, I am permitted to return the wine to the merchant, for he will be unable to sell my wine as undiluted wine and there is no possibility that potential buyers will be deceived. [1]**And if you say that** it is still forbidden to return the diluted wine to the merchant, because the merchant, if he is dishonest, **may add** undiluted **wine** to the mixture **to make it stronger, and** then **sell it** as ordinary wine — in which case potential buyers may be misled into thinking that the wine has not been diluted at all and buy it at the full price, making me an accessory to fraud — such reasoning is invalid. [2]For **if so, there is no end to the matter.** Such reasoning would lead to the absurd conclusion that it is forbidden to sell *any* wine to a merchant, since he may then dilute it and resell it as ordinary wine! The prohibition applies only to items that readily lend themselves to deceptive practices. Accordingly, the Gemara concludes that diluted wine may be resold to a merchant if the seller is reasonably certain that the merchant will be unable to pass it off as undiluted.

מָקוֹם שֶׁנָּהֲגוּ [3]The Gemara now turns to the next clause of our Mishnah: **"In a place where** merchants **are accustomed to add water to wine, they may add** water, **etc."** [4]Commenting on this Mishnah, a **Tanna taught:** "The amount of water which may be added in such places is **half** the amount of the wine, or **one-third, or one-fourth,** depending on the local custom."

אָמַר רַב [5]**Rav said: This Mishnah,** which permits the diluting of wine with water, **was taught** only with regard to wine still **in the winepresses** and which had not yet begun to ferment. At that point adding water to the unfermented grape juice does not cause it to spoil. However, once the juice ferments, it is prohibited to add water. Hence, if the merchant failed to dilute the wine in time, he may not do so later.

MISHNAH רַבִּי יְהוּדָה אוֹמֵר [6]The Mishnah now considers other business practices that border on deceit. **Rabbi Yehudah says: A shopkeeper must not distribute parched grain or nuts** or any other treat **to children** free of charge, **since he** thereby **accustoms them to come to him** and buy from him, and this is unfair competition. Competition between merchants should be based only on quality and price. Attracting customers by manipulating the minds of children is the same as defrauding the other merchants. **But the Sages permit this** practice.

יְדִיעַ. [1]וְכִי תֵּימָא דְּטָפֵי וּמְחַיְּילֵיהּ וּמְזַבֵּין לֵיהּ, [2]אִם כֵּן אֵין לְדָבָר סוֹף.

[3]"מָקוֹם שֶׁנָּהֲגוּ לְהַטִּיל מַיִם בַּיַּיִן, יַטִּילוּ וכו'". [4]תָּנָא: "לְמֶחֱצָה לִשְׁלִישׁ וְלִרְבִיעַ".

[5]אָמַר רַב: וּבֵין הַגִּיתּוֹת שָׁנוּ.

מִשְׁנָה [6]רַבִּי יְהוּדָה אוֹמֵר: לֹא יְחַלֵּק הַחֶנְוָנִי קְלָיוֹת וֶאֱגוֹזִין לַתִּינוֹקוֹת, מִפְּנֵי שֶׁהוּא מַרְגִּילָן לָבֹא אֶצְלוֹ, וַחֲכָמִים מַתִּירִין.

LITERAL TRANSLATION

well known. [1]And if you say that he may add [wine] and make it stronger and sell it, [2]if so, there is no end to the matter.

[3]"[In a] place where they are accustomed to add water to wine, they may add, etc." [4][A Tanna] taught: "By half, by one-third, or by one-fourth."

[5]Rav said: And they taught [this] in the winepresses.

MISHNAH [6]Rabbi Yehudah says: A shopkeeper must not distribute parched grain or nuts to children, since he accustoms them to come to him, but the Sages permit [this].

RASHI

וכי תימא מייתי חמרא חייא ומערב ביה – עד שלא יהא ניכר טעם המים. **אם כן** – דלכולי האי חיישינן. **אין לדבר סוף** – שאף המים לבדם אסור למכור לחנווני, שמא יערבם ביין. ולא חשו אלא בזמן שאני מוכר לו דבר העשוי לרמות בו כמות שהוא עכשיו. **למחצה לשליש ולרביע** – הכל כמנהג המדינה יטיל מים, אם מחצה, מחצה, אם שליש, שליש.

BACKGROUND

קְלָיוֹת **Parched grain.** This refers to grains of wheat or barley roasted while the ears were not completely ripe. The roasting process transforms some of the starch in the grain into sugar, and the grain becomes sweet. Such parched grain was sometimes processed into sweet flour for the baking of cakes. Usually, however, the parched grain was eaten as a sweet and was a natural choice for a shopkeeper who wanted to attract young children to buy his wares.

NOTES

אֵין לְדָבָר סוֹף **There is no end to the matter.** I.e., if we are so concerned that the wine may be adulterated, it should even be forbidden to sell *water* to a merchant, since he may use it to dilute wine (*Rashi*). *Ritva* explains the text to mean that if we are concerned that the wine will be tampered with, we should not be permitted to sell wine to a merchant under any circumstances.

לֹא יְחַלֵּק... וְלֹא יִפְחוֹת **Distributing parched grain and lowering prices.** The Mishnah did not combine these cases into a single sentence, i.e., "Rabbi Yehudah forbids distributing parched grain and lowering prices, while the Sages permit this," because they are different. According to the Sages, distributing parched grain is permitted, whereas lowering prices is praiseworthy (*Ein Yehosef*).

HALAKHAH

הַחֶנְוָנִי הַמְחַלֵּק קְלָיוֹת וֶאֱגוֹזִין **A shopkeeper who distributes parched grain or nuts.** "A shopkeeper is permitted to distribute without charge parched grain, nuts, etc., to children, in order to encourage them to buy from him. Similarly, he may charge less than other shopkeepers do," following the view of the Sages. See also *Arukh HaShulhan*, who suggests that it is only permitted to sell food at a discount, but not other merchandise. (Ibid., 228:18.)

BACKGROUND

גְּרִיסִים **Pounded beans.** Pounded beans were usually crushed with special instruments, after which other types of foods were prepared from them. Indeed, foods prepared from legumes of this sort were very popular among the general public.

SAGES

אַבָּא שָׁאוּל **Abba Shaul.** A Tanna of the third and fourth generations, Abba Shaul was a younger contemporary of Rabbi Akiva. The name "Abba" was an honorific title given to Sages of early generations. He is described as being "the tallest of his generation" — a description accurately reflecting both his physical appearance and the high regard in which he was held. Many of his Halakhic rulings — even when expressed as a minority opinion — became the basis for later Halakhic practice.

LANGUAGE (RASHI)

פרונ"ש* From the old French *prunes*, meaning "plums."

TRANSLATION AND COMMENTARY

[1]Likewise, according to Rabbi Yehudah, a shopkeeper **should not lower his prices** below the fair market value of his merchandise, since this too is considered unfair competition. It is unethical to try to drive one's competitors out of business by engaging in a price war. **But the Sages say** that if a shopkeeper lowers his prices, **he is remembered for good.** Thus, not only is it permitted to lower prices, but this is even considered praiseworthy, as the Gemara will explain.

לֹא יָבוֹר אֶת הַגְּרִיסִין [2]Likewise, a merchant **should not sift pounded beans** and then charge more for the beans than usual. **These are the words of Abba Shaul.** Abba Shaul forbids sifting pounded beans because the seller may then charge more for them than they are really worth, and the buyer, impressed by their appearance, may overestimate their value. [3]**But** in this case as well **the Sages permit this** practice. [4]However, even the Sages **agree that** a merchant **should not sift the top of** a pile of produce **in a bin** and leave the rest unsifted, **since this is only done to deceive.** Once the inferior produce at the top has been removed, the customers see only the superior produce, and they might be deceived into believing that the bin is filled with produce of the same superior quality.

אֵין מְפַרְכְּסִין [5]Similarly, a merchant **may not paint a person** (i.e., a slave), **an animal, or utensils** that he is selling, to deceive the buyer by improving their appearance.

GEMARA מַאי טַעֲמַיְיהוּ [6]The Gemara considers the first clause of the Mishnah, in which the Sages disagree with Rabbi Yehudah and permit distributing free treats to children. The Gemara asks: **What is the Sages' reasoning?** Why do they not agree with Rabbi Yehudah that competition should be based on quality and price alone?

[1]וְלֹא יִפְחוֹת אֶת הַשַּׁעַר, וַחֲכָמִים אוֹמְרִים: זָכוּר לַטּוֹב. [2]לֹא יָבוֹר אֶת הַגְּרִיסִין. דִּבְרֵי אַבָּא שָׁאוּל. [3]וַחֲכָמִים מַתִּירִין. [4]וּמוֹדִים שֶׁלֹּא יָבוֹר מֵעַל פִּי מְגוּרָה, שֶׁאֵינוֹ אֶלָּא כְּגוֹנֵב אֶת הָעַיִן.

[5]אֵין מְפַרְכְּסִין לֹא אֶת הָאָדָם, וְלֹא אֶת הַבְּהֵמָה, וְלֹא אֶת הַכֵּלִים.

גמרא [6]מַאי טַעֲמַיְיהוּ דְּרַבָּנַן?

LITERAL TRANSLATION

[1]And he may not lower the price, but the Sages say: He is remembered for good.

[2]He must not sift pounded beans. [These are] the words of Abba Shaul. [3]But the Sages permit [this].

[4]But they agree that he must not sift from the top of a bin, for it is only [done] to deceive the eye.

[5]One may not paint a man, or an animal, or utensils.

GEMARA [6]What is the reasoning of the Sages?

RASHI

משנה **ולא יפחות את השער** – למכור בזול, מפני שמרגיל לבא אצלו ומקפח מזונות חבירו. **זכור לטוב** – שמתוך כך אוצרי פירות מוכרין בזול. **גריסין** – פולין גרוסות ברחיים אחת לשתים. **לא יבור את הפסולת** – לפי שמתוך שנראות יפות הוא מעלה על דמיהם הרבה מדמי הפסולת שנטל מהם. **וחכמים מתירין** – טעמא מפרש בגמרא. **ומודים שלא יבור מעל פי המגורה** – למעלה, להראות יפות, ואת הפסולת שבתוכו לא בירר. **לפי שאינו אלא כגונב את העין** – בברירה זו. **ואין מפרכסין** – מפרש בגמרא. **לא את האדם** – עבד כנעני העומד לימכר.

גמרא **שיסקי** – *פרונ"ש. **מאי טעמא** – נקט "זכור לטוב", לשון ברכה.

NOTES

דִּבְרֵי אַבָּא שָׁאוּל **These are the words of Abba Shaul.** *Ḥiddushim HaMeyuḥasim LeRitva* had a slightly different reading here, namely: "This *follows* the words [i.e., opinion] of Abba Shaul" (כְּדִבְרֵי אַבָּא שָׁאוּל). The commentator observes that Abba Shaul was himself a merchant, and exceptionally strict about deceiving others, as we learn from other passages in the Talmud. Thus the Mishnah means that sifting pounded beans is forbidden "according to Abba Shaul's opinion," i.e., in accordance with his own personal practice.

פִּרְכּוּס אָדָם **It is forbidden to paint a person.** A woman may beautify herself in order to appear more attractive than she really is (and find a husband). However, she may not conceal visible physical defects, as this is outright deception (*Rabbi Ya'akov Emden*).

HALAKHAH

לָבוֹר מֵעַל הַמְּגוּרָה **Sifting from the top of a bin.** "A merchant may remove inferior produce from the top of a bin, so the rest of the produce will look better and the merchant will be able to charge more for it, so long as he also removes all the inferior produce below the surface of the bin." (Ibid., 228:17.)

יִפּוּי סְחוֹרָה **Improving the appearance of merchandise.** "It is forbidden to alter the appearance of merchandise (animals, utensils, or people) to make it look better than it really is. Thus it is prohibited to dye a slave's beard so that he will look younger, or to feed an animal with broth made from bran to make it look fatter (or to scrape it so that it will look better), or to dye old clothing so that it will seem new. However, it is permitted to dye or otherwise improve the appearance of new merchandise, since doing so does not mislead potential buyers (because the merchandise really is new — *Sma*). Likewise, it is forbidden to soak meat or to inflate an animal's entrails to make it look better (unless all merchants ordinarily do so — *Sma*)." (Ibid., 228:9,15.)

NOTES

"And others say . . ."

pp. 247–248 Commentary

On page 247 we finish off the story of Rava and Abaye and then move to the next phrase of the mishnah. (Note that p. 243, lines 2–3 of the mishnah aren't commented on. The Gemara doesn't feel compelled to add to everything the Mishnah says. It selects some items for attention and ignores others.) Here, the Gemara elaborates on the Mishnah's permission to follow local custom. Not only are we allowed to add water to wine but we may do it in the measure that is customary in local practice.

The last mishnah could be good for those on different ends of the political spectrum to discuss, for it highlights the differences between capitalist and communist systems. Which system is better for the consumer? Which is better for the merchant? How aggressive can one be in pursuing business? In this mishnah, the sages appear to be on the side of free enterprise, which they see as better for the consumer. Rabbi Yehudah is on the side of controlled competition, which is better for the merchants. (In fact, reading this, one begins to wonder if Rabbi Yehudah himself owned a store!) The sages are on the consumer's side, prohibiting *ona'ah* by overcharging but not by undercutting prices!

One is permitted by the sages to improve one's merchandise and, coincidentally, its appearance, as long as one doesn't do it in order to deceive (p. 248, lines 2–4). For example, you might be willing to pay more for skinned, boned chicken and a merchant is allowed to process his birds in order to entice you to buy them. However, the merchant is not allowed to present a package with boned, skinned chicken on the top and regular chicken on the bottom, for this is deceptive. The bottom line is, one cannot attempt to improve the surface appearance of anything for sale in order to deceive the consumer.

—JZA

Sages
Rabbi Yehudah

When the Mishnah speaks of Rabbi Yehudah without any further details it is referring to Rabbi Yehudah son of Rabbi Il'ai, one of the greatest *tannaim* of the fourth generation. He was one of the last five of Rabbi Akiva's disciples, and his father, Rabbi Il'ai, had been a disciple of Rabbi Eliezer. Rabbi Yehudah learned Rabbi Eliezer's teachings from his father. In his youth he studied with Rabbi Tarfon, and he transmits teachings in his name as well as in the names of the other sages of Yavneh: Rabbi Eliezer, Rabbi Yehoshua, Rabban Gamliel, Rabbi Elazar ben Azaryah, Rabbi Yishmael, and Rabbi Yose HaGalili. But Rabbi Yehudah's main teacher was Rabbi Akiva, according to whose teachings he laid the foundations for the halakhic exegesis of Leviticus in a work known as the Sifra (or Torat Kohanim). According to tradition, an unattributed statement in the Sifra is a teaching of Rabbi Yehudah. He was ordained by Rabbi Yehudah ben Bava and is frequently quoted in aggadic exegesis together with Rebbi Nehemyah. In differences of opinion between Rabbi Yehudah and Rabbi Meir, or between

Rabbi Yehudah and Rabbi Shimon, the Halakhah follows Rabbi Yehudah. Among his disciples were Rabbi Eleazer son of Rabbi Shimon, Rabbi Yishmael son of Rabbi Yose, and Rabbi Yehudah HaNasi. His son, Rabbi Yose son of Rabbi Yehudah, was also a famous sage.

—Rabbi Steinsaltz

Mishnah: Rabbi Yehudah says, A shopkeeper must not distribute parched grain or nuts to children, since he accustoms them to come to him. But the sages permit this.

The Gemara goes on to explain that the sages permit this because each shopkeeper is free to come up with his own "gimmick" to entice children to shop there. Rabbi Yehudah says that such a practice is misleading to children, who will shop there only because of the rewards.

Rabbi Yehudah would never get a job today working for a cereal maker. I remember the weekly supermarket trip when I was growing up, when I often selected a box of breakfast cereal not by whether I actually liked the food, but by which box had the better prize inside.

The Kedusha D'Sidra, a selection found at the end of the traditional weekday morning service, offers a blessing for shopkeepers and their customers:

"May God open our hearts to Torah, inspiring us to love, revere, and wholeheartedly serve God. Then we shall not labor in vain, nor shall our children suffer confusion."

—Mark Frydenberg

The spiritual
and material are one
in selling and self.

It is no mistake that the word *avodah* refers both to services dedicated to God and to work. In this way, we are reminded that we can serve God by being honest in the ways we earn our living.

—Naomi Hyman

Six Questions

A person is asked six questions at the final judgment. The first question is, "Were you honest in business?" (The other questions are as follows: 2. Did you set regular times for Torah [study]? 3. Did you engage in procreation? 4. Did you look forward to salvation? 5. Did you engage energetically in [the creation of] wisdom? 6. Did you understand one thing from another, i.e., did you learn about mysticism?) (B. Shabbat 31a)

—JZA

N O T E S

Gemara

¹דְּאָמַר לֵיהּ: "אֲנָא מְפַלֵּיגְנָא אַמְגוּזֵי, וְאַתְּ פָּלֵיג שִׁיסְקֵי". ²"וְלֹא יִפְחוֹת אֶת הַשַּׁעַר, וַחֲכָמִים אוֹמְרִים: זָכוּר לַטּוֹב וכו'". ³מַאי טַעְמָא דְּרַבָּנַן? [60B] ⁴מִשּׁוּם דְּקָא מַרְוַוח לְתַרְעָא.

⁵"וְלֹא יָבוֹר אֶת הַגְּרִיסִין. דִּבְרֵי אַבָּא שָׁאוּל. וַחֲכָמִים מַתִּירִין, וכו'". ⁶מַאן חֲכָמִים? ⁷רַבִּי אַחָא, דְּתַנְיָא: "רַבִּי אַחָא מַתִּיר בְּדָבָר הַנִּרְאֶה". ⁸"אֵין מְפַרְכְּסִין לֹא אֶת הָאָדָם וכו' וְלֹא אֶת הַכֵּלִים". ⁹תָּנוּ רַבָּנַן: "אֵין מְשַׁרְבְּטִין אֶת הַבְּהֵמָה, וְאֵין נוֹפְחִין בַּקְּרָבַיִים, וְאֵין שׁוֹרִין אֶת הַבָּשָׂר בַּמַּיִם". ¹⁰מַאי "אֵין מְשַׁרְבְּטִין"?

LITERAL TRANSLATION

¹Because he can say to him: "I am distributing nuts, and you may distribute plums."

²"And he may not lower the price, but the Sages say: He is remembered for good, etc." ³What is the reasoning of the Sages?

[60B] ⁴Because he eases the market price.

⁵"And he must not sift pounded beans. [These are] the words of Abba Shaul. But the Sages permit, etc." ⁶Who are the Sages?

⁷Rabbi Aḥa, for it was taught: "Rabbi Aḥa permits in [the case of] something which is visible."

⁸"One may not paint a person ... nor utensils." ⁹Our Rabbis taught: "One may not stiffen an animal, and one may not inflate the entrails, and one may not soak meat in water."

¹⁰What is "one may not stiffen"?

RASHI

גמרא שיסקי — *פרונ"ש. **מאי טעמא** — נקט "זכור לטוב", לשון ברכה. **משום דמרווח תרעא** — ואוצרי פירות יראו שהוזלו וימכרו בזול. **מתיר בדבר הנראה** — הלא יכול הלוקח לראות ולהבין מה דמי הפסולת הנברר מאלו, שישנו באחרים. וטוב לו להעלות בדמיהן של אלו יותר על כן מפני הטורח. **משרבטין** — לשון שרביט, כדמפרש לקמיה. שזוקף שער הבהמה כשרביט שתראה שמינה. **ואין נופחין בקרביים** — בני מעיים הנמכרים בבית הטבח שיראו רחבים וגדולים. **ואין שורין בשר במים** — שמלבין, והכחוש נראה שמן.

TRANSLATION AND COMMENTARY

דְּאָמַר לֵיהּ ¹The Gemara answers: **Because** the seller **can say to** any merchant who accuses him of unfair competition: **"I am distributing nuts** in order to attract customers, **and you can distribute plums!** No one is preventing you from doing the same or better."

וְלֹא יִפְחוֹת אֶת הַשַּׁעַר ²The Gemara proceeds to analyze the next clause in the Mishnah: "Likewise, according to Rabbi Yehudah, **he may not lower his prices** below the fair market value of his merchandise, **but the Sages say:** A merchant who lowers his prices is **remembered for good, etc."** ³The Gemara asks: **What is the Sages' reasoning?** Why do the Sages maintain that a merchant who lowers his prices is to be "remembered for good"?

[60B] מִשּׁוּם דְּקָא מַרְוַוח לְתַרְעָא ⁴The Gemara answers: **Because** a merchant who lowers his own prices also **brings down the** general market **price.** If one merchant lowers his prices, others will follow, leading to a general reduction in prices. According to the Sages, competitive prices are not only ethical, but they also benefit consumers.

וְלֹא יָבוֹר אֶת הַגְּרִיסִין ⁵The Gemara now takes up the next clause of the Mishnah: **"And he** must **not sift pounded beans** and then charge more for the beans than usual, because customers may be misled into paying more than the beans are actually worth. **These are the words of Abba Shaul. But the Sages permit** this, **etc."** ⁶The Gemara asks: **Who are the Sages** who disagree with Abba Shaul here? Whose opinion are they following and what is the basis of their argument?

רַבִּי אַחָא ⁷The Gemara answers: The Sages follow the opinion of **Rabbi Aḥa, as was taught in** the following Baraita: **"Rabbi Aḥa permits** improving the appearance of merchandise in the hope of attracting customers **in a case where** the change **is visible."** Rabbi Aḥa is of the opinion that it is permitted to attract customers by improving the appearance of merchandise, provided that the buyer sees what he is paying for. Thus, in the case of pounded beans, if the customer is willing to pay extra for sifted beans, it can only be to save himself the trouble of sifting them. Therefore, it is not considered unethical for the seller to sift them, even when he charges extra for this service.

אֵין מְפַרְכְּסִין ⁸The Gemara proceeds to discuss the next clause of the Mishnah: "A merchant **may not paint a person ... or utensils** to make them look better than they really are, thereby deceiving the buyer." ⁹The Gemara cites a Baraita which presents other rulings in a similar vein: **Our Rabbis taught: "A person** selling live animals **may not stiffen** the hair of **an animal** to make it look sleeker before presenting it for sale, **nor** may a butcher selling **entrails inflate** them to make them look bigger, **nor** may a butcher selling **meat soak it in water** to improve its appearance. These practices are forbidden because their purpose is to deceive.

מַאי אֵין מְשַׁרְבְּטִין ¹⁰The Gemara asks: Precisely **what** did the Baraita mean when it said: "One **may not stiffen** an animal's hair"?

LANGUAGE

שִׁיסְקֵי Plums. Various explanations of the etymology of this word have been offered. Perhaps the most convincing is that this is an Aramaic form of the Hebrew שֵׁיזָף — jujube, *zyzziphus vulgaris.*

LANGUAGE (RASHI)

פרונ"ש* From the old French *prunes*, meaning "plums."

REALIA

שִׁיסְקֵי Plums. שִׁיסְקֵי, more properly translated as "jujube," are from the buckthorn family (*Rhamnaceae*). Jujube trees are deciduous, and they have fine, thorny branches with serrated leaves. These trees are common in various parts of Asia; certain types of jujube are grown in Eretz Israel as well. The fruits of this tree are small and red and have a bittersweet taste. They were usually dried and eaten as candies.

TERMINOLOGY

מַאן חֲכָמִים רַבִּי פְּלוֹנִי Who are the Sages? Rabbi X. Sometimes, when a Tannaitic source ascribes a particular viewpoint to "the Sages" (חֲכָמִים), the Talmud may use this expression to prove that this is in fact the view of an individual Sage.

"And others say . . ."

p. 249 Commentary

The Gemara now comments on the difference between Rabbi Yehudah and the sages. Why do the sages allow such fierce competition? Because they think it is good for the consumer when free competition reigns.

In line 7, the Gemara discusses the example of pounded, sifted beans. This can be likened to shelled pecans today. You may be willing to pay more for shelled pecans since it saves you work. In addition, such a change also improves the appearance of the merchandise in such a way that deception is impossible. You would quickly be able to tell whether all the pecans being sold to you had been shelled or not.

In line 8, we explore the next clause of the mishnah and the Gemara cites a *baraita*. This *baraita* happens to have been included in the Tosefta. Now that we are almost at the end of this passage, you might want to compare the Tosefta (in the "Ingredients" Section) with the Gemara and see how the skeleton of our Gemara already existed twenty years after the Mishnah was finished.

—*JZA*

NOTES

LANGUAGE

סַרְבְּלָא Cloak. This word, which also appears in the Bible (Daniel 3:21, 27), refers to a certain type of trousers worn in Persia (the word is derived from the Persian *sal-var,* "trousers"). It seems that the same root is used here, even though it apparently means "mantle," or "cloak" in the present context.

פִּרְכּוּס Painting. The origin of this word is uncertain. Some scholars are of the opinion that it come from the Greek root περκάζω, *perkazo*, meaning to darken, in the sense of a beard becoming darker.

REALIA

צַלּוּמֵי גִּירֵי Painting arrows. A decoration embroidered on the hem of a Greek garment.

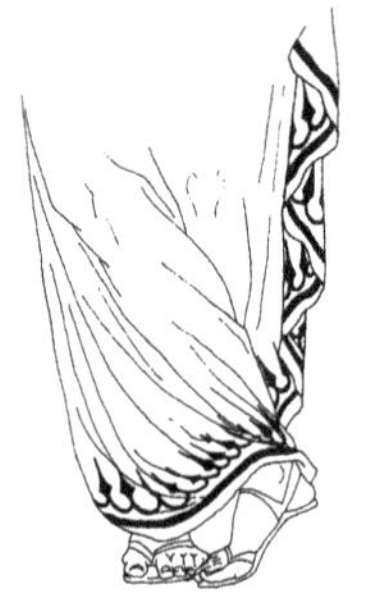

BACKGROUND

לְכַסְכּוּסֵי קְרָמֵי Scouring fine cloth. *Rashi* interprets קְרָמֵי as "colored garments," while *Arukh* explains that it means "thin, expensive clothes."

LANGUAGE (RASHI)

אשטלי״ר* From the Old French *estrelier*, "to comb, to brush animal hair."

פרנזי״ש** From the Old French *frenjes*, which means "fringes hanging from the corner of a garment."

אנפריישי״ר*** From the Old French *enpeser*, "wash, launder."

אוברי״ץ**** From the Old French *ovres*, which means "cloth with decorations and embroidery."

SAGES

זְעֵירִי Ze'iri. A second generation Babylonian Amora, Ze'iri was a student of Rav. After his teacher's death, Ze'iri apparently immigrated to

TRANSLATION AND COMMENTARY

הָכָא תַּרְגְּמוּ [1]The Gemara answers: **Here** in Babylonia, the Rabbis **explained** that a merchant may not feed animals **broth made of bran,** since this causes the animal's stomach to swell and its hair to stand up.

זְעֵירִי אָמַר רַב כָּהֲנָא [2]**Ze'iri said in the name of Rav Kahana:** The Baraita is referring to **brushing an animal's hair** to stiffen it and make the animal appear bigger than it really is.

שְׁמוּאֵל שְׁרָא לְמִרְמָא תּוּמֵי לְסַרְבְּלָא [3]Continuing its discussion of what constitutes prohibited misrepresentation of merchandise, the Gemara relates that **Shmuel permitted putting fringes on a cloak** to make it look more attractive. Similarly, **Rav Yehudah permitted scouring fine cloth,** to present it at its best. [4]Likewise, **Rabbah permitted beating rough cloth** — linen or canvas — to make it appear finer. **Rava permitted drawing** decorative designs on cloth, in the shape of little **arrows,** for example. [5]**Rav Pappa bar Shmuel permitted the drawing** of decorations **on baskets.**

וְהָא אֲנַן תְּנַן [6]Having cited the rulings of all these Amoraim, the Gemara objects that such conduct seems to contradict our Mishnah: **But surely we** have **learned** in our Mishnah: "One **may not paint a person or an animal or a utensil** to make it look better than it is, so as not to deceive potential buyers"!

לָא קַשְׁיָא [7]The Gemara answers: **There is no difficulty** resolving this contradiction between the Mishnah's ruling and that of the various Amoraim cited here. [8]The permissive rulings of the Amoraim only **apply to new** merchandise, whereas the Mishnah's prohibition applies **to old** merchandise. The Mishnah does not object to making merchandise look more attractive, provided no deception is involved. What the Mishnah forbids is misleading customers by painting old merchandise to make it look new. But if the merchant is not hiding anything, and the buyer is ready to pay more for a more attractive article, the merchant is permitted to enhance the appearance of his merchandise.

פִּרְכּוּס דְּאָדָם מַאי הִיא [9]The Gemara continues its discussion of the Mishnah by asking: **What** did the Mishnah mean by a seller **"painting a person"?**

[1]הָכָא תַּרְגְּמוּ: מַיָּא דְּחִיזְרָא. [2]זְעֵירִי אָמַר רַב כָּהֲנָא: מִזְקַפְתָּא. [3]שְׁמוּאֵל שְׁרָא לְמִרְמָא תּוּמֵי לְסַרְבְּלָא. רַב יְהוּדָה שְׁרָא לְכַסְכּוּסֵי קְרָמֵי. [4]רַבָּה שְׁרָא לְמֵידַק צְרָדֵי. רָבָא שְׁרָא לְצַלּוּמֵי גִּירֵי. [5]רַב פַּפָּא בַּר שְׁמוּאֵל שְׁרָא לְצַלּוּמֵי דִּיקוּלֵי. [6]וְהָא אֲנַן תְּנַן: "אֵין מְפַרְכְּסִין לֹא אֶת הָאָדָם, וְלֹא אֶת הַבְּהֵמָה, וְלֹא אֶת הַכֵּלִים"! [7]לָא קַשְׁיָא. [8]הָא בַּחֲדַתֵי, הָא בְּעַתִּיקֵי. [9]פִּרְכּוּס דְּאָדָם מַאי הִיא?

LITERAL TRANSLATION

[1]Here they explained: Broth [made] of bran.

[2]Ze'iri said in the name of Rav Kahana: Brushing up [the animal's hair].

[3]Shmuel permitted putting fringes on a cloak. Rav Yehudah permitted scouring fine cloth. [4]Rabbah permitted beating rough cloth. Rava permitted painting arrows. [5]Rav Pappa bar Shmuel permitted painting baskets.

[6]But surely we have learned: "One may not paint a man, nor an animal, nor utensils"!

[7]There is no difficulty. [8]This [applies] to new ones, this to old ones.

[9]What is painting a man?

RASHI

מיא דחיזרא – משקין אותה מי סובין, והם נופחין מעיה ושערה נזקף. **מזקפתא** = קירצוף, *אשטלי״ר בלעז. **למימרא תומי לסרבלא** – **פרנזי״ש, לייפותו עושין לו תלאי מחוטי משי סביב. **לכסכוסי** = ***אנפריש״ר בלעז, במי סובין. **קרמי** = בגדים המצויירים, ****אוברי״ץ בלעז. **למידק צרדי** – להדק בגדי קנבוס במקבות עץ, שיראה חוטן דק. **לצלומי גירי** – לצייר חיצים. **דיקולי** = סלים. **בחדתי** – מותר, שאינו אלא ליפות. והרוצה להוסיף על דמיהם בשביל יופיים, מוחל הוא. **בעתיקי** – אסור, שגונב את העין שנראים כחדשים.

NOTES

לְמִרְמָא תּוּמֵי לְסַרְבְּלָא Putting fringes on a cloak. *Ra'avad* explains that this refers to tying fringes which hang from the garment in pairs (the word תּוּמֵי being equivalent to the word תְּאוֹמֵי, meaning "pairs"), to make the garment stronger and more attractive.

צַלּוּמֵי דִּיקוּלֵי Painting on baskets. The word צַלּוּמֵי is cognate to the Hebrew צֶלֶם — "image" — and means "to draw" (patterns), while דִּיקוּלֵי — "baskets" — are woven baskets, which were usually made from palm leaves, but occasionally from willow branches and the like. The common denominator in all these cases is that the Rabbis permitted improving the appearance of merchandise even if potential buyers would not necessarily realize that such improvements had been made, as long as they were not deceived into thinking that they were buying top-quality merchandise.

בַּחֲדַתֵי וּבְעַתִּיקֵי New ones and old ones. Cosmetic improvements on new merchandise are permitted, because they cause only a slight increase in price. In fact, the price rises only because of the labor invested in improving the item, as a result of which it is more likely to attract potential buyers. However, it is forbidden to improve the appearance of old merchandise, because the improvements conceal existing flaws and make the merchandise look new, which

"And others say . . ."

p. 250 Commentary

The Gemara continues expanding on the Tosefta's commentary and then, in lines 3–5, gives five brief examples that illustrate how the sages ruled leniently in cases in which merchandise had been decorated. Were all sages lenient in this regard or did the editors of the Gemara simply choose to record lenient rulings? We cannot know, but it would appear that sages were consulted to some extent on matters of commerce and that in real life, the strict, idealistic vision of the Mishnah was interpreted with a great deal of latitude and with an understanding of the needs of people trying to sell goods. The *stamma*, aware of this contradiction, solves it in its characteristic fashion in lines 6–7, suggesting that all these lenient rulings were made with regard to new merchandise and that the Mishnah refers only to old stock.

These rulings may have been arranged to show a consistent trend on the part of Babylonian authorities to interpret this mishnah with great leniency. The sages whose rulings are cited here are all Babylonian and are listed in chronological order (which is by no means the usual case). According to Rabbi Steinsaltz (*Talmud Reference Guide*, p. 35), Shmuel is a first generation *amora*, Rav Yehudah a second generation one, Rabbah is of the third generation, and Rava is from the fourth. Rav Pappa bar Shmuel may have been appended to the end of this series because his story finishes off the whole chapter. In other words, the arrangement of these cases seems designed to show that such leniency was the accepted norm.

—JZA

Sages
Rav Yehudah (bar Yehezkel).

The name Rav Yehudah without any patronymic in the Gemara refers to Rav Yehudah bar Yehezkel, one of the greatest Babylonian *amoraim* of the second generation. He was the founder of the Pumbedita Yeshivah. According to tradition he was born on the day Rabbi Yehudah HaNasi died (Kiddushin 72b). His father, Rav Yehezkel, was an *amora* of the first generation, and Rami bar Yehezkel was his brother. He studied under Rav and Shmuel, and Shmuel used to call him *shin'nah*, "the sharp-witted one." Rav Sheshet was his colleague and among his students were Rabbah, Rav Yose, Rabbi Zera, and others. Eretz Israel was very dear to him, but he nevertheless strongly opposed the emigration of his students to Eretz Israel. The Hebrew language was also very dear to him, and he used it frequently.

—Rabbi Steinsaltz

Rabbah.

Rabbah bar Nahmani the Priest, called Rabbah for short, was one of the greatest Babylonian *amoraim* of the third generation. Rabbah studied under Rav Huna, Rav's disciple, and his entire method in the Halakhah followed that of Rav. He also studied Torah with Rav Yehudah and with Rav Nahman, and he was a student and colleague of Rav Hisda. While still a young man he was considered greater than all the others of his generation in his sharpness of mind, and he was called "the uprooter of mountains." After Rav Yehudah's death Rabbah was chosen, though still a young man, to be the head of the Yeshivah of Pumbedita, though he did not accept the full appointment until close to the time of his death. Rabbah was involved in halakhic discussions with all the great sages of his generation, and the famous controversies between him and his colleague, Rav Yosef (in which the Halakhah follows Rabbah in almost every instance), are an important element of the Babylonian Talmud.

Rabbah trained many students, and in fact all the sages of the following generations were his students, especially his nephew Abaye, his outstanding student. It is known that his private life was full of suffering, and his sons apparently died in his lifetime. He was also very poor and supported himself with difficulty by agricultural labor. The people of his city also treated him badly. Although Rabbah died relatively young, he established himself as one of the pillars of the Babylonian Talmud. His son, Rava, was also an important sage in the following generation.

—Rabbi Steinsaltz

Rava.

A great Babylonian *amora* of the fourth generation, Rava was a colleague of Abaye. His father, Rav Yosef bar Hama, was also a famous sage. Rava's outstanding teacher was Rav Nahman bar Ya'akov, and he was also a student of Rav Hisda, with whom he studied together with his colleague Rami bar Hama. Rav Hisda's daughter married Rami bar Hama, and when Rami bar Hama died, she married Rava. Rava also studied with Rav Yosef. He founded a yeshivah in Mehoza. In all the many halakhic controversies, between him and Abaye, the Halakhah follows him, except for six cases. After Abaye's death, Rav was appointed head of the Pumbedita Yeshivah, which he transferred to his home city of Mehoza. Among his students were Rav Pappa and Rav Huna, the son of Rav Yehoshua. A great number of sages transmit teachings in his name: Rav Zevid Mar the son of Rav Yosef, Rav Mesharshiya, Rav Pappi, Ravina, and others. After his death the yeshivah of Mehoza split in two, and Rav Nahman bar Yitzhak filled his place as the head of the Pumbedita Yeshivah, while Rav Pappa established a yeshivah of his own in Neresh.

—Rabbi Steinsaltz

NOTES

NOTES

TRANSLATION AND COMMENTARY

כִּי הָא דְּהַהוּא עַבְדָּא סָבָא [1]The Gemara explains that this refers to **cases like** that described in the following story. There was **a certain old slave** whose hair had turned white, and **who went and dyed his head and his beard** black, to make himself look younger. [2]The slave then **came before Rava and said to him: "Buy me** as your slave." [3]In reply Rava **said to** the slave: **"Let the poor be members of your household"** (*Avot* 1:5), meaning that he preferred to employ poor Jews as domestic servants for wages, because the livelihood of paupers takes priority over that of slaves. [4]Seeing that Rava was not interested in buying him, the slave **came before Rav Pappa bar Shmuel, who bought him.** [5]**One day** Rav Pappa bar Shmuel **said to** his new slave: **"Give me** some **water to drink."** [6]Rather than perform this simple task, the slave **went and whitened his head and beard** by washing off the dye. [7]The slave then **said to** Rav Pappa bar Shmuel, his master: "You can now **see that I am older than your father!** It is not proper for you to make me perform menial tasks." [8]When Rav Pappa bar Shmuel heard this, **he said of himself,** paraphrasing a Biblical verse (Proverbs 11:8), **"The righteous is delivered out of trouble, and another** (the original text reads: "the wicked," but Rav Pappa did not wish to call himself wicked) **comes in his stead."** Thus Rava — the "righteous" of the verse — preferred to employ the poor and was saved from trouble, while Rav Pappa bar Shmuel — the "other" who "came in Rava's stead" — was punished by buying a worthless slave.

[1]כִּי הָא דְּהַהוּא עַבְדָּא סָבָא דַּאֲזַל צְבַעֵיהּ לְרֵישֵׁיהּ וּלְדִיקְנֵיהּ. [2]אֲתָא לְקַמֵּיהּ דְּרָבָא, אֲמַר לֵיהּ: ״זִיבְנָן״. [3]אֲמַר לֵיהּ: ״יִהְיוּ עֲנִיִּים בְּנֵי בֵיתְךָ״. [4]אֲתָא לְקַמֵּיהּ דְּרַב פַּפָּא בַּר שְׁמוּאֵל, זַבְנֵיהּ. [5]יוֹמָא חַד אֲמַר לֵיהּ: ״אַשְׁקְיַין מַיָּא״. [6]אֲזַל חַוְּורֵיהּ לְרֵישֵׁיהּ וּלְדִיקְנֵיהּ. [7]אֲמַר לֵיהּ: ״חֲזִי דַּאֲנָא קַשִּׁישׁ מֵאֲבוּךְ״. [8]קְרֵי אַנַּפְשֵׁיהּ: ״צַדִּיק מִצָּרָה נֶחֱלָץ, וַיָּבֹא אַחֵר תַּחְתָּיו״.

הדרן עלך הזהב

LITERAL TRANSLATION

[1]Like that [case] of a certain old slave who went [and] dyed his head and his beard. [2]He came before Rava [and] said to him: "Buy me." [3]He said to him: "Let the poor be members of your household." [4]He came before Rav Pappa bar Shmuel, [and] he bought him. [5]One day he said to him: "Give me water to drink." [6]He went [and] whitened his head and his beard. [7]He said to him: "See that I am older than your father." [8]He said (lit., "read") of himself: "The righteous is delivered out of trouble, and another comes in his stead."

RASHI

צבעיה — שהיה זקנו לבן וצבעו שחור, ונראה כבחור. **זיבנן** — קנה אותי לעבד. ונכרי היה, דעבד עברי אסור לאחר חורבן, שאין היובל נוהג. **ויהיו עניים בני ביתך** — משנה היא (אבות פרק א משנה ה). טוב לי לפרנס עניי ישראל ושמשוני. **דיקניה** — זקנו. **צדיק מצרה נחלץ** — זה רבא.

הדרן עלך הזהב

Eretz Israel, where he became an outstanding student of Rabbi Yoḥanan. Despite his youth, Ze'iri was honored by Rabbi Yoḥanan and Resh Lakish as a great man (indeed, Rava remarked that any Mishnah which Ze'iri did not explain was not explained properly). Ze'iri may have returned later to Babylonia, and his Halakhic teachings were transmitted by the students of Rav Huna.

Some scholars hold that there were two Ze'iris, one of whom was a colleague of Rav. At any rate, Ze'iri is definitely not identical with the later Amora Rabbi Zera (or Ze'ira, as he is sometimes known in the Jerusalem Talmud).

רַב פַּפָּא בַּר שְׁמוּאֵל Rav Pappa bar Shmuel. A Babylonian Amora of the third and fourth generations, Rav Pappa bar Shmuel studied with Rav Ḥisda and Rav Sheshet, and later engaged in Halakhic discussions with Abaye and Rava. Rav Pappa bar Shmuel lived in Pumbedita, where he was a Rabbinical judge. Indeed, the Gemara states elsewhere (*Sanhedrin* 17b) that Talmudic references to "the judges of Pumbedita" refer to Rav Pappa bar Shmuel. The Gemara also relates that Rav Pappa bar Shmuel instituted a new unit of measurement, which was used in the city of Papunya.

NOTES

it is not. Indeed, this is forbidden even if the buyer is informed that the merchandise is old; otherwise, it is obvious that deceiving people this way is forbidden (see *Ḥiddushim HaMeyuḥasim LeRitva*).

הַהוּא עַבְדָּא סָבָא A certain old slave. *Rashi* explains that the old man was a non-Jew who sold himself to a Jewish master. *Rashi* argues that the Gemara could not have been referring to a Jewish slave (i.e., a Jew who sold himself into slavery because of poverty; see Leviticus 25:39), because Jews were not sold into slavery after the destruction of the Temple. (Jewish slavery was only practiced while the Jubilee Year was observed, and observance of the Jubilee Year ceased with the destruction of the Temple.)

Rashba, however, claims that *Rashi*'s interpretation is impossible: If the old man was a non-Jewish slave, he could not have sold himself to a new master, since he still belonged to his previous master. Nor could the old man have been a non-Jewish slave who had already been emancipated, since such a person would be treated like any other Jew (according to the Halakhah, a non-Jewish slave automatically becomes a Jew once he is freed). Accordingly, *Rashba* explains that the old man was an ordinary non-Jew who wanted to sell himself to work for Rava or Rav Pappa bar Shmuel.

Ra'avad offers yet another explanation. According to him, the old man was a Jew. However, when he said, "Buy me," he did not mean "Buy me as a slave," but rather "Hire me for a long period of time" (i.e., three years or more), since being hired for such a long period is tantamount to being sold.

דַּאֲנָא קַשִּׁישׁ מֵאֲבוּךְ That I am older than your father. When Rav Pappa bar Shmuel heard this, he realized that it was inappropriate to ask the slave for a drink, since all elderly people deserve honor and respect (*Maharsha*).

צַדִּיק מִצָּרָה נֶחֱלָץ The righteous is delivered out of trouble. *Iyyun Ya'akov* explains that Rav Pappa bar Shmuel considered Rava "righteous" because he followed the Mishnah's teaching that "paupers should be members of one's household," and hence Rava was "delivered out of trouble."

HALAKHAH

יִהְיוּ עֲנִיִּים בְּנֵי בֵיתְךָ Let the poor be members of your household. "It is better to invite orphans and poor persons to join one's household, to avail oneself of their services and to support them, rather than to buy slaves for this purpose." (Ibid., *Yoreh De'ah* 251:6; see *Shakh* and *Taz* ad loc.)

"And others say . . ."

p. 251 Commentary

We end this chapter of Bava Metzia with two contrasting cases of the way a painted person was treated. In this story, a slave dyes his hair in order to appear younger and thus more salable. The slave goes to Rava, who says that he would rather hire a poor person than a slave. In other words, it might be more economically advantageous to hire a slave but it is better for the community to give a poor person a job so that he needn't descend into slavery. Rav Pappa bar Shmuel agrees to buy the slave, but when Rav Pappa discovers that the slave is older than himself, he cannot bring himself to order the slave about. The passage thus ends with a fitting anecdote that summarizes the themes of its last three *mishnayot*: the need for absolute integrity in business and concern for people's feelings.

Rav Pappa chides himself by quoting Proverbs 11:8. Just as Rabbi Eliezer was "blessed" instead of having the word "excommunicated" applied to him (p. 237, line 5) so, here, Rav Pappa calls himself "another one" rather than "an evil one." This is a summation meant to fill us with hope: The righteous will be saved from trouble and the evil will take their place.

When we finish studying a chapter of Talmud, we conclude by saying the formula in Hebrew found in the middle of the page, *Hadran alach 'Hazahav'* which means, "We will return to you, [the chapter beginning with the word] "The Gold." In this way, we reinforce the idea that we are never done studying and that we've never fully plumbed the depths of any one chapter of Gemara. We will put it by for a while, in order to study further, but we will return to it.

—JZA

Painting a Person

By changing the outer appearance you negate the inside of a person. God has made the balance fit. Like a scale, our outside reflects our life experiences, our joys, our sorrow, our growth, our insights, all reflected by the lines, the fat, the whole aging process. When we alter our outward appearance surgically, we challenge God and we dilute the blessed years that God has given us on this earth.

If a person chooses plastic surgery for ego satisfaction there is no difficulty, but if a person chooses this procedure in order to deceive, entice, or fool a "buyer" (e.g., lover, employer, etc.) then that person is guilty. The Talmud teaches, it is forbidden to mislead by altering or misrepresenting our merchandise or ourselves.

—Steffie Odle

Conclusion to Chapter Four

This chapter examines many of the fundamental principles governing the acquisition of movable property. According to the accepted view (that of Rabbi Yoḥanan), movables can be acquired by Torah law by paying for them. By Rabbinic decree, however, monetary payment cannot serve as an instrument of acquisition; consequently, even after payment is made, the object still belongs to the seller, and both parties may still retract. Movables can be acquired by drawing them into one's possession (*meshikhah*), after which neither party may retract and the buyer is obligated to pay for his purchase. Even though payment by itself cannot effect a binding sale, if one of the parties wishes to retract after payment has been made, the other party may demand that the courts pronounce a curse upon him. Moreover, there are times when even the violation of a mere verbal agreement is prohibited, so that one who reneges on such an agreement is labeled dishonest.

For a sale to be binding, *meshikhah* must be performed on the merchandise being bought, and not on the money used as payment. When two parties exchange coins, "money" is defined in relative terms, so that one type of coin is treated as the merchandise and the other as the money used as payment. Thus, coins minted from metals other than silver are considered "merchandise" in relation to silver coins, even though such coins are considered "money" vis-à-vis other objects.

This chapter also presents many of the laws regarding *ḥalifin* — the exchange of one article for another. According to the accepted view, coins cannot effect *ḥalifin*, nor can they be acquired through *ḥalifin*. Produce cannot effect *ḥalifin*, but can be acquired through *ḥalifin*. *Ḥalifin* can only be effected with a utensil that belongs to the buyer, even if the utensil is not worth a *perutah*.

The chapter continues with the laws pertaining to *ona'ah* — overcharging and underpaying. These laws apply to most types of property, but not to land, slaves, promissory notes or property consecrated to the Temple. If one overcharged or underpaid by less than one-sixth, the difference between the market price of the article and the price charged is waived. However, if one overcharged or underpaid by exactly one-sixth of what the merchandise is worth, the surcharge must be refunded, though the sale is not canceled. If one overcharged or underpaid by more than one-sixth, the sale is canceled completely if one of the parties so wishes. Likewise, if one overcharged or underpaid by even the slightest amount for something sold by weight, measure or number, the sale is canceled. Just as a seller is forbidden to overcharge for merchandise, so too is a buyer forbidden to underpay. However, the amount of time given to each party to cancel the sale varies, depending on which of the two parties was defrauded. The *ona'ah* laws apply not only to ordinary people, but even to professional merchants, despite the fact that they presumably know the worth of the merchandise they sell.

The last part of the chapter discusses "verbal wrongdoing," i.e., hurting other people's feelings, which is deemed a graver offense than monetary fraud, both because it cannot be rectified by monetary means, and because it is directed against one's person rather than one's property. Anyone who puts his fellow to shame is subject to divine retribution, and not to court-administered penalties. Anything that causes the listener distress is considered "verbal wrongdoing," whether it be an outright insult or rebuke, or merely a joke or facetious comment. While it is prohibited to insult anyone, this offense is particularly serious if the person offended was a convert, since the Torah added a special prohibition against wronging such a person. The chapter concludes by teaching that it is forbidden to mislead potential buyers by touching up the merchandise one sells, or otherwise misrepresenting it.

"And others say . . ."

Rabbi Steinsaltz's summary (p. 254, last paragraph)

We have covered a wide range of subjects in these few pages: hurting people's feelings, the story of David and Bathsheba, relations between husband and wife, which prayers go directly to God, the purity of a certain oven, an intense fight in the Academy, sifted beans and shelled pecans, wine and concentrated orange juice, hair coloring, and respect for one's elders! And yet this vast variety of subjects was woven together in a beautiful, logical, and meaningful way by the Gemara. The value of human integrity, whether in a verbal or a monetary interchange, was upheld as one of the highest values in Judaism. Indeed, upon studying this passage a student made the following reminder for her classmates about the importance of observing the ban on *ona'ah*:

Where do you go from here? If you made your way through this chapter you've made a good start. You can move on to other passages in the Steinsaltz Talmud. Or you can use the Artscroll, El Am, or Soncino translations. Or you might want to concentrate on your Hebrew. The main thing is to keep going and develop a daily discipline of study so that you continue using the literary, halakhic, and spiritual skills you have acquired by studying this passage. I wish for you the joy of returning, again and again, to the wonder of the Talmud!

—JZA

NOTES

How to Use Dictionaries and Other Tools of the Trade

If you are going to take the invitation to study more Talmud to heart, you're going to need a few aids along the way. Besides a text of the Talmud you ought to have the following.

1. *Introduction to the Talmud and Midrash*, by H. L. Strack and G. Stemberger (Edinburgh, Scotland: T&T Clark, 1991). This is an exceptionally fine, one-volume introduction offering the fruits of scholarly research into rabbinic literature. Its only drawback is it use of abbreviations in almost every sentence.

2. *Aids to Talmud Study*, by Aryeh Carmell (New York: Feldheim, 1980). This slim, inexpensive volume is a user-friendly introduction to Talmudic terminology, grammar, and realia.

3. *A Dictionary of the Targumim, the Talmud Babli and Yerushalmi, and the Midrashic Literature*, by Marcus Jastrow (Israel, 1903). Though this dictionary is nearly one hundred years old it is still the best dictionary we have for studying rabbinic literature.

To look up a word in Jastrow you need to know the three-letter root, or *shoresh*, that is at the heart of every Hebrew or Aramaic word. (One word of encouragement: the roots can be well hidden and you may go through ten tries before you find them, so don't despair.) Once you've found the root, Jastrow will first list the Hebrew and then the Aramaic (signified by the abbreviation "ch." for "Chaldean," another name for the Aramaic language) meanings of the word. In entries for nouns, the dictionary tells what gender the word is (masculine or feminine). It also quotes some sources. For example, in Jastrow's entry for the word *anach* he suggests the pun we explored on the similarity of *anach* to *ona'ah* (pages 232–233).

4. Any recent work by Jacob Neusner. Neusner is one of the greatest contemporary scholars of rabbinic literature and his insights are very important for understanding this corpus of work.

5. *The Mind of the Talmud: An Intellectual History of the Bavli*, by David Kraemer (New York: Oxford University Press, 1990). Professor Kraemer takes you through the levels of the Bavli and shows you its nuances.

Rashi Script

Author's Note: The following two pages are reprinted from *The Talmud: The Steinsaltz Edition: A Reference Guide.*

Rashi Script

Rashi script is one of the most common forms of Hebrew writing in printed Hebrew texts. Almost all commentaries on the Talmud (and the Bible) and Halakhic works are printed in this script. The ability to read this script with ease is an essential skill for studying this literature. Actually, Rashi script is simply the printed version of the Sephardi cursive Hebrew script. Rashi and his students, the Tosafists (whose commentaries are normally printed in this script), did not use it; instead they used Ashkenazi cursive writing, from which contemporary cursive Hebrew script developed. Rashi script received its name because of its use in the history of Hebrew printing. The first books printed in Hebrew were published by Sephardi Jews, and when they printed the Hebrew Bible with commentary, in 1475, they distinguished between the Biblical text and its commentaries by printing the former in regular, square Hebrew letters, and the latter in a different typeface. Since Rashi's commentary was printed in this typeface it came to be called "Rashi script." Another typeface, very closely resembling Rashi script, was used among Ashkenazi Jews; this typeface, which has a somewhat Gothic appearance, is called "teitsch." Teitsch letters were used primarily in Germany, particularly for Yiddish-German translations and notes. As can easily be seen from the table of Rashi script that follows, there is little difference between printed Hebrew writing and Rashi script.

The most noticeable differences are to be found in the letters א, ב, צ, and ש. Certain letters in Rashi script are quite similar to one another, and it is therefore important to distinguish between them in order to avoid confusion:

א-ח These two letters are very similar; the difference between them is that א has a small projection on the upper left-hand side, whereas ח does not.

ח-ת The left foot of the ת has a small projection at the bottom facing outward, whereas ח does not.

ט-ע In certain typefaces, these letters look very similar; they can be distinguished, however, by the fact that the ע has a projection on the outward facing left-hand side.

ל-צ The similarity between these two letters is apt to be particularly confusing, as there is no similarity whatsoever between ל and צ in regular Hebrew script (or print). Note, therefore, that the upper part of the ל in Rashi script points straight up, whereas the upper part of the צ is tilted to the right.

ם-ס These two letters are similar not only in Rashi script, but in printed texts as well. The difference between ם and ס in Ashkenazi cursive writing is the opposite of the difference between these letters in Rashi script. Note, therefore, that the ם in Rashi script is round and smooth at the bottom, while ס has a small projection on the lower left side.

ע	ע	י	י	6	א
פ	פ	כ	כ	ג	ב
ף	ף	ר	ר	ג	ג
ﬞ	צ	ל	ל	ד	ד
ן	ץ	מ	מ	ה	ה
ק	ק	ס	ם	ו	ו
ל	ר	נ	נ	ז	ז
ﬨ	ש	ן	ז	ח	ח
ת	ת	ס	ס	ט	ט

NOTES

The Downfall of Rabbi Eliezer*

The stories we read in the Yerushalmi and the Bavli regarding Rabbi Eliezer's excommunication are dramatic ones—so dramatic, in fact, that they inspired Rabbi Steinsaltz to write his own version of the events as reported in the Bavli. He puts himself, and you, right into the action. (As an exercise, you can imagine writing a similar version of Rabbi Eliezer's story based on the Yerushalmi.) This is another example of a commentary on an often told tale that addresses many inspiring and important issues.

I t is impossible ever to forget that day, the greatest day of Rabbi Eliezer's life and the most lamentable, the day he rose to the peak of his existence and then fell, so completely that we never set eyes on him again. To be sure, those of us who witnessed the events of that day have, like myself, often wondered whether they really happened—even though over the years they seem to become more clearly focused than ever. Even while it was all taking place, we experienced the same mixture of wonder and incredulity, as though we were in two worlds at once. To this very moment, I cannot tell where we were. Altogether, there is something awkward and painful about the whole

* From *The Strife of the Spirit* by Adin Steinsaltz (Jason Aronson Inc. 1988).

thing and, being now an old man, I may even be mistaken about certain details. But since there are few of us left to tell of it and no one, so far, has ever divulged the scarcely-to-be-believed facts, let me try to render as complete an account as I can.

The whole thing started as something quite inconsequential; it was one of those minor debates in the *Bet Midrash*, most of them leaving nothing more behind than case material for the students to learn by rote. The subject was a contrivance of some sort, an invention by a potter, or rather a craftsman working with clay and bricks, who had a new idea about making a baking stove. Now this potter, whose name was Akhnai, or something like that, had conceived an ingenious way of getting around the strict regulations concerning the purity of an oven. He constructed it in sections, and between the sections he poured sand, which was then plastered over. The whole oven could be taken apart and put together again. It could thus be considered a broken vessel and, according to strictly legal tradition, broken pottery was in the nature of material returned to earth and was not subject to rules concerning purification. In that sense, it remained legally pure no matter how much uncleanness it gathered. Akhnai considered that making and selling them could turn into a profitable enterprise. Before proceeding further with the development of his invention, however, he thought it would be advisable to get the opinion of Rabbi Eliezer.

The industrial-minded potter was probably a decent enough fellow, with a smattering of learning and perhaps even with some pretensions at artistic as well as technical innovation—which doesn't explain why he chose to consult Rabbi Eliezer of all people, especially since Rabbi Eliezer was known to be contemptuous of new ideas and could, as likely

as not, reject this oven out of hand. It may have been a provocation, of course, on the part of some of the more mischievous pupils, a deliberate misguidance. Or, the potter may have been led by circumstances we cannot now fathom. Whatever it was, the oven was brought to Rabbi Eliezer and, to everyone's surprise, Rabbi Eliezer's verdict—in no uncertain terms—was that it was pure and would always remain legally pure, because it was not in the category of implements. The inventive manufacturer was himself dumbfounded. On the one hand, he could now sell any number of such ovens to his fellow villagers, on the other, he was more perplexed and uncertain than ever about the legal purity of his oven. He therefore decided to bring his contrivance to the *Bet Midrash* to get it confirmed by the sages of that worthy assembly.

In those days, the problems dealt with by the *Bet Midrash* were numerous and varied, and we lived in the exhilarating conviction that it was all very important somehow, that whatever we decided was precedent and would become *halachah* for generations to come.

When this oven-maker appeared—a rather broad-chested, simple artisan with a Galilean accent—we were inclined to make light of the whole thing. We of the back rows, the scoffing novices, felt that this was an obvious trick, a device to get around the *halachah* regulations of purity. Those in the front rows with outstanding memories restated the words of earlier sages on the matter of an oven constructed in sections, and how it had been clearly condemned as something that accumulates uncleanness. It was all in good humor, and I recollect the phrase used by someone of the House of Betira, who still spoke a lot of Babylonian: *"Hukha Vetlula,"* he said, and when one of us asked what it meant, he jokingly translated it as "stuff and nonsense." Anyhow, as this would indicate, there didn't seem to be much to concern or trouble us. We were even wondering whether a vote was needed when Rabban Gamaliel, who presided over the assembly, rose to sum the matter up.

He was tall and autocratic and a trifle impatient. "Is there anyone who disagrees that this oven is impure?" he asked. Whereupon, to our consternation, Rabbi Eliezer stood up. He wasn't called Eliezer the Great for nothing, for he was immensely tall but unlike his princely brother-in-law, Rabban Gamaliel, he was very heavy and ponderous. What is more, he was extremely grave and dignified; one hardly ever saw him smile, and when he spoke, his voice had an impressively sonorous tone.

"I have declared this oven pure," he said, "and I still maintain that it is pure." A few moments of shocked surprise followed. An Elder, who sat a couple of rows ahead of me and who was already a little hard of hearing, blinked his eyes and, turning from side to side, called aloud, "Eh, what? Pure?" The astonishment in his voice reflected the feelings of the rest of us, especially since we were well aware that Rabbi Eliezer never jested in the *Bet Midrash*, and if he said something, he really meant it.

The occupants of the front rows looked at one another to see who would speak up and, when no one did so, the same Babylonian of the House of Betira, who had previously called it all a *"Hukha Vetlula,"* now rose and suggested that, with due respect to the previous speaker, the oven had to be considered unclean. He then proceeded to reiterate all the arguments that had already been given—about the need to preserve purity in respect to vessels of clay and the various precedents—and supported them by the weight of words spoken by the sages of the House of Betira

and things learned from the great Rabban Yochanan ben Zakkai and other sayings ascribed to earlier sages such as the son of Hillel the Elder. All of which was presented out of respect to Rabbi Eliezer; a lesser dignitary would have been exposed to a snort of contempt from Ben Betira for daring to defy the assembly. Finally, he admitted he could not help wonder how anyone could conceivably declare this oven to be pure.

Rabbi Eliezer, who had been listening quietly, waited to make sure he was finished, and then uttered only one word. He spoke without bothering to get up, in his rich, clear voice, and this somehow goaded the others to answer vehemently.

Another worthy of the House of Betira, a cousin I believe of the first, quickly came to the defense of his relative. Not that any of us were ignorant of the past greatness of the Betiras nor did anyone cast any doubt on their piety and erudition. Anyhow, when he had had his say, another sage felt compelled to voice his opinion on the matter, and he was followed by a whole rush of arguments on the part of additional front row sages—some long-winded, a few brief and concise.

Rabban Gamaliel sat throughout all this with more than his usual tranquility, indicating with a word or a gesture who was to be the next speaker. Some of the rest of us, especially those in the back rows, I'm sorry to admit, were keen to hear how Rabbi Eliezer would react to the weight of the arguments against him. Too many of us had known the lash of Rabbi Eliezer's contempt for all innovation or novelty.

Of course, there were a few personal pupils of Rabbi Eliezer who tried half-heartedly to defend him. There was one, I remember, we used to call the little Eliezer, or Elai, a name that later became famous on account of his son, the great scholar, Yehuda ben Elai. Anyhow, this Elai now endeavored to lend some support to his teacher by insisting that the appliance being discussed was of a different nature than the usual oven, because of the sand between the sections and so on. All very commendable as an act of devotion to a teacher, but hardly convincing.

Rabbi Eliezer himself sat in his customary calm, listening with the attentiveness he gave to everything that had to do with Torah, but also showing that cold noncompliance we were used to seeing in him whenever he was opposed. As the arguments against him became a deluge, his face became stonier and more set.

Rabban Gamaliel remained serene and quiet, the tense glow of his intelligence evident in his eyes, which shifted up and back from interpreter to speaker, and alighted on someone in the second row, whose chief claim to recognition lay in his hoary age. It was from this moment that the whole matter began to assume a different aspect. This old man of the second row was originally from Alexandria and was said to have been a pupil of Yedidiah, or Philo, as he was called. Like most of that school, he was an extremely pious fellow, very scrupulous about observing the *mitzvot* but not too knowledgeable, so that even though he was well on in years he sat in the second row, and even that was more in deference to his being related by marriage to the family of Nakdimon ben Gurion than to his wisdom. It was no secret that Rabban Gamaliel preserved a certain respect for all the first families of old Jerusalem, the Jerusalem before the destruction, even those that had fallen from their greatness or their wealth. He would go out of his way to show his regard,

such as in this instance of the elderly fellow now being allowed to speak, who was someone we knew as a bore and a sermonizer.

He used to deliver Sabbath afternoon sermons in the synagogue on Aggadah, somewhat in the style of the Philo school. Although he knew Hebrew very well, his accent remained Greek and it was remarked, rather slyly, that the suspect Greek philosophy also spoke through him. At the same time, as mentioned, he was punctiliously observant about his religious duties and was a loyal follower of the school of Hillel. He would occasionally run diplomatic errands in which his fluency in Greek was useful. On the other hand, he didn't speak much in the *Bet Midrash*, and when he did he used to talk like one of the extremists of the Hillel School, arousing the secret scorn of many and not only the survivors of the School of Shammai. To be sure, no one said anything, perhaps because he was a relative by marriage of Hyrcanus the elder, father of Rabbi Eliezer, who, incidentally, because of his own age, he addressed by his first name, Eliezer.

This old man now began his speech by quoting *halachah* precedents, not omitting several that had been thoroughly expounded by previous speakers, and adding words of wisdom he had heard from Hillel the Elder. Some of the more roguish novices around me winked and smiled at each other whenever he repeated what the Elder Rabban Gamaliel had said (it was the one *halachah* he remembered of that sage and it later became fixed in his name in the Mishnah scripture). His tone, at any event, was that of a patronizing older person addressing a younger colleague, his being related by marriage to Rabbi Eliezer giving him a right to do so somehow.

It would all have passed without leaving

much trace—everyone having become restless and eager to finish the whole affair without further ado—except that, for some reason or other, the old bore suddenly veered away from the routine *halachah* framework and began to talk about what he called the inner content of the discussion, "the idea," in Greek.

With this his speech assumed the enthusiastic tone of his sermons in the synagogue and he forgot that he was not talking to the simple folk of the congregation of Alexandria but to the sages of Israel. He got carried away and said that the things spoken by Rabbi Eliezer were an example of that mode of thought that we, the pupils of Hillel the Elder, had proven to be of no value whatever. Such notions were remnants of the repudiated approach of the School of Shammai and it was indeed to be wondered at, how someone like Rabbi Eliezer, a pupil of Rabban Yochanan ben Zakkai, could let himself fall into such a patently wrong reasoning, because it was so obvious to all that the oven was impure. Rabbi Eliezer was merely an example of that formalistic legalism that did not accord with the inner spirit of the Torah, which teaches us that we should not let ourselves be beguiled by trivialities or outer details but should go along the way of truth of the inner spirit of things, for we cannot follow after the play of logic or build the *halachah* on the basis of an idea or a formal arrangement that does not take into consideration the essential reality of things.

Truth to tell, we pupils did not pay much attention to all this; we felt we had already heard it before. We were only astounded at his daring to tell it to Rabbi Eliezer to his face. After all, we were not too concerned about the principles of the matter. But when I lifted my head, I saw that Rabbi Eliezer's face was more fiercely negative and noncompliant than ever. As we knew from experience, when Rabbi Eliezer became hurt and angry, it was not like anybody else suffering a personal affront; it was the wrath of the Torah, the response of sublime purity to offense or disrespect.

He had been known even to burst out at Rabbi Akiva in words afterwards recalled with dread and anguish, and now that he showed all the signs of such a fierce inner rage, we all trembled a little. The old man, as soon as he also became aware of it, dropped his voice and concluded his speech almost in the middle of a sentence. Whereupon, without even waiting for permission to do so, Rabbi Eliezer rose to his full height, more impressive and grave than ever, and in the taut silence that ensued his voice boomed forth.

"What is the meaning of this thing you call formalism?" Here it may be mentioned that Rabbi Eliezer had himself grown up in a Greek-speaking household and in his youth had studied with a master who was learned in Greek philosophy. He was, thus, far more sensitive to the nuances of the criticism leveled at him than were many of the ordinary members of the *Bet Midrash* who, although they were familiar with the Greek terms, did not grasp the full import of the concepts involved.

Now it was no longer a matter of a simple stove but a matter of the relation to Torah. "What is formalism?" he asked and answered his question by quoting something Rabban Yochanan ben Zakkai had said to the Sadducees. We were all familiar with the whole story, of how the great teacher had said, "Can the Law of the Torah be compared to your rules of nature and your logic, your whole shaky philosophy, the philosophy with which you sow confusion among us?"

He continued, "Torah is an essence unto itself

and everything in it is independent of the world. By what authority do you say that, according to the Torah, this oven is a deception, an attempt to get around the rules of purity? The Torah is altogether made up of pathways and signs, all its words are guidelines for the world, and it is far beyond the stupid laws of the earth. Whatever the Torah makes obligatory, whether it seem possible or impossible, is not to be questioned. Do not try to make the Torah an instrument for human needs, for it is not the Torah that serves the world but the world that serves the Torah. We cannot be responsible for the blunders of the ignorant, and we cannot adjust the Law of Torah to accommodate man or nation. What, then, is the meaning of formalism here? There is Torah, the unswerving obedience to Torah, and that's all. We sit here, and we study Torah only for this purpose and not to discuss or argue or consider public opinion. Whether a thing is right or wrong, correct or incorrect, will be decided by Torah; I will not accept any other authority!"

Thus it was that Rabbi Eliezer let himself go, and we who should have perhaps restrained him, heard him out with growing dismay. Indeed, he went too far in denying the connection between Torah and life, and in rejecting all the many laws and regulations passed by the *Bet Midrash* itself, which had the power of Scripture over the lives of the people. He had gone too far and had exceeded all bounds, not only of the subject under discussion but of good manners.

Even Rabban Gamaliel showed extreme displeasure at this subversive attack on himself as well as on the School of Hillel; and Rabbi Yehoshua, who almost never was upset by anyone or anything, was provoked to bursting point. Rabbi Tarfon, whom we would expect to ease the tension with a quip or jest,

seemed to have curled up in himself as though personally insulted. There was a strong feeling in the *Bet Midrash* that what had been uttered should not have been and could not have been said.

When the sages of the house finally rose up to speak, we heard much that was memorable and rare. Several of the speakers expounded not only on *halachah* matters but also on the way each one understood the *halachah*. Rabbi Tarfon, for instance, rose up finally and spoke eloquently. A stirring talk was delivered by the young Rabbi Elazar ben Azaria, whom we already recognized as one of the great minds of the generation, even though his beard was hardly grown.

Some of the addresses were drawn out, others were brief, but all of them without exception insisted that it was impossible, it was forbidden, to think of the Torah as not being alive and as not being connected with the ongoing existence of the world. Torah could not be considered by itself, separate from the world, as though what it had to say did not relate to, and guide, the course of events.

In a variety of ways it was mentioned that Rabbi Eliezer's approach could have been correct in a vastly different world. One of the speakers said that at the End of Days, long after the rebuilding of the Holy Temple, it might perhaps be possible to adopt such an approach.

I remember that Rabbi Akiva also spoke, and in his speech there was a vague hint of something we gathered was of an esoteric nature, so that not all of us knew what he meant. He, too, asserted that the Torah has to be bound up with the essence of things. His words had the ring of authenticity. I will admit I never did get to the bottom of Rabbi

Akiva, even then when he was still at the beginning of his greatness.

At the conclusion of his talk, Rabbi Yehoshua got up, and as he began to speak, one was, as always, reminded that he was one of the poets of the *Bet Midrash*. His voice, too, was soft and pleasant, and the way he ordered his ideas was clear and convincing. At first sight, he may have seemed small, dark, and even ugly, but to us, who listened to him talk, he was enormously enchanting and delightful. Although he repeated some of the things that had already been stated, about the Torah and the way of Torah, he did not linger over them. He made a point of speaking *halachah*, as though there was nothing at stake but the matter of Akhnai's stove. Clearly he wished to restore the discussion to a definite subject and to the halachic framework of normal *Bet Midrash* activity. At the same time, he very decidedly indicated that it was out of the question to consider this stove as anything but a deception and consequently impure.

Even though the followers of the School of Shammai were few in number, they stubbornly clung to a certain conservative point of view. Now that the issue of a basic approach was let out of the bag, these followers of the School of Shammai did not wish to be cheated of a chance to express themselves. I recall especially Yochanan ben Hyrcanus, sturdy and youthfully alert in spite of his gray head of sixty years. His nickname, so apt it was known to us from his very first years at home, was "Devil boy." At any rate, he now spoke at length, bringing up various arguments, most of them out of place, and tried to get to the root of the matter, the root of *halachah* itself. I must admit I understood only a little of what he said; although his logic and wit made one feel it was all very clear, there was also the feeling that it wasn't quite the whole truth, that there was something twisted in what he said. It was almost as though he were trying to lead one astray.

Afterwards, several of Rabbi Yehoshua's disciples tried to go into more detail on the specific issue at hand, but neither Yochanan ben Hyrcanus nor any other followers of the School of Shammai responded in kind. They simply were pulled back to the old conflict and the spirit of dissension between the Schools of Hillel and of Shammai, which we had thought was long since over and done with.

The day waned and twilight set in. We had extended the discussion far beyond the usual time and Rabban Gamaliel decided to come to a conclusion. The interpreter, Hutzpit, called everyone to silence, and Rabban Gamaliel, in his customary tone of address, no different from that heard at the end of any ordinary controversy in the *Bet Midrash*, said, "Gentlemen, we will count the votes. All those who grant this stove ritual purity will say so, and those who disagree will declare that they do not grant it purity."

Rabban Gamaliel was very careful about his choice of words and never uttered any expression of blame if he could possibly help it, so that he never said "uncleanness" if he didn't have to; and now he launched the vote by saying, "Gentlemen, I myself do not grant purity." After him all those present rose up, one after another, and gave vent to their opinion, I among them. In fact, only Rabbi Eliezer and one other sage of the first row voted to grant purity. It was years since such a decisive majority had been expressed in a vote.

I don't know whether the matter would have ended there, peacefully enough, had it not been for an unexpected outpour on the part of one of the veteran disciples of Rabban Yochanan ben Zakkai. This elderly person, never conspicuous for his wisdom, now got up, and without being given permission, began to speak very agitatedly. "You see, dear sirs, at the conclusion of all the very sharp and deep words that have been uttered here, the overwhelming majority has been able to judge correctly and to find the truthful halachic solution."

He then continued to tell us how the words of sages were like firm stakes in the ground, like trees planted by the waters, and so on; how the truth must always win, as it did here in this discussion; and he finished with a saying that used to be quoted by certain scholars when they completed their addresses. "Behold, my friends, just as this great tree stands firmly rooted in its place and does not budge, so is this halachah fixed and immovable; just as the water flowing in this channel does not move backwards, so does truth never flow back."

This tree, which he now pointed to, was a giant carob tree, heavy with age. It stood next to the Bet Midrash, and the pupils would frequently sit under its leafy branches, studying, their backs against the broad trunk and their faces turned toward the shallow channel of water that ran nearby and irrigated the tree, making it grow to such proportions. This tree was thus one of the landmarks of the Bet Midrash; and even though it did not give much fruit, no one ever dared to think of cutting it down. I must confess, too, that as we glanced out at the tree in response to the last remarks made about it, and saw the light of the setting sun leave its golden imprint on the upper branches, and heard the soft rush of the water on the channel nearby, we were all reassured somehow, by its stability and serenity.

Rabbi Eliezer's voice suddenly broke the stillness—an altogether different voice. There was something else present in his face, too, something that made us suddenly afraid to look at it. He was no longer with us in this place, discussing halachah; he was more like someone who sees that which is taking place at a great distance, and we who were near him were invisible. He seemed to be somewhere else, on a different level. We were aware that Rabbi Eliezer was one of those who had gone deeply into the occult mysteries of the Chariot, and his whole appearance now betokened some such inner vision.

Suddenly, before he even began to speak, we were overcome by a nameless fear—a fear of the hidden and the esoteric, of those mysterious things known only to the initiated and as terrible in their power as prophecy. Although in a certain respect he seemed to be removed and distant, and extremely tall, indeed towering above us in every way, he remained bound somehow to that which had been happening here before. And in a voice that was not his—after all, his characteristic voice was familiar enough—in a voice that was resonant with other forces, alien powers and unknown worlds, he turned to the ancient carob tree: "This carob shall testify that the halachah is with me!"

Whereupon something happened, and although I saw it with my own eyes, I am not sure whether it was a seeing such as men usually see. We had not stirred from our seats, but before us something happened that shook the very foundations of our certainty in all that existed. Nothing was clear or definite any more, because this enormous tree moved suddenly from its fixed spot, and we all saw it move, trunk and branches together, sliding along the earth away from the wall of the Bet Midrash to a point about a hundred cubits away, where it came to a halt and stood still. It must be admitted that not only I, but all those present—even though we never spoke of it, except perhaps for the glance of astonishment we exchanged with our eyes—felt that never again could we rely on the law and order of nature. Rabbi Eliezer had called upon the powers above this world to help him prove his point. And whether we agreed with him or not, we could not but be shaken to the core by the feeling that we no longer knew what the truth was.

It was the sound of Rabban Gamaliel's voice that now woke us out of this strange, uncanny state. With the same cool tone of the most ordinary daily affairs, he said, "Despite which, no proof can be drawn from the carob tree."

Although Rabbi Eliezer did not seem to be listening, he stirred, and in that vibrating, prophetic voice he called out, "The channel of water shall testify that the halachah is with me!" And now the open conduit that had become completely exposed with the shifting of the carob tree, this same rushing channel of water now became still and then, before our incredulous eyes, the water began to flow in the opposite direction, up the slope of the rise, light, easy waves running up the conduit of water.

Once more the cool tone of Rabban Gamaliel's voice broke the silence: "There is no proof in the channel of water!" This time Rabbi Eliezer turned his face away from the window, through which, as I mentioned, he was looking without seeing. Scanning the entire assembly with those frightening, unseeing eyes, he called out: "The walls of the Bet Midrash shall testify that the halachah is with me!" Whereupon we heard the walls of the Bet Midrash begin to stir. The structure

was not exceptionally massive, but it was a building that had been made to last, and we now witnessed the thick walls shifting and cracking and leaning from the horizontal outward and then more and more inward. Were we terrified? I can't be as certain of our physical fear as of our terror of the nature of the event. The power of Rabbi Eliezer's words frightened us beyond the sudden dread of being crushed by a falling building. After the shifting of the tree from its place, nothing was self-evident and certain anymore, and I personally was no longer able to be astonished by anything; all was possible and at the same time, it seemed as though I, and only I, survived within a dream, and as in a dream, I could not budge, could not remove myself from the scene. Those who sat next to the walls were likewise frozen into immobility, although they felt the walls bending over them more tangibly than the rest of us.

But the whole thing did not last more than a moment. In the instant of our panic, we heard the voice of Rabbi Yehoshua speaking to the walls. Strange that a man should address walls, and even more strange that he should do so in the same way that one rebukes young pupils or children who take advantage of a master's kindliness. However that may be, this chiding tone, even though the subject of it was so utterly unbelievable, was in itself extraordinary in its very ordinariness. We dearly loved Rabbi Yehoshua, knowing that he never really got angry and that he only pretended to be vexed, like a good-hearted father who could not hide the affection from his soft and pleasant voice even when he was reprimanding us.

But now, as he admonished the walls, his voice carried an additional quality, of mystery and power, a resonance beyond this world, on planes and levels of being beyond the known and ordinary. "If scholars contend with one another about the *halachah*, what is that to you?" he asked. And just as children will fall back, discomfited at being scolded, so did these walls now recede shamefacedly, to their erect position. What we think is an unbridgeable difference between man and things was suddenly obliterated, and the walls were very definitely hesitating, wobbling aslant for an interval in time before deciding to remain firmly erect.

The only one who had remained unmoved throughout all this, standing as though to gather all his forces, was Rabbi Eliezer. He now lifted his gaze upward and called out, in a mighty voice: "The Heavens shall testify that the *halachah* is with me!"

Whereupon we heard the Voice. This was the first time in my life I had ever heard a *Bat Kol*, a voice from Heaven. When others used to tell me about it, I understood only the words, because there is no way of describing what a heavenly voice is. It is not like the sound of speech, and yet it is a voice. If there is anything to which it can be compared, it would be more like the reverberating echo of a cry in the mountains. And even though the sound of it is clear enough, one cannot locate it; it doesn't come from any definite place, or from any creaturely throat, and the effect of it is indeed indescribable. At any event, that which was uttered by the Voice cannot be forgotten: "What have you against Eliezer, my son, with whom the *halachah* is always in accord?"

It was more than a reverberation of sound from all sides; this that was beyond anything that can be called a voice made us feel with an absolute certainty that whatever it said was true and could not possibly be otherwise.

We remained stunned and petrified into silence. The *Bat Kol* had uttered its injunction from Heaven, shattering all our convictions and prejudices. Thereupon, once again, the voice of Rabbi Yehoshua was heard, and this time in the accents of prayer: "Lord of the Universe, You revealed Yourself in all Your glory on Mount Sinai. There You gave us the Torah, the one and only Law, and in it You spoke the Truth and the Judgment and the Right, and in Your Torah You wrote saying that in council one should follow the decision of the majority. But what if the majority do not agree with Rabbi Eliezer? Are we not to abide by that which is right?"

What happened after this was so very simple, it is difficult to put it on the same level as the Heavenly voice. Even though there was absolutely no sound, no voice or great crackling thunder, we all experienced the vivid sensation of the passing of the *Bat Kol* from the *Bet Midrash*, as though it had been renounced by some greater power above—as though, if I may dare to say so, the Holy One, Blessed by He, Himself had agreed with Rabbi Yehoshua. Because after all these dramatic events, the world was restored to us, a different world, but still the world of Torah, and we understood the holiness of this Torah in our possession, a holiness derived not from heaven but from that which was here and now, from this *Bet Midrash*. When the sages, whether great or wise or whether simple and ordinary, studied the Torah, the Torah they pored over was Truth, the words of the living God.

At this moment, then, we were restored to the *Bet Midrash*, to the walls that no longer seemed to slant, to the channel of water that again flowed as usual, to the sun that was setting as usual—and everything was as it had always been. We were relieved to know that the Heavens did not coerce us, did not compel us to make one decision rather than another, that the obscurity of doubt was suddenly cleared away and it was we, in our freedom of the majority vote, who decided the substance of truth. It was a feeling of immense relief shared by all of us, even Rabbi Eliezer I think, because he did not turn and take his seat with dignity but sank down into it, sweating profusely, stricken with sorrow and fatigue.

When Rabban Gamaliel spoke, we were back in the customary *Bet Midrash* atmosphere as I said, even though it could never again be the same. Nevertheless, the usual tone of Rabban Gamaliel helped us to feel right, as he said, "Members of the Assembly, since we have decided that this oven is impure, its bread is hereby declared unclean, for it was not prepared in accordance with the laws of purity, and so the attendants will gather all the loaves and burn them in the compound next to the *Bet Midrash*."

The attendants gathered up the loaves of bread and took them outside. The Galilean inventor of the oven disappeared, but no one saw him take his departure. A few of the younger pupils went out to gather wood to burn the loaves of bread. We had witnessed enough such halachic proscriptions—on cakes of meal and offerings, and the subsequent burning in the compound—so that there was no reason this should be as different and strange as it seemed to us. Perhaps the whole ordinariness of the world had changed: the attendant carrying the loaves, the pupils preparing the fire, and the fire itself. Smoke began to rise. It was already dark when we heard Rabbi Eliezer give vent to his anger. His anger was full of a terrible bitterness, an abysmal humiliation.

"How dare you alter the decision of Heaven!"

Wrapped in this fierce mortification, he rose and left the *Bet Midrash*. But it seems that he was not the only one to feel anger. Rabban Gamaliel, always so wonderfully self-controlled, now raised his voice an octave, so that it was just a trifle more decisive, and yet profoundly sad.

"Men of the Assembly," he said, "we cannot tolerate such a refusal to accept the decision of the Sanhedrin of Israel. If the Sanhedrin decides, then no one, not even if it be Rabbi Eliezer ben Hyrcanus . . ." Here he hesitated, almost as if he were about to add "my brother-in-law," and he continued, "can say such things as were heard just now."

Then, almost as an afterthought, he added, "There is the precedent of Akabia ben Mahalalel." We all knew about this Akabia, a great mind, one of the outstanding men of his generation, who had defied the decision of the majority, with the result that he was excommunicated. Indeed, many years had passed since any of the great sages had been excommunicated; there were other ways of keeping them in line. But now, precisely because of the prestigiousness of Rabbi Eliezer, the hint was clear.

No one offered to say anything. Everyone waited for one of the sages to express it more explicitly. The old men, who had spoken so glibly a while ago, were now silent, and even those in the first row waited for someone else to speak up. All eyes were gradually focused on Rabbi Yehoshua—Rabbi Yehoshua of the kindly disposition, the one who was the close friend of Rabbi Eliezer from their difficult years at school together. There was a long pause. At last he stood up and said it:

"It seems we have no choice. We cannot divide the one Torah into two Torahs." A long, hushed interval, and he continued, "I am of the opinion that we have to consider whether to excommunicate him."

Once the word was uttered, it was clear that it would be so. There was no more desire to discuss the matter. And Rabban Gamaliel, unable now to hide the extremity of his emotion, was obviously torn; he had to force himself to remain calm. It was, however, in a clear and firm voice, hiding all his personal feelings (as befits a leader of Israel), that he called out, "Stand and be counted!"

Now, too, there was a majority, and the majority decided to excommunicate Rabbi Eliezer.

About the Author

Judith Z. Abrams is a woman with a mission: She wants to bring the beauty of Talmud to as many people, and with as much depth, as possible. To that end, she has published many books on rabbinic literature, including *Judaism and Disability: Portrayals in Ancient Texts from the Tanach through the Bavli* (Gallaudet University Press), which was the recipient of the Koret Jewish Studies Publication Program Publication Subsidy for 1998, *The Talmud for Beginners,* Volumes I, II, and III (Jason Aronson Inc.), and *Learn Talmud: How to Use the Talmud: The Steinsaltz Edition* (Jason Aronson Inc.). Rabbi Abrams and her husband, Steven, have co-authored *Jewish Parenting: Rabbinic Insights* (Jason Aronson Inc.) and she has also written a number of children's books. Rabbi Abrams earned her Ph.D. in rabbinic literature from the Baltimore Hebrew University and teaches across the country. She is the founder and director of Maqom: A School for Adult Talmud Study, where anyone can learn Talmud, regardless of their background. Maqom study materials are available on the Internet (http://www.compassnet.com/~maqom). Rabbi Abrams and her husband live in Houston with their three children, Michael, Ruth, and Hannah.

www.ingramcontent.com/pod-product-compliance
Lightning Source LLC
Chambersburg PA
CBHW050414110426
42812CB00006BA/1885
* 9 7 8 0 7 6 5 7 6 0 4 7 0 *